D0388222

The Myth
of the Male Breadwinner

Conflict and Social Change Series
Series Editors
Scott Whiteford and William Derman
Michigan State University

The Myth of the Male Breadwinner: Women and Industrialization in the Caribbean, Helen I. Safa

Roads in the Sky: Hopi Indians in a Century of Change, Richard O. Clemmer

Ancestral Rain Forests and the Mountain of Gold: Indigenous Peoples and Mining in New Guinea, David Hyndman

"I Am Destroying the Land!" The Political Ecology of Poverty and Environmental Destruction in Honduras, Susan C. Stonich

More Than a Living: Fishing and the Social Order on a Polynesian Atoll, Michael D. Lieber

The Culture of Protest: Religious Activism and the U.S. Sanctuary Movement, Susan Bibler Coutin

Computing Myths, Class Realities: An Ethnography of Technology and Working People in Sheffield, England, David Hakken with Barbara Andrews

Literacy, Power, and Democracy in Mozambique: The Governance of Learning from Colonization to the Present, Judith Marshall

Gender, Sickness, and Healing in Rural Egypt: Ethnography in Historical Context, Soheir A. Morsy

Life Is a Little Better: Redistribution as a Development Strategy in Nadur Village, Kerala, Richard W. Franke

¡Óigame! ¡Óigame! *Struggle and Social Change in a Nicaraguan Urban Community,* Michael James Higgins and Tanya Leigh Coen

Manufacturing Against the Odds: Small-Scale Producers in an Andean City, Hans C. Buechler and Judith-Maria Buechler

The Bushman Myth: The Making of a Namibian Underclass, Robert J. Gordon

Surviving Drought and Development: Ariaal Pastoralists of Northern Kenya, Elliot Fratkin

The Myth
of the Male Breadwinner

Women and Industrialization
in the Caribbean

Helen I. Safa

Westview Press

BOULDER • SAN FRANCISCO • OXFORD

Conflict and Social Change Series

Cover and frontispiece art by Dominican artist Silvano Lora

All rights reserved. No part of this publication may be reproduced or transmitted in any form or by any means, electronic or mechanical, including photocopy, recording, or any information storage and retrieval system, without permission in writing from the publisher.

Copyright © 1995 by Westview Press, Inc.

Published in 1995 in the United States of America by Westview Press, Inc., 5500 Central Avenue, Boulder, Colorado 80301-2877, and in the United Kingdom by Westview Press, 12 Hid's Copse Road, Cumnor Hill, Oxford OX2 9JJ

A CIP catalog record for this book is available from the Library of Congress
ISBN 0-8133-1211-6 — ISBN 0-8133-1212-4 (pbk.)

Printed and bound in the United States of America

The paper used in this publication meets the requirements of the American National Standard for Permanence of Paper for Printed Library Materials Z39.48-1984.

10   9   8   7   6   5   4   3   2   1

*To Manouchehr, who for
thirty-two years sustained me with
so much love and commitment
to last a lifetime*

Contents

Tables and Illustrations

Tables

xi

Photographs

Preface

This book has taken a long time to complete. I started the research in Puerto Rico in 1980, a year that marked a fundamental change in my life because I left the New York area, where I had lived most of my life, to take a position as director of the Center for Latin American Studies at the University of Florida. The flood of administrative duties, which lasted five years, meant I could not devote much time to the research, but my interest in the impact of paid employment on the status of women workers continued and expanded to include the Dominican Republic. Dominican free trade zones clearly were becoming the showpiece of the 1980s Caribbean Basin Initiative and reinforced the need to examine the implications of the newly industrializing female labor force in export manufacturing.

I was beginning to write comparative analyses of these two Caribbean countries when the possibility of doing research in Cuba appeared in 1986. I could not resist the opportunity to compare the impact of paid employment on women industrial workers in two capitalist countries (with different development trajectories) with the same trend in the first socialist country in the Americas. Starting research in Cuba in 1986 probably delayed the final writing for several years, but I think it was worth it, particularly because in 1994 Cuba found itself in such economic distress. There are virtually no other ethnographic studies of Cuban women during the period when the revolution was still thriving, and I think it is important to analyze its accomplishments as well as its shortcomings, which will undoubtedly be stressed in years to come.

While I did not contemplate a comparative study at the beginning of my research, I have learned a great deal in the process. Comparative research has stimulated my interest in broader issues concerning the relationship between race, class, and gender and its impact on family formation and gender ideology. It has also made me more aware of the similarities and differences in gender relations in each Caribbean society that stem not only from recent development strategies but from earlier historical patterns. Unfortunately, I came to recognize the importance of race in terms of its impact on employment, marital patterns, and gender ideologies too late to incorporate a full analysis here, but its importance suggests a fruitful field for future research barely touched in the Hispanic Caribbean. Over time, I also came to realize the importance of focusing on gender issues in my analysis rather than focusing exclusively on women, since a full comprehension of women's status can only be obtained through a comparison with men. This need for comparison can be seen most clearly in the area of labor force participation, where the changes in women's status can be explained not only by the increase in women's employment but also by the deterioration of male employment, in terms of lower rates of growth, higher unemployment, lower wages, and other factors that have contributed to the weakening of the myth of the male breadwinner. This "global feminization of labor" extends far beyond the Caribbean, as Standing (1989) has shown, and appears to contribute to the global rise in female heads of household and to growing poverty worldwide.

Through the forty years I have spent living and doing research in the Hispanic Caribbean, I have been able to observe many of these changes firsthand. Thus, my knowledge of these three countries is informed not only by the results of the studies presented here but also by intense personal involvement with the people of these countries over the years. I started living and working in Puerto Rico in 1954, when Operation Bootstrap was in full swing. At the time, I believed this type of reform could redress poverty and inequity. After I began graduate studies in anthropology at Columbia University with a fellowship from the University of Puerto Rico, my skepticism grew. My dissertation research, which culminated a decade later in my first monograph, *The Urban Poor of Puerto Rico,* is a critical analysis of the successes and the shortcomings of Operation Bootstrap for the Puerto Rican poor. The data presented here represent my first formal research in the Dominican Republic, although I have visited the country many times since my initial trip in 1954, when Trujillo was still dictator. Despite a formal return to democracy after Trujillo's death in 1961, the Dominican Republic never achieved genuine economic and social reform and is now following the export industrialization strategies that brought only temporary economic growth to Puerto Rico decades ago. I have published earlier versions of the Puerto Rican and Dominican data in several edited volumes and journal articles.

My work in Cuba started later, after I was first invited to visit in 1977, and I have made repeated trips since then. In 1983, as president of the Latin American Studies Association, I helped initiate the first exchange program between Cuba and the association, with funding from the Ford Foundation, and the visits grew more frequent. I am sure that my previous visits and the knowledge of my research and publications assisted me in gaining the support of the Federation of Cuban Women for my research on women industrial workers in Cuba. Because U.S. Treasury Department regulations prohibit payment to Cubans, the federation agreed to take on the expense of all the field work in Cuba, including the computer analysis. This agreement represented a considerable sacrifice of money and staff time for them, and it was an honor for me to have gained their confidence, since this was the first time they had collaborated with a scholar from the United States. Though socialism is now widely discredited, I learned a great deal from working in a socialist country where a genuine redistribution of resources had taken place. I cling to a belief that greater social justice must prevail and that this cannot be achieved without the empowerment of the working class, including women.

Many people have contributed to the research findings presented here, but I bear responsibility for the interpretation. The study in Cuba was conducted by a highly motivated and energetic team of Cuban researchers who worked for or were contracted through the Federation of Cuban Women, including Marta Núñez, Rita María Pereira, Margarita Flores, Rosa María Cartaya, and Raúl Ramos. Vilma Espín, president of the federation, and then director of foreign relations Ester Velís took a personal interest in the study and provided sage advice as well as logistical support. I hope that they profited from the experience as much as I did.

I am grateful to the Wenner-Gren Foundation for Anthropological Research and its former director, Lita Osmundsen, for funding my research in Cuba as well as providing support for the in-depth interviews in Cuba, Puerto Rico, and the Dominican Republic. These in-depth interviews were particularly helpful because I had not participated in the interviews for the survey research in any of these countries, and it gave me an opportunity to come to know some of the women I have written about here on a more personal basis. They reinforced in me the idea of the importance of family, especially children, and of women's indomitable will to struggle against all odds. The sincerity and generosity they showed me are deeply appreciated, and I hope this book may in small measure contribute to some improvement in their lives.

Much of the survey research in Puerto Rico was conducted by Carmen Pérez H., then a graduate student in anthropology at Rutgers University, where I taught previously. The Puerto Rican research was funded through a small grant from the National Institute of Mental Health. The opportunity to compare the data from Puerto Rico with those from the Dominican Republic came through the Center for Research for Feminist Action (CIPAF), whose director, Magaly Pineda, graciously provided me with the results of their study of women workers in the Dominican free trade zones. Three graduate students at the University of Florida, Lorraine Catanzaro, Quintina Reyes, and Milagros Ricourt, used this data for their M.A. theses in Latin American Studies, and I have benefited from their analyses. Francis Pou of the Fundación García Arévalo assisted me in conducting the in-depth interviews in the Dominican Republic, and the team of Cuban researchers helped me in Cuba.

Many graduate students at the University of Florida also helped me in computer analysis and transcription and coding of the in-depth interviews, including Elizabeth Brailowsky, Kathleen Gladden, Quintina Reyes, and Thea de Wet. With her usual skill and dedication, Carmen Meyers from the Center for Latin American Studies took on the tedious task of formatting and typing final drafts, while Kathleen Grant, my assistant; Richard Phillips of the Latin American Collection of the University of Florida library; and many other staff at the center and university helped in numerous ways. I am also grateful to colleagues who provided data and commented on earlier drafts, particularly Carmen Diana Deere, Isis Duarte, Susan Eckstein, Alice Colón, Frank Moya Pons, Alejandro de la Fuente, Emilio Pantoja, Luz Alba de Acevedo, and June Nash, my close friend and collaborator for many years. Finally, my thanks go to my family, and especially my late husband, Manouchehr, for their endless patience and support during these many years. This book marks the culmination of fifteen years of empirical research and reflection, which is my way of thanking the people, especially the women, of the Caribbean for all they have given to me. I hope it will be of some assistance in their everyday struggle for survival.

Helen I. Safa

1

Gender and Industrialization in the Caribbean Basin

Juana Santana works in the free trade zone of La Romana in the Dominican Republic and sustains her family of three children on her weekly salary of DR$57 (in 1986 about U.S.$20), which must cover household costs including food, rent, the baby-sitter, and her own expenses such as transportation and lunch. Her husband earns some money driving a taxi (*público*) owned by his family, but like many of the men living with the women workers in the free trade zones, he does not have a stable job. With three children to support, her husband's unstable income, and the high cost of living, Juana knows she has to continue working. She notes: "Anyway, I have to work, either in the zone or in a private home [as a domestic], anyway, because I, I cannot be dependent on my husband. Because what he earns is not enough, to help my family and to help me here at home."

Juana's situation is typical of what many women workers in the free trade zones face—low wages, poor working conditions, lack of inexpensive and adequate child care, limited job alternatives, partners who offer limited assistance or none at all, and an increasingly high cost of living. She also expresses women's increasing consciousness that they need to work and can no longer depend on a male breadwinner. The concept of the male breadwinner is becoming a myth as women worldwide become increasingly important contributors to the household economy.

The myth of the male breadwinner reflects many changes that have taken place as a result of the new international division of labor that started in the 1960s. Increased international competition from Japan and other newly industrializing countries (NICs) in Asia—such as Hong Kong, Taiwan, South Korea, and Singapore—and the high cost of labor in advanced industrial countries such as the United States led to the relocation of parts of many manufacturing processes to cheaper wage areas overseas, particularly in labor-intensive industries such as garments and electronics (Safa 1981). The search for cheap labor intensified in the 1980s as a result of the debt incurred by developing countries to foreign banks and multilateral lending institutions such as the World Bank. In order to pay off this debt and reduce their growing balance of payments deficit, developing countries encouraged exports and restricted imports. The redistributive welfare state was sharply curtailed both in advanced industrial and in developing countries as public services were reduced and privatized, placing additional burdens on households already suffering from lowered wages, rising inflation, and unemployment. The need for additional income forced growing numbers of women into the labor force, especially married women who were commonly assumed to be supplementary wage earners. From 1950 to 1980, the size of the female labor force in Latin America and the Caribbean increased threefold, with participation rates for women growing from 18 to 26 percent, a rate even faster than that for men and including all age groups (Safa 1992: 71–72). This increase reflected both a growth in the supply of women workers due to higher educational levels, lower fertility, and heavy rural-urban migration and an increasing demand for women in the growing service and export-processing sectors. From 1980 to 1988, women's share in the Latin American and Caribbean labor force as a whole rose from 33 percent to 38 percent (ECLAC 1992: 59), reflecting the continued higher rates of increase for women than for men.

Standing (1989) demonstrates that this pattern of "global feminization" of labor with increased female and declining male labor force participation is not confined to Latin America and the Caribbean but is found in many developing as well as advanced industrial countries where international competition, labor deregulation, and structural adjustment measures have weakened workers' bargaining power. Labor market deregulation cheapens wages by explicitly abandoning formal labor regulations or by simply weakening their implementation, as in the case of informal agreements between the state and multinational corporations to prohibit unionization in export-processing zones. Deregulation is manifest in a global shift from full-time wage and salary workers with fixed wages and fringe benefits to unprotected casual or temporary workers employed in export processing, subcontracting, and home work in the informal sector, all of which favor female employment. Women workers are preferred in export processing because they are cheaper to employ, less likely to unionize, and have greater patience for the tedious, monotonous work characteristic of assembly operations. Lim (1990: 105) estimates that in the mid-1980s there were approximately 1.5 million women directly employed in export manufacturing in developing countries, between a third and half of them in wholly or partly foreign-owned enterprises. Such enterprises include not only multinationals from the United States and other industrialized countries but also firms from other newly industrializing countries such as South Korea or Hong Kong. Most of these women are employed in Asia, with an increasing percentage in Latin America and the Caribbean. In 1983, Asia accounted for 55 percent of the world's employment in export processing, while Mexico, the Caribbean, and Central America represented 31 percent (Wilson 1992: 10). In 1993, the International Ladies' Garment Workers' Union (ILGWU) estimated that there were a half million workers in export manufacturing in Mexico and 320,000 more in the Caribbean and Central America, the majority in apparel and related trades (Justice 1993: 8).

Export-led industrialization actually represents the third stage in the international division of labor, which began in Latin America and the Caribbean in the colonial period with the export of primary products such as minerals and agricultural commodities such as sugar and coffee in exchange for manufactured goods from the United States and western Europe. To overcome this dependency and unequal exchange, Latin America embarked in the period following World War II on an ambitious program of import substitution industrialization, which was designed to promote national industries' providing consumer goods to their domestic markets. Import substitution industrialization was successful in promoting economic growth but ran into increasing difficulty, both because of the small size of the domestic markets and the low level of technology. These problems became more acute as import substitution tried to expand from labor-intensive industries such as food processing and textile manufacturing into capital-intensive industries, which required higher levels of technology and machinery that still had to be imported from abroad. In addition, national industries protected by high tariffs often tended to maintain inefficient productive processes, resulting in more costly and lower-quality consumer goods than those produced in more advanced industrial countries.

The debt crisis of the 1980s in Latin America and the Caribbean brought on by the increasing price of oil, deteriorating terms of trade with the United States and other advanced industrial countries, and spiraling interest rates caused a severe balance of payments deficit, which had to be reduced through exports. The need to export led to a shift in development strategies away from import substitution industrialization toward export manufacturing as a means toward industrialization and economic growth. But import substitution industrialization and export processing had very different implications for workers in developing countries. Import substitution required the development of an internal market through an increase in the purchasing power of workers, which favored wage increases, the strengthening of labor, and the development of the redistributive state. The market for export-led industrialization is external and demands the maximum reduction of production costs, principally wages, to compete effectively on the international level. Foreign investment is given priority over national industry and the domestic market shrank considerably in the 1980s as lower wages, inflation, and unemployment reduced purchasing power. As import substitution industrialization became more capital intensive, it also favored skilled male workers over unskilled females, but export processing employs more women, particularly in labor-intensive industries such as garment and electronics. The shift from import substitution industrialization to export-led industrialization thus contributed to a gender recomposition of the labor force, which weakened the dominance of the male breadwinner.

Studies of women workers in the export-processing industry provoked an intense debate over its impact on women's status, some arguing that it integrates women into the development process and others insisting that it exploits women as a source of cheap labor (Tiano 1986, Lim 1990, Fernandez-Kelly 1983). Recently, this debate has become less dichotomous, particularly as studies have gone beyond the labor process to examine the impact of wage labor on gender relations in the household. Paid employment has long been viewed as one way of breaking down women's isolation and dependence on men. Paid employment is expected to give women greater economic autonomy, to increase their authority in the household, and to develop their consciousness of gender and class subordination. However, there are many obstacles to achieving such goals, including the segregation of women into poorly paid, unstable jobs (such as export processing), their double burden of wage work and domestic labor, and a gender ideology that continues to portray women as "supplementary" workers, even when they are becoming increasingly important economic contributors to the household economy.

This book will compare the impact of paid industrial employment on women workers in Cuba, Puerto Rico, and the Dominican Republic, three countries that share a common cultural heritage rooted in Spanish colonialism, Catholicism, and a plantation economy focused on sugar. All were subjected to U.S. hegemony after the Spanish-American War in 1898. However, the three countries followed quite different patterns of industrialization in the post–World War II period. Export-led industrialization started in Puerto Rico in the late 1940s and was not adopted in the Dominican Republic until the 1960s, growing tremendously with the advent of the debt crisis in the 1980s. The Cuban revolution in 1959 led to a radical transformation to a socialist economy whereby the state took over most forms of production and focused primarily on sugar exports and import substitution industrialization. There has been an increase in female employment in all three countries since the 1960s, but in Puerto Rico and the Dominican Republic this has been accompanied by declining or stagnating rates of male employment. Import substitution industrialization, sugar production, and a policy of full male employment provided men with jobs in Cuba until the economic crisis in 1990 that resulted from the collapse of Cuba's trade with the former socialist countries of Eastern Europe and the Soviet Union, which occurred after this research was conducted. However, the redistributive policies of the Cuban socialist state also led to a decline in dependence on the male breadwinner, even within a context of full male employment.

All three countries have undergone a rapid transformation from an agrarian to an urban industrial economy since 1960, with profound consequences for the gender restructuring of the labor force. Though most previous studies of women workers in export-processing industries have focused on increasing female employment, I argue that a *gender* perspective is important both at the national and the household level in examining the impact of paid employment on women's status. Women gain little from increased employment if they are merely substituting their earnings for those of men. Unfortunately, this is often the case where development strategies favor female workers over men, as in the assembly-type export enclaves found in Puerto Rico and the Dominican Republic. Cuba's policies of promoting female employment within a context of full male employment were aimed at encouraging more egalitarian and stable gender relations, but the outcome has been somewhat different.

This study is based primarily on household surveys and in-depth interviews conducted in all three countries at various time periods. In 1980 I supervised a survey of 157 women workers in three Puerto Rican garment plants of the same manufacturer. In 1981, Centro de Investigación y Promoción de Acción Femenina (Center for Research and Promotion of Feminist Action) (CIPAF), a private Dominican women's research center, conducted a survey of 231 women workers in the three oldest export-processing zones of the Dominican Republic. In 1986 I conducted in-depth interviews with a sub-sample of working women surveyed in both countries, which enabled me to examine the effects of the economic crisis that occurred in the intervening period, particularly in the Dominican Republic. In 1986 a survey of 168 women workers in a large textile factory in Cuba was carried out by a team of re-searchers from the Federation of Cuban Women (FMC) under my super-vision, and I returned in 1987 to conduct in-depth interviews with a sub-sample of these women. Although there are considerable differences be-tween the garment and textile industries, my analysis focuses less on the labor process than on the impact of different development strategies on rates of male and female labor force participation and on changing gen-der roles in the household.

State Policy and Export-Led Industrialization in the Caribbean

In the smaller countries of Central America and the Caribbean, export promotion has long been the primary development strategy, ever since their incorporation into the world economy in colonial times. However, starting in the 1960s, in addition to traditional agricultural exports such as sugar, coffee, and bananas, there was an increase in manufacturing, following the "industrialization by invitation" strategy initiated by Puerto Rico a decade earlier. Import substitution industrialization, which was initiated in the post–World War II period to stimulate domes-tic industry in Latin America, never achieved the same levels in the Ca-ribbean Basin as in the larger countries of Latin America because of an even more acute lack of capital and technology. The small size of the Ca-ribbean Basin countries, combined with their low purchasing power, also limited the possibilities of developing a viable internal market, which is critical for import substitution. In order to gain access to for-eign markets, capital, and technology, Caribbean countries are much more dependent than larger Latin American countries on multinational corporations.

In recent years, spurred on by the debt crisis and growing unemploy-ment, the competition among Latin American and Caribbean countries for foreign investment in export manufacturing has been intense. Gov-ernments attempt to encourage foreign investment by lifting trade barri-ers and by offering tax holidays, subsidized credit, and export subsidies. Many countries in the Caribbean also allow unrestricted profit repatria-tion. Special export-processing zones are constructed at public expense for export manufacturing plants, complete with water, electricity, roads, and other services. Thus the state has played a major role in fostering ex-port manufacturing, often aided by the U.S. Agency for International Development (AID), which in the 1980s made this a key development strategy throughout Latin America and the Caribbean (Joekes with Moayedi 1987). This AID policy of financing and advertising free trade zones has recently come under sharp attack and has been subjected to some restrictions by the U.S. Congress as a result of U.S. labor unions' investigations into these practices and their denunciation of the consequent job loss for U.S. workers (Bradsher 1992: 5). From 1980 to 1993, the U.S. apparel industry lost nearly 300,000 jobs, and half of them are estimated to have moved to Mexico, the Caribbean, and Central America (Justice 1993: 8). This movement is expected to accelerate under the North American Free Trade Agreement (NAFTA).

Two key factors prompted U.S. government support for export manufacturing in the Caribbean region. As noted earlier, increasing competition from foreign imports, particularly from the newly industrializing countries in Asia, forced U.S. firms to cut labor costs by shifting the labor-intensive phase of production to cheaper wage areas abroad (Safa 1981). Though this process started with labor-intensive industries such as garments and electronics, it now includes heavy industries such as automobile assembly. Many of these are relocating to the U.S.-Mexican border—and they employ more men (Shaiken 1994). U.S. government policy also viewed export manufacturing as a way of improving the stagnant economies of the Latin American and Caribbean countries, where the debt crisis of the 1980s has been described in terms of a "lost decade." Political instability, particularly in Central America and the Caribbean, was also a prime consideration in promoting "security through development" (Deere et al. 1990: 154).

Special tariff programs were instituted to promote the relocation of labor-intensive phases of manufacturing abroad as early as the beginning of the 1960s through items 806.30 and 807 of the U.S. Tariff Codes, which reduced duties on imports with U.S. components assembled or processed abroad. These items aided the competitive position of U.S. industry by limiting U.S. tariffs to the "value added" upon goods assembled abroad, thus substantially reducing labor costs. Item 807 in particular provided the basis for the *maquiladora* (export-processing) plants under the Mexican Border Industrialization Program and stimulated the growth of assembly plants in the Caribbean as well, where manufacturing exports grew rapidly during the 1960s and 1970s (Deere et al. 1990: 143–144). The Generalized System of Preferences (GSP) enacted in 1974 authorizes the President to grant duty-free treatment to eligible products from third world countries for a period of ten years, provided that at least 35 percent of the products' total value comes from direct processing costs in those countries.

U.S. government support for export manufacturing in the Caribbean Basin was enhanced by the 1983 enactment of President Reagan's Caribbean Basin Initiative (CBI). The CBI enables qualified Caribbean Basin countries to acquire one-way, duty-free access to U.S. markets for certain exports for a 12-year period. Although textiles and garments have been excluded from the CBI, due to opposition from U.S. labor, certain Caribbean countries have been granted special import quotas by the United States through the Guaranteed Access Levels (GALS) program, sometimes referred to as 807A. Apparel imports to the United States under the GALS program have grown by 76 percent annually between 1987 and 1991, but they are limited to garments made entirely from U.S.-made and -cut fabric (Deere and Meléndez 1992).

Partly in response to early tariff incentives, U.S. investment in the Caribbean Basin between 1977 and 1982 was growing at a faster rate than in any other world region. According to a U.S. Department of Commerce survey released in 1988, the leading countries in terms of reported investments were the Dominican Republic, Jamaica, and Costa Rica, with 54 percent of the value of new investments of U.S. origin and 24 percent of Caribbean origin. The remainder represents increasing Asian investment in the region, concentrated in the garment sector, stemming in part from rising production costs at home and from the exclusion of South Korea, Singapore, Taiwan, and Hong Kong from the Guaranteed System of Preferences (GSP) program due to higher per capita income. Through relocation in the Caribbean Basin, Asian firms hope to regain privileged access to the U.S. market.

The composition of U.S. investment in the region also changed dramatically after 1984, mainly due to sharp cuts in investment in traditional commodities such as sugar in the Dominican Republic, bauxite in Jamaica, and petroleum in Trinidad. As a result, although mining and mineral products constituted over half of U.S. imports from Caribbean Basin countries in 1984, this had shifted to manufacturing by 1990 (Table 1.1). The shift toward export manufacturing in the Caribbean Basin implies a profound restructuring of the countries' economies away from these traditional commodities, which had been their principal exports for many years, into serving as a source of cheap labor for U.S. light industry.

The nature of this transformation differed in all three countries, due to differences in development strategies and social policy. Cuba's import substitution industrialization strategy was designed to fulfill domestic consumer demands and to boost sugar production, the primary source of foreign exchange. Socialist goals of redistribution were given priority over productivity, particularly in the first decade of the revolution, through programs of full employment, agrarian and urban reform, and ambitious programs to wipe out illiteracy and improve the health of the Cuban population. Puerto Rico also managed to achieve dramatic improvements in the areas of health, education, and housing, but much of

TABLE 1.1

Composition of U.S. Imports from CBERA[a] -Beneficiary Countries, 1984 and 1990
(Current U.S.$000's)

Sector	1984		1990	
	U.S.$000's	Percentage	U.S.$000's	Percentage
Agriculture and fishery	2,222.6	25.3	1,982.5	26.3
Mining and mineral products	4,459.2	50.8	1,520.0	20.2
Manufacturing	1,937.7	22.1	3,763.2	50.0
Other	162.2	1.8	259.5	3.5
Total	8,781.7	100.0	7,525.2	100.0

[a] Caribbean Basin Economic Recovery Act.
Source: Derived from U.S. Department of Labor, Bureau of International Labor Affairs, "Trade and Employment Effects of the Caribbean Basin Economic Recovery Act, Seventh Annual Report to the Congress" (Washington, DC: U.S. Department of Labor, 1991), Table 4. Reproduced from Deere and Meléndez 1992:70.

this was financed by U.S. federal funds to sustain a population with growing levels of unemployment. Industrialization in Puerto Rico was never able to absorb the surplus labor generated by the collapse of the sugar economy, particularly since many of the jobs created in labor-intensive industries were for women, and as a result, many Puerto Ricans migrated to the United States. The collapse of the market for traditional agricultural commodities, especially sugar, in the Dominican Republic led to an export promotion strategy focusing both on export manufacturing and non-traditional agricultural exports such as root crops, vegetables and horticultural crops, and tropical fruits, particularly pineapples. In both areas, the Dominican state played a key role, leasing cheap state-owned land to non-traditional agricultural exporters and keeping minimum wages low for both industry and agriculture (Raynolds 1994). However, neither of these efforts offset the lost foreign exchange earnings from sugar, and they made the economic crisis starting in the early 1980s particularly difficult for the Dominican population suffering from growing levels of unemployment, low wages, and cuts to already minimal state services.

My focus will be on the period since 1960, when the real impetus to industrialization began in the Dominican Republic and Cuba, though Puerto Rico's industrialization program began a decade earlier. This period accentuated divergences in state policy. Socialist Cuba broke all economic ties with the United States, which declared an embargo on all trade with the island, and became dependent on trade and aid from the former Soviet Union and other socialist countries in Eastern Europe. Puerto Rico, on the other hand, became increasingly dependent on U.S. investment, markets, and technology to support its export industrialization program and by the 1980s was already becoming a postindustrial economy. The Dominican Republic, like Cuba, remained dependent on sugar exports for foreign exchange earnings until the early 1980s, though a drive toward import substitution industrialization was started under Trujillo and accelerated in the 1960s and 1970s (Moya Pons 1990). Export manufacturing expanded rapidly in the 1980s, mainly due to the cut in the U.S. sugar quota and the need to find another source of foreign exchange. The reduction in Dominican labor costs due to the economic crisis and currency devaluation also represented real cost advantages to U.S. manufacturers, who were seeking to meet international competition. Thus, export-led industrialization in the Dominican Republic and Puerto Rico has increased U.S. hegemony, while the Cuban revolution broke U.S. control of that island's economy but resulted in increased dependence on trade and aid from the former Soviet Union.

In this study, I shall focus on the garment and textile industry, which along with electronics has been the area of greatest growth in export manufacturing in the Caribbean Basin. Between 1983 and 1986, textile and apparel imports into the United States from the region grew by an average annual 28 percent, increasing to 39 percent in 1987 and accounting for approximately one-fourth of all imports. Most of the growth in garment exports from the region is occurring under the provisions of items 807 and 807a (GALS), with exports from the Dominican Republic, Haiti, and Jamaica having increased by more than 20 percent annually during the 1980s (Deere et al. 1990: 167). In 1988, garments represented 78 percent of all manufacturing exports from the Dominican Republic, with a total value of U.S.$183.8 million, an increase of 333.4 percent since 1981. The Dominican Republic is now the leading source of garment manufacture in the Caribbean Basin (Dauhajre et al. 1989: 39–40, 98).

Garment and textile manufacturing have commonly represented the first stage of industrialization in both advanced industrial and developing countries, whether in earlier forms of industrialization in the nineteenth century or the more recently initiated export manufacturing. Developing countries have a comparative advantage in labor-intensive industries such as garment manufacture because they require relatively low levels of capital and technology but an abundance of cheap labor, provided chiefly by women. However, the enclave pattern of export-led industrialization in the Caribbean, combined with low investment in research and development and tariff regulations requiring the use of U.S. materials, results in little skill or technology transfer to these developing countries and dampens rather than stimulates domestic production. In a study of the Caribbean clothing industry, Steele argues that it "is the obvious intent of the U.S. administration to make it impossible for participating countries to build up substantial apparel industries which are not just offshore assembly operations for U.S. contractors but self-sufficient manufacturing enterprises such as those developed in the Big Three [Hong Kong, Taiwan, and South Korea] and other major garment supplying countries" (Steele 1988: 58). These tariff regulations were in part designed to appease U.S. labor unions opposed to offshore production.

In Puerto Rico and the Dominican Republic, most garment export manufacturing firms are direct subsidiaries of U.S. multinationals rather than domestic producers subcontracted to these foreign investors. In 1988, 63 percent of the export-processing firms in the Dominican Republic were owned by U.S. capital, compared to 10 percent Dominican (Abreu et al. 1989: 76), although the percentage of Dominican-owned plants has increased in recent years. There has also been growing investment from Korea and Hong Kong, since quotas imposed by the United States on these East Asian countries have limited their direct access to the U.S. market. U.S. investment is equally dominant in Puerto Rico, although the percentage of locally owned apparel firms has increased in recent years as the U.S.-owned garment industry went into decline (Priestland and Jones 1985). This heavy dependence of the garment industry on U.S. capital, technology, and markets plus the lack of linkages to the domestic economy in all areas but labor significantly reduce the country's ability to generate capital and more indigenous and capital-intensive forms of industrial production, either in export processing or in the domestic economy, as Asia was able to do. It also limits the growth of male employment. Unlike the Asian export model, export-led industrialization in the Caribbean increases dependence on the U.S. and contributes little to the general economic development of these small and open economies.

In the Caribbean, the state's principal role in export manufacturing is to create a favorable climate for foreign investment through investment incentives and the control of wages and labor. Most workers in Caribbean export-processing zones are entitled to the minimum wage, but can boost their wages by surpassing their production quotas, since they are paid on a piece-rate system. Hourly minimum wages vary considerably between countries, with a high in 1988 of $4.28 an hour in Puerto Rico (where the federal minimum wage applies) to a low of $.55 an hour in the Dominican Republic (Table 1.2). Labor control can be achieved through outright repression or prohibition of unions in free trade zones, as in the Dominican Republic, or through cooptation of labor, as in Puerto Rico. Both repression and cooptation lead to a weak and frag-

TABLE 1.2

Comparative Hourly Wage Levels in the Caribbean Region, 1988

Country	Hourly Rate in U.S.$ [a]
Dominican Republic	.55
Haiti	.58
Grenada	.75
St. Lucia	.75
Dominica	.83
Belize	.85
Jamaica	.88
St. Kitts	.90
Montserrat	.92
St. Vincent	1.15
Antigua	1.25
Trinidad-Tobago	1.80
Netherlands Antilles	1.80
Bahamas	2.10
Barbados	2.10
Puerto Rico	4.28
U.S. Virgin Islands	4.50

[a] Hourly wages include fringe benefits; the data are for semi-skilled labor in export processing industries.

Source: The Bobbin Consulting Group (Columbia, SC), 1988, pamphlet. Reproduced from Deere et al. 1990:149.

mented labor movement that increases the vulnerability of women (and male) workers in both countries.

Both labor and the state were further weakened by the economic crisis that hit most of the Caribbean in the mid-1970s and 1980s. The economic crisis has made Caribbean countries even more dependent on export promotion to address the decline in the balance of payments, to service their debts, and to reduce growing unemployment. Many Caribbean and Latin American states have been forced to adopt International Monetary Fund (IMF) structural adjustment policies, which further reduce their control over the economy and usually involve a cut in government services and personnel. Labor is also weakened by structural adjustment measures that generally result in higher levels of unemployment and lower real wages.

State policy toward export-led industrialization differs somewhat in Puerto Rico because of its continued colonial status as a U.S. territory. This status assures Puerto Rico of free access to the U.S. market but restricts the range of permissible economic and political activity and makes the economy very dependent on federal transfer payments to sustain an increasingly impoverished population. U.S. corporations located in Puerto Rico pay no federal corporate income tax, though they are subject to a 10 percent Puerto Rican tollgate tax if their profits are re-patriated immediately. The Dominican Republic has greater political autonomy but is increasingly dependent on U.S. market forces to sustain its economy. State economic policy has basically been set by a "predatory state" instigated by the dictator Trujillo, who ruled the country from 1930 to 1961. Despite elections and lip service to increasing democratic participation, the state has continued to serve the interests of the agrarian and industrial elite with little attention to the needs of the poor.

All three countries have experienced increased female labor force participation rates. However, in Cuba the increase in female labor force participation is due not so much to the demand for female labor in industrial jobs, as in the Dominican Republic and earlier in Puerto Rico, as to wage and consumer policies of the Cuban state instituted in the 1970s, which promoted women's incorporation into paid employment. The increasing percentage of women in the labor force and other social policies have also contributed to changes in gender roles at the household level, but women are not replacing men as the principal breadwinner among the women workers studied, as in Puerto Rico and the Dominican Republic. I shall show the impact of the different development strategies in these three countries on male and female participation rates in the following pages.

The Rise and Decline of Operation Bootstrap

Puerto Rico's export-led industrialization program, known as Operation Bootstrap, started much earlier than similar programs in other Caribbean countries, stimulated by free access to the U.S. market. The first industrial incentives act passed in 1947 was part of an ambitious program to diversify the economy away from monocrop agriculture (basically sugar) and to improve the level of living through increased employment and heavy investment in housing, health care, and education. Operation Bootstrap actually went through three stages, changing in focus from labor intensive to capital intensive in the mid-1960s and initiating a third stage of high-tech industrialization in the mid-1970s. Although different in emphasis, no one stage eclipsed the other, so that labor-intensive industries such as apparel continued to provide the major source of female employment in manufacturing in the 1980s. The industrialization program was initially designed to provide employment to men displaced from agricultural employment, but women became the primary labor force in the labor-intensive factories attracted in the first stage such as apparel and food processing.

Although growth in manufacturing output more than tripled from 1950 to 1980, it still could not offset the enormous declines in agriculture over this period. In 1940, agriculture employed 44.7 percent of the labor force and manufacturing 10.9 percent; in 1980, agriculture had declined to 5.2 percent, while manufacturing nearly doubled to 19 percent (Dietz 1986: 258). Some of this surplus labor was absorbed in services and particularly in public administration, but many workers migrated to the United States. Migration peaked in the 1950s, precisely when Operation Bootstrap was taking off, and continued at high levels until 1970, totaling in this 20-year period about 605,550 persons, a figure equivalent to 27.4 percent of the 1950 population (Dietz 1986: 286). Men slightly outnumbered women, and most were in the most productive age groups between 15 and 39. Given the "safety valve" of migrating workers, unemployment rates declined somewhat from 1950 to 1970. But the decreasing and in some years reverse flow of migration in the 1970s increased unemployment rates considerably in 1980, especially for men (Table 1.3). Unemployment rates continue to be higher for men than for women, and in our sample survey of garment workers, 90 percent say it is easier for a woman than for a man to find a job. In addition, male labor force participation rates declined about 20 percent between 1950 and 1980 (Table 1.3), reflecting both the precipitous decline in agricultural employment and declining out-migration after 1970. Increasing levels of higher education also kept young men (and women) out of the labor market. However, women were affected less negatively than men, and after an initial decline from 1950 to 1960, their participation rates rose again to 31.4 percent in 1990. Women were absorbed into export manufacturing, particularly during the first stage of labor-intensive industrialization in the 1960s, and later into growing trade and public administration sectors (Acevedo 1990: 240). Overall participation rates also declined 10 percent during this 40-year period, as Puerto Ricans withdrew entirely from the labor force, relying on transfer payments or unreported work in the informal sector.

Growing male unemployment, higher wages, and the increasing cost of transportation were factors that prompted the inauguration in the mid-1960s of the second stage of industrialization, focusing on capital-intensive industries such as petrochemicals and pharmaceuticals, which employed more men (Ríos 1990). Higher wages reflected the rising cost of living as well as efforts on the part of U.S. unions to close the wage gap between the mainland and the island. In 1950, the average hourly wage in manufacturing was only 28 percent of the U.S. wage, but the full extension of U.S. minimum wage laws to Puerto Rico in 1981 considerably reduced wage differences. In apparel, for example, the dif-

TABLE 1.3

Rates of Labor Force Participation and Unemployment for Females and Males
in Puerto Rico, 1950-1990
Percentages

	Females		*Males*		*Both*
	Ages 14+	*Ages 16+*	*Ages 14+*	*Ages 16+*	
Labor force participation rates:					
1950	30.0	--	79.8	--	54.6
1960	20.1	--	71.5	--	45.5
1970	--	28.0	--	70.8	48.0
1980	--	27.8	--	60.7	43.3
1990	--	31.4	--	61.6	45.4
Percent of the civilian labor force unemployed:					
1950	13.1	--	15.3	--	14.7
1960	10.4	--	12.7	--	12.1
1970	--	10.2	--	11.0	10.7
1980	--	12.3	--	19.5	17.1
1990	--	10.7	--	16.2	14.2

Source: Estado Libre Asociado de Puerto Rico, Departamento del Trabajo y Recursos Humanos, 1991 *Serie Histórica del Empleo, Desempleo, Grupo Trabajador en Puerto Rico 1947-1990.* These figures rely on sample population surveys conducted by the P. R. Department of Labor, but are generally deemed more reliable than the census.

ferences ranged from 35 percent of U.S. earnings in 1955 to 75 percent in 1983 (Priestland and Jones 1985: 26). Despite these increases, apparel remained the lowest-paying industry on the island, with an average hourly wage in 1985 of $3.95 an hour.

Capital-intensive industries were adversely affected by the oil crisis of the 1970s, which virtually eliminated the petrochemical industry, and the economic crisis that hit Puerto Rico and the United States in 1974. Capital-intensive industries also did little to alleviate unemployment, even for men, and remained heavily dependent on U.S. investment. Investors, primarily external, absorbed an average of 75 percent of the net income from these capital-intensive industries and failed to develop backward or forward linkages to the Puerto Rican economy, so that these industries constituted an export enclave similar to the garment or sugar industries that preceded them. Though capital-intensive industries employed more men than women, the total number of jobs generated was small, due to a higher capital-labor ratio. The indirect employment effects were also minimal (Dietz 1986: 254).

In an attempt to attract more stable industries catering to a highly skilled and more well-paid labor force, Puerto Rico in the mid-1970s initiated the third stage of industrialization, focusing primarily on high-tech industries such as electronics and scientific instruments. However, at this stage, manufacturing played a secondary role to the growth of the service sector, and industrial incentives were extended to include export-service industries such as investment banking, public relations, insurance, and computer services. Puerto Rico's role as the leading financial, administrative, and trade center for the Caribbean was reinforced in 1976 by Section 936 of the U.S. Internal Revenue Code, which allowed U.S. subsidiaries in Puerto Rico to repatriate their profits free of federal taxes. Profits were still subject to a 10 percent Puerto Rican tollgate tax, but this could be reduced by reinvesting or depositing these funds in Puerto Rican banks for a certain period. Section 936 made Puerto Rico into a major tax haven for manufacturing multinationals within the United States, which included sheltering profits derived from production elsewhere (Pantojas-García 1990). This continued dependence of Puerto Rican export manufacturing on U.S. investment and inputs failed to generate self-sustained growth, despite the move into capital-intensive and high-tech industries.

Each of these stages in the industrialization process affected female employment. Women constituted the primary labor force in the early stages of labor-intensive industrialization, which required large supplies of cheap labor. More than half of all new jobs created between 1960 and 1980 went to women, and in 1988 they still constituted 47 percent of all workers in the manufacturing sector (Santiago-Rivera 1993: 147). Though capital-intensive industries favored male workers, women were also attracted to better-paying white-collar jobs, particularly in the government, which had become the principal source of employment in Puerto Rico by 1980. It seems that Puerto Rican women may be experiencing a bifurcation in the labor force, with younger, more educated women entering these newer white-collar professions, while older, less-educated women remain in declining manufacturing industries and low-paying service jobs (Acevedo 1989: 12). This helps account for the older age of our Puerto Rican sample, where over 75 percent of the women garment workers are over 30 years old and two-thirds are married. This contrasts sharply with the average profile of women workers in export manufacturing, most of whom are young (as in the Dominican Republic) and single.

The relatively high educational levels and low fertility levels among the Puerto Rican women in our sample result in part from conscious state policies to upgrade the labor force and reduce population growth. In 1980, when this survey was conducted, 39 percent of all Puerto Rican women were high school graduates, which corresponds to the percentage in our sample, while fertility rates had declined to 2.8 births per woman, again approximately the same as the rates among our sample (Presser and Kishor 1991: 60–61). This had declined again to 2.2 births per woman by 1990.

Both higher educational levels and lower fertility levels contributed to an improvement in the female occupational profile and to their higher labor force participation rates. In addition, women have been working more because of the rising cost of living and increasing unemployment and declining real wages among men, making it necessary for both husband and wife to contribute to the household economy. Nearly three-fourths of our sample of Puerto Rican women garment workers claim their families could not survive without their working, and the woman's salary never represents less than 40 percent of the total annual household income, even among single women, and is usually higher among married women and especially female heads of household. Thus, Puerto Rico's form of export-led industrialization, by providing more jobs for women than for men, has contributed to the weakening of the man's role as primary breadwinner in many Puerto Rican households, leading to new patterns of authority and gender roles.

However, the increasing incorporation of women into the labor force could not meet the economic needs of many of the Puerto Rican poor, particularly given high unemployment and a rising cost of living. The percentage of households headed by women also rose from 16 to 19 percent from 1970 to 1980, and to 23.2 percent in the 1990 census.[1] This was due in part to a high divorce rate, to which the marginalization of men may have contributed. As a result, many poor families, including the working poor employed in low-wage industries such as apparel, became increasingly dependent on transfer payments to support themselves. These are primarily federal funds in the form of social security and food assistance payments, which grew from 12 percent of personal income in 1950 to 30 percent by 1980. Food stamps, or *cupones* as they are known in Puerto Rico, began in the mid-1970s and the program grew to reach 58.4 percent of the population in 1980 (Dietz 1986: 299), declining to 47 percent in the 1990 census. In our 1980 sample, only 19 percent of the households received food stamps, chiefly large families with many young children or households headed by women. While seen as subsidies to workers, these transfer payments are also aids to low-wage industries like apparel that do not pay an adequate wage and might otherwise leave the island because of wage increases or a shortage of cheap labor. By providing alternative or supplementary sources of income, transfer payments further reduce a woman's dependence on a male wage but increase her dependence on the state. Transfer payments, combined with slow job growth and migration, also contributed to declining overall participation rates so that by 1983, over one-half of all families were without any resident wage earner (Amott and Matthaei 1991: 278).

These social support measures, in addition to ambitious government programs in housing, education, and health, helped to underwrite the costs of social reproduction for the working class as well as to contain class conflict. State policy was directed at containing and coopting the labor movement rather than repressing it as in the Dominican Republic and other Latin American countries. Industrialization also led to a profound recomposition of the working class and paradoxically, to a weakening of the labor movement, since the strength of the militant labor union among sugar cane workers was sapped by the decline of the sugar industry and the increasing fragmentation and diversification of the industrial labor force. Fragmentation and competition between labor unions was accentuated by the rapid growth of AFL-CIO affiliates, in which the ILGWU played a leading role. Though unionized, most women workers in our sample regard the ILGWU as a company union that does little to defend their interests or invite rank-and-file participation. The union's primary interest is in containing worker demands to retard the flight of garment plants to cheaper wage areas elsewhere, but as we shall see, they have not been very successful. In addition, the proportion of unionized workers in Puerto Rico as a whole dropped from 20 percent in 1970 to 6 percent in 1988, which can be partially blamed on unions' neglect of women workers (Santiago-Rivera 1989: 93).

The final blow to the labor movement and to the industrialization program came with Puerto Rico's loss of its comparative advantage as a source of cheap labor to Mexico and other Caribbean countries, who also offered tax incentives and even lower wages. In the 1960s, many countries such as Mexico, Jamaica, the Dominican Republic, and the newly industrializing Asian countries began to copy Puerto Rico's export-led industrialization strategy. High wages plus duty-free access to the United States, which most Caribbean countries acquired in 1983 through the Caribbean Basin Initiative, eliminated Puerto Rico's one remaining competitive advantage, particularly in labor-intensive industries in which labor costs are a prime consideration. Puerto Rico has tried to counter this competition in manufacturing with the establishment of twin plants, utilizing funds accumulated under Section 936; these plants are similar to those along the U.S.-Mexican border, where the final and more skilled stages of the manufacturing operations are carried out on the island, with the initial assembly stages in the Dominican Republic, Haiti, and other Caribbean islands.

Competition from cheaper wage areas brought about a sharp decline in the Puerto Rican garment industry, as its percentage of total manufacturing employment decreased from 25 percent in 1977 to 21 percent in 1984 (Priestland and Jones 1985: Table 1). As the garment industry declined, the structure of production also shifted from transnational to local capital, often subcontracted to larger U.S. firms. In 1983, 50 percent of garment plants were locally owned and were usually smaller and less capitalized than U.S. plants, employing 31 percent of the total labor force in the garment industry (Priestland and Jones 1985: Tables 2 and 3). In 1983, it was estimated that $50 million, or one-fourth of the value of local production, was manufactured in *marquesina* or carport operations, that is, small workshops in the underground economy (Priestland and Jones 1985: 20). Women are the principal workers in these illegal operations. In the early 1980s they were paid as little as $1.00 per hour and were given no fringe benefits, which also reduces the cost to employers. However, since much of this income is unreported, it may be more easily combined with transfer payments such as public assistance, unemployment insurance, or social security, and it is also not subject to taxation. As in the United States, this type of underground economy lowers both the labor and infrastructure costs of production (Fernandez-Kelly and Sassen 1995). The growth of the underground economy is symptomatic of the decline in the established garment industry and may be contributing to it through additional competition.

Despite its problems, Operation Bootstrap transformed Puerto Rico from an agrarian to an urban, industrial economy, with a ten-fold increase in per capita Gross National Product (GNP) between 1950 and 1980 (Dietz 1986: 244). With its transformation into an increasingly important financial center, Puerto Rico now has been totally integrated into the U.S. economy, as external investment has shifted from sugar plantations, to manufacturing, and now to banks and other commercial institutions. But even with massive migration and transfer payments, Operation Bootstrap failed to provide sufficient income or jobs to sustain the population. Gross inequalities in income remain, with 55 percent of working families in the 1990 census falling below the poverty level. Most families can no longer survive on a single wage, so that even when men are employed, their wives are generally also working. Women must often assume full economic responsibility if they are female heads of households or when their husbands are unemployed. Thus, not only did the industrialization program create an initial demand for female labor, but the continuing poverty of much of the population has made it necessary for women to work. Both demand and supply factors have weakened the man's role as breadwinner and have resulted in women becoming major contributors to the household economy. A similar change has occurred as a result of the export-led industrialization program in the Dominican Republic, as shown in the following pages.

The Dominican Republic: Export Manufacturing and the Economic Crisis

Although both countries underwent a rapid transformation from an agrarian to an industrial economy, the development process in the Dominican Republic has differed considerably from that of Puerto Rico. The Dominican Republic remained dependent on agricultural exports, principally sugar, until the early 1980s, when the United States drastically cut its sugar quotas. Still, employment in the agricultural sector began to decline in 1960, with a decrease from 60.6 percent to 25.3 percent in 1990, while industrial and particularly service and commercial employment increased substantially (Table 1.4). Services include domestic service, which in 1991 still employed nearly one-third of the economically active Dominican women. Despite its decline, agriculture has continued to be the primary source of employment for men, and in 1991 employed 36 percent of the economically active Dominican men (Ramírez 1993: 15).

Industrialization started much later in the Dominican Republic than in Puerto Rico and focused largely on import substitution until the massive and rapid expansion of export manufacturing in the 1980s, resulting largely from the reduction in the cost of labor due to the economic crisis and currency devaluation. Manufacturing exports grew 307.4 percent between 1981 and 1988 to U.S.$502.1 million, with textiles and garments averaging 35.8 percent of the value of exports during this period (Dauhajre et al. 1989: 38–39). The number of free trade zones and workers rose spectacularly between 1985 and 1992, when there were a total of 140,000 workers in 27 free trade zones in various regions of the country (Table 1.5). In 1992, about 60 percent of these jobs were held by women, and about half were still employed in the three original free trade zones studied here (Consejo Nacional de Zonas Francas de Exportación 1993).

The sharp increase in export manufacturing is directly attributable to currency devaluations mandated by the International Monetary Fund, which lowered the cost of labor and other expenses in the Dominican Republic to one of the lowest levels in the Caribbean. Despite several increases in the minimum wage, the real hourly minimum wage in the Dominican Republic declined 62.3 percent between 1984 and 1990 (Fundapec 1992: 32). From 1981 to 1991, about one-fourth of the population were unemployed, and unemployment continues to be much

TABLE 1.4

Sectoral Composition of Economically Active Population[a]
Dominican Republic 1970-1991
Percentages

Activity	1960	1970	1981	1991
Agriculture	60.6	45.3	23.6	25.3
Industry[b]	11.4	10.9	18.2	20.6
Commerce, restaurants, and hotels	6.7	6.4	10.8	19.9
Services	18.1	17.9	23.9	34.2
Unspecified	3.2	9.5	23.6	--

[a] Economically active population, 10 years and over, and only including the employed and those of the unemployed actively seeking employment.

[b] Manufacturing, sugar, construction, minerals, and electricity.

Source: Ramírez 1988:45 and for 1991, Ramírez 1993:15.

higher for women than for men (46.7 percent vs. 11.8 percent respectively in 1991) (Ramírez 1993: 10). However, two-thirds of the economically active women are salaried, compared to 46 percent of the men, showing that women are surpassing men in formal wage labor. In contrast, a higher percentage of men than women are self-employed (38 percent vs. 24 percent) (Ramírez 1993: 19), suggesting that men in particular are being absorbed in the informal sector. Underemployment in the Dominican Republic is very high and in 1980 was estimated at 43 percent (Ramírez et al. 1988: 47). The economic crisis also led to an extraordinary growth in international migration from 1985 to 1989, mostly to the United States. Migrants are generally younger, urban residents, and about half are women, many of whom are in professional or clerical jobs (Ramírez 1992: 110).

The steady reduction in U.S. sugar quotas from the Dominican Republic starting in the early 1980s aggravated the economic crisis and the need for foreign exchange and additional sources of employment. The Dominican Republic accounts for roughly half the U.S. sugar quota from the Caribbean Basin, and its reduction resulted in a decline in sugar export revenues from a high of U.S.$555 million in 1981 to U.S.$191 million in 1989 (Raynolds 1994: Table 1). Agriculture for domestic consumption and import substitution industrialization also stagnated, which had a negative effect on employment, particularly for men. Private domestic investment fell after 1983 while foreign investment grew, especially in tourism and export manufacturing (Fundapec 1992: 43), both of which employ large numbers of women. However, export manufacturing contributes less to gross domestic product (GDP) than sugar production, since the value-added component of sugar is estimated to be as high as 90 percent, while garments assembled from

TABLE 1.5

Growth in Employment in Dominican Free Trade Zones

Year	Number of Employees
1981	19,456
1982	19,236
1983	21,387
1984	25,099
1985	22,720
1986	48,603
1987	72,735
1988	85,000
1992	140,000

Source: Corporación de Fomento Industrial. 1992 figures from Consejo Nacional de Zonas Francas de Exportación, Dominican Republic, 1993.

U.S.-made and -cut cloth average, at most, 27 percent (Deere and Meléndez 1992: 63–66).

Export manufacturing was attracted by the abundance of low-cost female labor in the Dominican Republic. Female labor force rates in the Dominican Republic quadrupled from 9.3 percent in 1960 to 38 percent in 1990 (Table 1.6). Several factors in the development process favored this dramatic increase, including urbanization, the growth of the service sector, and the growth of export processing. Internal migration has increased considerably in the Dominican Republic since 1950, and in 1990, 59 percent of the population lived in urban areas. Female labor force rates are considerably higher for women in urban areas, and the unemployment rates are lower, which helps explain why women migrate in larger numbers. Male labor force participation rates declined 10 percent between 1950 and 1960, reflecting increased enrollment at higher educational levels and slow job growth, and then they stabilized. Male unemployment, lower wages, and inflation increased the pressure on women to work to add to the household income.

Demographic changes also have been taking place in the Dominican female population since 1960 that make women more employable, including rising educational levels and marked decreases in fertility. It is estimated that total fertility rates have declined from 7.3 births per woman in the 1960/1965 period to 3.3 from 1990 to 1995. Educational levels have grown as fast for women as for men, and in 1981, 15.5 percent of employed women had a university education (Báez 1991: 2–4). Despite a generally low level of public expenditure in social services, there have been notable gains in the health and educational levels of the population. From 1950 to 1980, illiteracy decreased from 57 percent to 25 percent, the gross general mortality rate was reduced by 60 percent,

TABLE 1.6

Female and Male Labor Force Participation in the Dominican Republic
Percentages

	1950	1960	1970	1980	1990
Female	16.0	9.3	25.1	28.0	38.0
Male	85.1	75.9	72.6	72.0	72.2
Total	50.6	42.8	48.8	49.5	54.7

Source: Ramírez 1988:41. 1990 figures from Báez 1991. Includes economically active population 10 years and older.

and the infant mortality rate decreased 43 percent, while life expectancy increased from 43 to 61 years (Ramírez et al. 1988: 143). However, the economic crisis in the early 1980s cut government expenditures in health, education, and other services considerably. The rural population still suffers from inferior schooling, lower literacy rates, and less access to public services such as piped water and electricity. Income distribution remains highly unequal, with 10 percent of the population receiving more than one-third of all income from 1967 through 1984 (Ramírez et al. 1988: 49). Disparities in income distribution have been aggravated by the economic crisis, and in 1991, 1.8 percent of the households receiving the highest monthly per capita income of more than DR$5,000 accounted for 22.2 percent of all income (Ramírez 1992: 120).

By 1981 women already constituted 40 percent of the workers in the non-sugar manufacturing sector, most of them concentrated in the free trade zones (Duarte et al. 1989: 124). In the 1990s, export manufacturing constitutes one of the most important sources of urban employment for women. Garment firms employing a largely female labor force have always predominated in the Dominican free trade zones, and they constituted 67 percent of all firms in 1992 (Consejo Nacional de Zonas Francas 1993). Clearly export manufacturing is a key component of Dominican development strategy and has had a major impact on women's incorporation into the labor force.

Working women are becoming major economic contributors to the household, and in our sample of Dominican women workers in export manufacturing, 38 percent consider themselves to be the major economic provider. Like most women workers in export manufacturing worldwide, Dominican women in our sample are young rural migrants (75 percent are under 30 years of age), and two-thirds have no previous work experience, which increases their vulnerability. However, contrary to global patterns, more than half of the Dominican women workers sampled are married, and over one-fourth are female heads of household, who carry the heaviest financial responsibility since most are the principal or sole economic provider. As in Puerto Rico, the percentage of Dominican female heads of household has increased, standing at 24.1 percent in 1984 (Gómez 1990: 27) and at 29.5 percent in 1991 (Ramírez 1992: 120), which may again be partially attributed to the economic marginalization of men. The inability of men to fulfill their role as economic provider may be contributing to marital instability in both countries.

Popular protests against the IMF and the effects of structural adjustment have grown during the crisis and point to the weak ability of organized labor to channel workers' anger, mainly due to labor's own disunity. Seven labor confederations emerged in the 1980s, each tied to different political parties or factions of parties, while levels of unionization remained low, never representing more than 10 or 15 percent of the labor force (Espinal 1988: 26–27). A decline in sugar prices and the drastic reduction of U.S. sugar quotas in 1985 and 1986 led to the closing of six state-owned sugar mills, representing the most highly organized labor sector, and the loss of thousands of jobs as well as much-needed export revenues. Although not legally prohibited, few unions operate in the free trade zones, and workers are fired and blacklisted with other firms for participation in union organizing.[2] Discontent is expressed in turnover or eventual withdrawal rather than through labor organizing. Dominican women workers in export manufacturing receive little support from the government in their struggle for better wages and working conditions, and those who have tried to take complaints of mistreatment or unjust dismissal to the Ministry of Labor have generally been rejected in favor of management.

Despite the spectacular increase in export manufacturing in the Dominican Republic, the contribution it makes to economic development is questionable. Though export manufacturing was designed to alleviate unemployment and to produce badly needed foreign exchange, neither goal has been adequately achieved. The jobs created in the free trade zones have been primarily for women and have contributed to an increase in their labor force participation without reducing unemployment for men, many of whom are being absorbed in the informal sector. The wages paid these women workers are extremely low and thus generate few demand linkages to the rest of the economy. Moreover, because of heavy reliance on imported inputs, Dominican export manufacturing is an inefficient generator of foreign exchange compared to traditional agricultural products such as sugar. As a result, despite the five-fold increase in the total value of exports from the Dominican free trade zones from 1980 to 1988, from $117 million to $517 million, the economy remained virtually stagnant, with average GDP growth rates reaching only 1.1 percent per annum during this period (Deere and Meléndez 1992). The fundamental reason is to be found in U.S. trade policies, which reduced export manufacturing in the Dominican Republic (and throughout the Caribbean Basin) to assembly operations, with very few domestic inputs. Since the tariff programs under which most of these export manufactures (and particularly apparel) enter the United States mandate the use of U.S. materials, the dutiable portion of 806-807 imports has not exceeded 32 percent of total import value since 1985, while under the GALS program, the dutiable portion on apparel imports is even lower, 26 to 27 percent. The Dominican Republic is the largest source of 806-807 imports from the Caribbean Basin, and U.S. imports from that country grew at the rate of 8.4 percent a year from 1984 to 1990, but basically the country served as a source of cheap labor for U.S. export platforms. If one adds to this the cost to the government of building infrastructure for the free trade zones, lost fiscal revenues due to tax holidays, and the guarantee to investors of unrestricted profit repatriation, then this form of export manufacturing appears unlikely to promote self-generating growth and development in the Dominican Republic.

Cuba: Gender Equality and the Revolution

In Cuba, state policy is more important in shaping the increase in female employment than the supply and demand factors in the capitalist economies of Puerto Rico and the Dominican Republic. As a socialist economy, almost 95 percent of Cuban workers are employed by the state, which has nationalized virtually all sectors of the economy except for 20 percent of agricultural land that remained in the hands of small private farmers (Mesa Lago 1981: 112). The state is committed to a policy of full employment for men and has actively promoted women's incorporation into the labor force as a means of promoting greater gender equality. Class inequality has played a far more important role in the Cuban revolution than gender, and the redistribution of wealth through measures such as free health and education, low-cost housing, agrarian reform, and rent reduction coexists with the dual goal of greater productivity. It is the tension between redistribution and productivity or between equity and growth and their respective correlates in moral and material incentives that marks the different stages of the Cuban revolution, each of which has had a differential impact on women's labor force incorporation.

In 1955, prior to the revolution, women's labor force participation was only 13 percent (Table 1.7), very low for a relatively modernized country with high levels of urbanization and literacy. As in the case of the Do-

TABLE 1.7

Cuban Male and Female Labor Force Participation Rates, 1955-1990
Percentages

| Year | *Labor Force Participation Rates* | | |
	Women	Men	Both
1955	13.0	78.8	43.3
1970	15.9	67.4	42.3
1975	21.1	63.0	42.3
1980	26.7	61.0	44.0
1985	30.0	62.9	46.6
1990	34.8	67.8	51.3

Source: Valdés and Gomariz, eds., *Mujeres Latinoamericananas en Cifras*, 1992:38. 1990 data based on estimations made by CELADE (the Latin American Demographic Center) using census data for the population aged 15 and over, These are considerably lower than Cuban data.

minican Republic in 1960, this low figure can be explained partly by the emphasis on sugar exported primarily to the United States. Though 53 percent of Cubans lived in urban areas, agriculture still provided the principal source of employment to men but employed only 5.7 percent of all working women, since most agricultural work was heavy manual wage labor for men on sugar plantations (Pérez-Stable 1993). One-fourth of working women were employed in domestic service, and only one in six were professionals (mostly teachers), although educational levels were nearly equal for both sexes. Very few married women worked outside the home, particularly among the elite despite their comparatively advanced education, because it signified that their husbands could not afford to maintain them. Again as in the Dominican Republic, the sharpest disparities were between the urban and rural areas, particularly between Havana and the rest of the island, on several social indicators such as schooling, literacy, health, housing, and income distribution. Though in Cuba as a whole, illiteracy in 1953 stood at 23.6 percent and infant mortality at 37.6 per thousand births (among the lowest rates in Latin America), these figures were much higher in the rural areas, where there was less access to schooling and health facilities, and malnutrition and poverty were widespread. Poverty in the rural areas was mainly due to high levels of rural unemployment and underemployment, particularly in sugar production, which only provided massive employment during the harvest season. This helps explain why the 1953 census, conducted during the harvest, revealed a comparatively low (8.4 percent) level of unemployment, while average annual unemployment ran between 16 and 20 percent and had remained unchanged for 15 years (Pérez-Stable 1993). About one-fourth of the economically active population were also self-employed, many of them small farmers often earning a precarious existence. Sugar production provided Cuba with the engine of growth but also the deterrent to greater economic diversification and economic autonomy, which the revolution sought to eliminate.

The Cuban revolution in 1959 was aimed at achieving social justice and economic and political autonomy through a total break with the past in terms of dependence on sugar and on the United States. The government embarked on an ambitious program of industrial development in the early 1960s, but it was short-lived as sugar again took over the economy. From 1963 to 1970, the entire economy was geared toward sugar production for export for capital accumulation, as seen most dramatically in the failed attempt at reaping a 10-million-ton harvest in 1970. More than half this sugar was sold (usually in kind) to the former Soviet Union, which became Cuba's principal trading partner after the U.S. blockade eliminated all forms of economic exchange with the United States. Key redistributive mechanisms were initiated during this first decade, including agrarian and urban reform, employment expansion, wage increases, and universal social security coverage, which reduced the retirement age of men to 60 and women to 55. Redistribution reveals the revolution's commitment to the poor and to the reduction of inequality, as well as Fidel Castro's and Che Guevara's desire to develop *conciencia* or consciousness through moral incentives. By emphasizing social justice (and national defense), the revolutionary government hoped that Cubans would give up striving for individual gain and material incentives and concentrate on the collective welfare. The government also hoped paid employment would integrate women into the revolution and develop their consciousness as workers.

In the first decade alone, notable achievements were made in areas such as education, health, and income distribution. By 1962, the income share of the richest 10 percent of the Cuban population had been reduced to 23 percent from 38.8 percent in 1953 (Brudenius 1990: Table 10.3). However, redistributive measures also reduced the need to work, since less purchasing power was required to secure items provided free or at reduced cost by the state, and this contributed to absenteeism, high turnover, and low productivity. Entrance into the labor force was also delayed because of prolonged schooling, while exit was facilitated by early retirement, so that the percentage of economically active men actually decreased somewhat from the prerevolutionary period, in which employment ensured survival (Table 1.7). As a result of all these factors, domestic productivity dropped, adding to the shortage of consumer goods provoked by the U.S. blockade.

Despite the Cuban revolutionary government's efforts to increase female labor force participation during the first decade of the revolution, by 1970 the rate for women had risen to only 16 percent (Table 1.7). The reasons for this lie primarily in the lack of material incentives rather than a lack of demand for female labor. During the first decade of the revolution, there were few consumer goods available, despite increasing demand due to wage increases and expanded employment. There was also a shortage of support services that would have eased the double burden on women of paid work and domestic chores. Various mechanisms were instituted to reduce these barriers to female labor force participation, including support services specifically directed toward working women, such as day care centers, shopping plans (Plan Jaba)[3] and communal laundromats. The Family Code of 1975 specifically mandated that couples share in domestic chores and child care as well as the cost of running the household. Women were also guaranteed the same salary as men for equal work, paid vacations, and generous maternity benefits, and the employment of women in certain sectors was promoted, although some heavier manual jobs were reserved for men. The FMC, one of the mass organizations created in 1960 to mobilize for the revolution, shifted away from recruiting women for volunteer labor, as in the Literacy Campaign, to giving greater attention to incorporating women into the labor force. The FMC had already assisted in the retraining of domestic servants, who were virtually eliminated from the labor force in the postrevolutionary period, which also contributed to declines in female employment. Rising educational levels contributed to an increasing supply of skilled women workers in Cuba. However, these policies did not have any real impact until the 1970s, when wage and consumer policies reinforced women's desire to become wage earners.

The failure to attain the goal for the 1970 sugar harvest and the decline in world sugar prices forced a shift in state policy away from redistribution and moral incentives toward greater productivity and material incentives. Sugar continued to be the primary export, but efforts were made to diversify and modernize the economy, in both the agricultural and industrial sectors. Mechanization was introduced by the revolutionary government in 1965, and linkages were established between sugar and other sectors, particularly industry. Import substitution industrialization was pushed primarily to modernize agriculture and to increase consumer goods through the production of capital goods, especially agricultural machinery. Import substitution industrialization helped reduce the percentage of consumer goods imported, particularly in food, which declined as a proportion of total imports by almost 50 percent (Pérez-Stable 1993: 87). The share of sugar and its by-products in total exports fell from 83.7 percent in 1980 to 77 percent in 1986, although some of this decrease is attributable to Cuban reexports of Soviet oil, an attempt to garner greater hard currency for the Cuban economy (Zimbalist 1990: 132–133). Cuba enjoyed preferential treatment from the former Soviet Union and Eastern Europe, particularly after its 1972 entrance into the Council of Mutual Economic Assistance, the socialist trading bloc (CMEA). This included high preferential prices for Cuban sugar, which increased sugar's comparative advantage.

During the 1970s, Cuba's rate of growth stood at 5 percent per capita, the highest levels achieved in the postrevolutionary period (Pérez-Stable 1993). In 1976, a new system of economic management and planning (SDPE; El Systema de Dirección y Planificación de la Economía) modeled after the Soviet Union attempted to decentralize the economy by making each firm accountable for its profitability and by increasing the role of workers and unions in the workplace (Fuller 1992). Wage increases were linked to productivity and skill levels, and monthly production and service assemblies, in which workers participated, were held in each workplace. Consumer durables and housing were distributed through the workplace on the basis of need and merit. The introduction of free peasant markets from 1980 to 1986 in which small farmers could sell their surplus crops at market prices contributed to the rapid expansion in the availability of consumer goods. Rationing was reduced from 95 percent to 30 percent of consumer items from 1970 to 1980 (Zimbalist and Eckstein 1987: 14). This increased the incentive to work, and it was reinforced by a 1981 reform of retail prices, which increased somewhat the cost of living. Men were also subject to a compulsory work law passed in 1971, but women were exempted.

These wage and consumer policies contributed to a rise in the female labor force participation rate to 35 percent by 1990 (see Table 1.7). Additional factors contributing to an increase in female employment included women's rising educational level and reduced fertility, facilitated by state policies providing free access to birth control and legalizing abortion. In 1988 the total fertility rate stood at 1.88 births per woman, below replacement levels and among the lowest in Latin America (FMC 1990: 14). Primary school enrollment is almost universal for both sexes, and female workers are better educated than male workers. By 1985, more than 46 percent of working women compared to 34 percent of working men had attained a high school education (Pérez-Stable 1993: 141). As in the case of Puerto Rico and the Dominican Republic, these factors increased the supply of women workers, particularly in more highly skilled jobs. By 1988, women constituted over 58 percent of technicians and 85 percent of administrative workers, while the percentage

TABLE 1.8

Cuban National Occupational Profile by Gender and Sector, 1986
Percentages

Sector	*Distribution by Gender*		*Sectoral Composition by Gender*	
	Women	*Men*	*Women*	*Men*
Industry	22.6	33.2	29.5	70.5
Construction	3.6	13.7	–	–
Agriculture and cattle raising	5.9	12.6	14.0	86.0
Forestry	.4	1.3	17.4	82.6
Transportation	3.0	8.1	18.5	81.5
Communications	1.1	.7	47.5	52.5
Commerce	14.8	9.4	49.0	51.0
Other productive activity	.6	.6	39.3	60.7
Personal and commercial services	4.0	3.4	41.9	58.1
Science and technology	1.1	.7	48.0	52.0
Education	21.1	6.3	67.2	32.8
Culture and art	1.4	1.1	43.3	56.7
Public health and social assistance	12.2	3.3	69.5	30.5
Finance and insurance	1.1	.3	69.7	30.3
Administration	6.0	4.6	44.7	55.3
Other non-productive activity	1.1	.7	47.1	52.9
Total	100.0	100.0	38.0	62.0

Source: Federación de Mujeres Cubanas, *Integración Económica de la Mujer Cubana a las Actividades Socio-económicas y Políticas,* 1989:27.

of women in executive positions also increased to 26.5 percent (FMC 1990: 73). In 1986, the share of women in the industrial sector had increased to 29.5 percent, but women were still concentrated in education, public health and social assistance, and finance and insurance, more traditional female sectors (Table 1.8).

The Cuban state hoped that rising educational and occupational levels for women would result in stable, nuclear families in which husband and wife shared the support of their children as well as domestic chores, as envisaged in the Family Code. However, as in Puerto Rico and the Dominican Republic, the percentage of female-headed households grew, responding in Cuba not to male unemployment but to the redistributive policies of the state, which made it easier for a woman to raise children on her own. In 1988, 43 out of every 100 marriages ended in divorce, principally among the young (FMC 1990: 22), while teenage pregnancies also rose, increasing the need for women to seek paid employment. Cuban single mothers must work because, unlike in Puerto Rico, no special supports are provided for Cuban female-headed households.

Changes in the structure of the economy and rising educational qualifications also contributed to a change in the composition of the male labor force, so that by 1986, the percentage of economically active men employed in industry was over 20 percent higher than that for men employed in agriculture (Table 1.8). After the initial decline in male labor force participation rates following the revolution, male rates increased substantially in 1975 and then stabilized (Table 1.7). Despite the continued importance of sugar, the percentage of the total economically active population employed in agriculture in 1981 was only 23.2 percent, due in part to mechanization, while the industrial sector grew to 28.7 percent and the service sector to 48.1 percent, primarily among women (Valdés and Gomariz 1992: 41).

The continued emphasis on sugar exports benefited Cuba as long as it could trade with the socialist countries and particularly the Soviet Union, on whom Cuba had grown as dependent as it had been earlier on the United States. The United States accounted for 68 percent of total Cuban trade during the 1950s, while the Soviet Union during the 1980s represented 66 percent, although high sugar prices further inflated this figure (Pérez-Stable 1993: 89). Although Cuba sold most of its sugar to the CMEA or socialist bloc countries at preferential prices, it still depended for 10 to 40 percent of its sales on the world market as a source of hard currency (Zimbalist 1990: 132). A sharp decline in the world price of sugar and oil (reexported from the Soviet Union) in 1986 led to a severe balance of payments deficit. Trade deficits combined with domestic corruption led to another change in policy known as *rectificación,* which reduced the move toward greater decentralization and a market economy. Market reforms were discontinued and the emphasis shifted back to moral incentives and *conciencia.* Worker and union input into decision making was reduced and the free peasant markets were closed.

These measures accelerated after the collapse of the CMEA and the virtual elimination of trade and aid from the socialist bloc, which dealt a sharp blow to the Cuban economy, from which it is still trying to recover. Cuban imports fell almost 60 percent while the world price of sugar continued to fall and Cuba's sugar harvest decreased, due partly to the shortage of imported inputs (Zimbalist 1992). The redistributive mechanisms initiated earlier and the reintroduction of universal rationing and a new food self-sufficiency program have staved off mass unemployment and malnutrition. However, both increased after 1990, due in part to the dramatic decline in the availability of consumer goods and the closing of factories and other workplaces due to the lack of fuel, electricity, and other necessities. This "special period," as it is known in Cuba, presents particular difficulties for women, in terms of shortages of food, water, electricity, and public transport, which has undoubtedly affected their labor force participation. While national-level employment data have not been released after 1989, absenteeism and turnover are known to have increased, and many workers have been reassigned to agriculture and home industries. This downturn is particularly difficult after the decade of rising expectations from the mid-1970s to the mid-1980s.

Conclusion

The rapid transformation from an agrarian to an urban, industrial economy in Cuba, Puerto Rico, and the Dominican Republic has brought about an increase in female labor force participation in each country. The increase is considerably higher in Cuba and the Dominican Republic than in Puerto Rico,[4] where migration and transfer payments have reduced the need for employment. The increase is not only the result of industrialization, although export manufacturing has certainly increased the demand for female labor in Puerto Rico and the Dominican Republic. In all three countries, there has also been an increase in the supply of qualified women workers, due to rising educational levels and lower fertility. These changes have been reflected in improvements in the occupational profile of women workers in each country, as growing numbers of women enter the professions, clerical work, and the burgeoning service economy. The increase in Cuban women's labor force participation also reflects the revolutionary government's efforts to encourage their incorporation and the wage and consumer policies pursued in the 1970s and early 1980s, which increased the material incentives for women to work.

The economic crisis has also accentuated the need for women to work in the Dominican Republic and Puerto Rico. In both countries, women are assuming increased economic responsibility for their households because higher rates of labor force participation for women have coincided with declining job opportunities for men. In Puerto Rico, men displaced from agricultural employment have suffered high levels of unemployment, while many have migrated to the United States or withdrawn from the labor force. Transfer payments have eased the transition and provided an alternative source of income to Puerto Rican households while increasing dependency on the state. No such social support mechanisms exist in the Dominican Republic, where the sudden cutback in sugar production has led growing numbers of men to enter the informal sector, and the proportion of both sexes migrating to the

United States is also increasing. Dominican labor was further weakened by the economic crisis and structural adjustment policies, which through currency devaluation lowered wages and increased the cost of living as well as cutting government expenditures in health, education, and other areas. The labor movement was weakened by fragmentation and strong state control over labor in both Puerto Rico and the Dominican Republic to ensure the political stability needed for foreign investment. It could be argued that a weak labor movement is necessary to the success of export-led industrialization, because cheap wages and lack of labor unrest are a critical component for international competition (Deyo 1986). This is one of the reasons women are favored as a source of cheap labor in both countries.

Though export-led industrialization provided an important source of foreign exchange and alleviated the debt crisis in the Dominican Republic, it has not led to self-sustained growth and has intensified dependence on the United States. In Puerto Rico as well, despite initial high growth rates, the economy has become increasingly dependent on transfer payments, migration, and federal funds to compensate for high unemployment and low activity rates. Thus, in both countries, export-led industrialization has maintained and even deepened the historically hegemonic role U.S. capital has always played in the region, starting with the export of primary commodities such as sugar in the Dominican Republic. Domestic industry in the Dominican Republic absorbed only 1.2 percent of the increase in the economically active population from 1980 to 1991, compared to 12.6 percent in the free trade zones (Fundapec 1992: 43). U.S. tariff regulations and the lack of linkages to the domestic economy in all areas but labor discourage the move away from labor-intensive industries such as garment into capital-intensive industrialization, which would have provided more jobs for men. Puerto Rico did shift into capital-intensive and high-tech manufacturing, but the value added is still low because of the lack of domestic inputs. The assembly type of export manufacturing promoted in both countries reduced the incentive for endogenous development and the demand for male labor. Thus, it is not export manufacturing per se which is at fault, but the enclave type of export promotion pursued both in Puerto Rico and the Dominican Republic.

Though the newly industrializing East Asian countries are often presented as models of development for the Caribbean, the export promotion strategies they follow are quite different from those in the Caribbean and point up the importance of state policy in determining the growth potential of export-led industrialization (Gereffi 1990; Jenkins 1991). Taiwan, South Korea, and Singapore relied heavily on state intervention in the economy, including control over foreign capital and technology, and cannot be seen as an example of free market policies, as some have suggested. The state has taken a leading role in the shift toward more capital-intensive forms of export-led industrialization, including heavy investment in research and technology and in manpower training programs. The state has not allowed assembly industries to dominate, as in Puerto Rico and the Dominican Republic. Domestic inputs in export-processing zones in South Korea and Taiwan rose substantially as early as the 1970s (Wilson 1992: 23), while in the Dominican Republic only 4 percent of local costs were spent on raw materials in 1986 (Dauhajre et al. 1989: 51).

In this way, East Asian states prevented the dependency on the United States to which the Dominican Republic and Puerto Rico and much of Latin America and especially the Caribbean have been subject. Consequently, they were able to move into the second stage of high-tech and more capital-intensive export-led industrialization. Between 1980 and 1987, South Korea and Taiwan maintained average annual growth rates of 8.6 and 7.5 percent respectively (Gereffi 1990: 11), much higher than the average GDP growth rate of 1.1 percent per annum in the Dominican Republic over the same period. In addition, East Asian emphasis on capital-intensive industrialization for the domestic as well as the export market has maintained the incorporation of men into the labor force, enabling them to retain their control over the household and maintaining the dominance of the male breadwinner.

Cuba has also failed to achieve self-sustaining growth, but for quite different reasons. Cuba's economic growth continues to depend on sugar exports, which maintains its vulnerability to the world market, despite the nationalization of the economy and the growth of tourism and other sectors. The Cuban revolution broke U.S. hegemony over the island, but continued dependence on sugar exports to the former Soviet Union and Eastern Europe sustained trade dependency and left Cuba with no alternative now that the socialist bloc has disintegrated.

The more gradual decline in agricultural employment in Cuba and the absorption of men into import substitution industrialization have provided a source of male employment that prevented the massive displacement of men that occurred in Puerto Rico and the Dominican Republic. However, Cuba's redistributive mechanisms reduced the reliance on wages and purchasing power as primary determinants of standards of living and made it easier for women to raise children on their own. Therefore, dependence on a male breadwinner also declined in Cuba, contributing to the formation of an increasing percentage of female-

TABLE 1.9

Selected Social Indicators of Development in Puerto Rico,
Dominican Republic, and Cuba

	Puerto Rico	Dominican Republic	Cuba
Life expectancy	76	67	76
Illiteracy (percentage of population 15 years and over)	10.4[a]	17	6
Infant mortality (per 1,000 live births)	14	54	11

[a] 1990 U.S. Census of Population and Housing. Summary of Social, Economic and Housing Characteristics, Puerto Rico.
Source: Social Indicators of Development in Puerto Rico, Dominican Republic, and Cuba, 1993. Washington, DC: The World Bank, 1993.

headed households, as in Puerto Rico and the Dominican Republic, chiefly because of male unemployment.

Economic growth in the 1970s led to rising expectations, which were severely damaged by the blow to the Cuban economy of the cutoff of trade with the socialist bloc in the 1990s. Despite the negative effects of the economic crisis the country is now undergoing, Cuba's achievements under socialism cannot be denied. By 1990, Cuba's life expectancy was the highest in Latin America while infant mortality and illiteracy were the lowest. These figures rank high above the Dominican Republic and are comparable to those in Puerto Rico, where health and education are heavily supported by federal funds (Table 1.9). The reformist policies of Puerto Rico could not match the revolutionary policies of Cuba in terms of reducing inequality, where the state became the principal employer and source of wealth.

Although the Cuban revolution in 1959 is commonly recognized as a major societal transformation from capitalism to socialism, all three countries underwent a major change in state policy in the post–World War II period. Puerto Rico's Operation Bootstrap signified a final blow to the absentee sugar corporations that had held economic power since the U.S. occupation in 1898, and ushered in a period of increased state intervention focusing on modernization, industrialization, and improvements in the standard of living. The death of Trujillo also resulted in partial democratic and economic reforms in the Dominican Republic and opened the country to increasing local and foreign (mainly U.S.) investment with limited state redistribution. Thus, the Cuban revolution, Operation Bootstrap, and the fall of Trujillo in the Dominican Republic all led to increasing state intervention and the formation of a redistributive state, which reached its apogee in socialist Cuba, took the form of a capitalist welfare state in Puerto Rico, and was most confined in the Dominican Republic.

In this book, I shall examine the linkages between these macro-level development strategies and gender relations in the household, with particular attention to changes in male and female labor force participation rates. In all three countries, women's paid employment has become a more visible and necessary component of the household economy, leading to women's increased authority and consciousness of gender and class subordination. Consciousness of gender subordination is expressed by the increasing economic autonomy of women in all three countries, in which incorporation into paid wage labor has played an important role. However, the myth of the male breadwinner persists and continues to influence gender roles, the labor process, and state policy, as I will discuss in the following chapters.

Notes

1. This is the most conservative estimate of female heads of household because it excludes women living alone or as household head with a husband present. I am indebted to Alice Colón for this clarification.

2. A new Dominican labor code passed in 1992 strengthened workers' rights to collective bargaining in the free trade zones, but most workers are still intimidated.

3. Plan Jaba was designed to reduce women's domestic burden by cutting down the time required for shopping.

4. The figures are not exactly comparable because they are based on different age groups and measurement techniques in each country, but I have reduced this variability as much as possible.

2

The Male Breadwinner and Women's Wage Labor

The massive increase in women's wage labor both in advanced industrial and in developing countries has generated intense debate over its effects on women's status. Does wage labor merely exploit women as a source of cheap labor and add to the burden of their domestic chores? Or does wage labor give women greater autonomy and raise their consciousness regarding gender subordination?

Curiously, similar questions are seldom raised in reference to men's involvement in wage labor. It is always assumed men will be employed, while for women, employment is still considered an option. Why? How did the image of the male breadwinner originate? Is the image still valid or, as I maintain, a myth now that increasing numbers of women are contributing to the household? These are the questions I shall explore in this chapter.

The myth of the male breadwinner is a powerful norm in Western industrial society that is rooted in women's dual productive/reproductive role. Women, even if they are employed, are assumed to be responsible for domestic chores and child care, while male responsibilities in the household are minimized in favor of their primary role as breadwinner. Designating men as the primary breadwinner maintains male control over female labor, which is largely confined to the home and reproductive sphere. Domestic labor under capitalism serves to maintain and reproduce the labor force, but because labor within the home is unpaid, it is increasingly devalued as income-earning activities in the public sphere confer greater status and prestige. Even when they are employed, women are at a distinct disadvantage in the labor market because of their dual productive-reproductive role. Women can thus be exploited as a source of cheap labor because their salaries are deemed supplementary to the primary male breadwinner.

The myth of the male breadwinner has ideological as well as material roots and is based on patriarchy as well as capitalism. Patriarchy may be broadly defined as male control over female labor and sexuality (Hartman 1981), that is, over women's productive and reproductive role. Patriarchy predates capitalism, but it is a dynamic concept that differs historically and cross-culturally. Systems of male dominance range from the high levels found in the classic patriarchy of the Middle East, South Asia, and East Asia to the relative autonomy of mother-child units evidenced in sub-Saharan Africa (Kandiyoti 1991). Classic patriarchy is sanctioned by kinship and religious systems that conferred total authority over women and youth to senior men in patrilocal corporate kin groups in return for male protection and support. In African polygynous systems, women's dependence on male support is quite low and is overshadowed by both sexes continuing reciprocal obligations with their own corporate kin groups. In bilateral kinship systems, which will be the major concern here, corporate kin groups are weakened and the nuclear household and conjugal unit assume greater importance, but men still control women's labor and sexuality through their economic power as primary breadwinner. Capitalist penetration and colonialism blurred these differences and imposed patterns of male hegemony not predicated on traditional kinship relations upon relatively egalitarian societies such as those found in precolonial Latin America, Africa, and other indigenous societies. Male hegemony eroded female autonomy by denying women access to productive resources such as land and wage labor (Boserup 1970; Etienne and Leacock 1980; Nash 1988).[1] In other areas capitalism reinforced patriarchy by utilizing preexisting hierarchies based on gender (and race and class) to facilitate the creation of an exploitable labor force, such as the slave system of the Caribbean that I shall discuss later.

Marxist feminists see capitalism in alliance with patriarchy as a source of women's subordination, but they differ as to which is primary and on the relationship between them (Walby 1986). Those emphasizing capitalism focus on class exploitation of labor by capital in the production process, while those emphasizing patriarchy emphasize gender exploitation through male domination over women in the family as the primary source of women's subordination. Feminist scholars like Barrett (1980: 211), for example, argue that the family is "the central site of the oppression of women." According to Barrett, gender ideology is formed principally within the family through a woman's dependence on a male wage and is reflected at other levels of society such as the workplace and the polity.

I argue, however, that a woman's dependence on a male breadwinner is not only reflected in but reinforced by certain policies at the workplace and from the state that continue to undervalue women as wage earners. Thus, there are various levels of gender subordination—in the family, the workplace, and the state—which while linked, need to be kept analytically separate. Patriarchy as manifest in male control over female labor operates at different levels: in the home, where women are charged with domestic responsibilities; at the workplace, where women are segregated into poorly paid, unstable jobs; and at the state, where legal mechanisms and public policy restrict women's right to hold property and earn wages, and in other ways sustain their status as dependent minors rather than full citizens. All three levels reinforce the role of man as primary breadwinner. But I shall argue that the primary locus of patriarchy has shifted with the development of industrial capitalism from the home to the workplace and the state, or from the private to the public sphere.

Changes in the Form of Patriarchal Control

Historical analysis reveals that the relationship between patriarchy and capitalism shifts over time. In the early stages of capitalism, patriarchy resides primarily in individual male heads of household, who maintain control over women's labor and sexuality. The home is the primary locus of production and reproduction and is the primary agent of women's subordination. With the development of industrial capitalism and the growth in importance of the nation-state, patriarchy shifts from being primarily in the private realm of the family to the public sphere of the workplace and the state (Mann 1986; Walby 1990). The development of advanced capitalism also results in the increasing importance of women as wage earners and challenges the status of men as principal breadwinners.

In agrarian societies dating from the first written records to the eighteenth century, there was a clear separation between the public and private spheres, and the household was the primary social unit. The male patriarch of the household had absolute power over all junior males, females, and children and was the sole representative of the household in the public sphere. With industrialization, as production moved outside the home into factories and offices, the household declined in economic and political importance, and many family functions such as education, health, and even child care were taken over by the state. Women began to enter the public sphere as they acquired individual rights as citizens in the emerging nation-state, though these rights were generally confined to women of the propertied classes. The household declined in size and the nuclear family became predominant, as extended families and kin ties were weakened by increased residential and social mobility. This shift was marked by increasing tension between the state, private capital, and individual men over women's labor and sexuality and was reflected in increasing state intervention in the economy against capital (e.g., protective legislation, minimum wages) or against individual male heads of household (e.g., laws guaranteeing women's property rights or rights to divorce and child custody). However, the state continued to recognize the man as head of the household and primary breadwinner, thus reinforcing his role.

Mann (1986) argues that patriarchy no longer exists in advanced industrial societies because the distinction between the public and the private sphere has been eroded through massive wage labor by both men and women, through universal citizenship, and through the nation-state's intervention in the private household, although he admits that patriarchal values still permeate many aspects of the state. I would argue that with the primacy of the public over the private sphere, the primary locus of patriarchy has shifted, so that the state may now uphold patriarchal values at the same time that it restricts the rights of individual men over women. There are many forms of the state, as there are of patriarchy, and Mann's model is more applicable to advanced industrial societies like Britain than to developing countries, where the distinction between the private and public sphere is still sharper. In most developing societies, as in advanced industrial societies earlier, the notion of separate spheres for men and women maintains gender differences and defines women as family members whose work roles are secondary (Kessler-Harris 1990).

Women were not passive victims of patriarchal control but actively resisted it in the home, workplace, and the polity. Many of the rights women won such as suffrage and legal equality in family law were due to women's pressure on the state to reconstitute their status as dependent minors with that of equal citizens. These pressures, in turn, were partly a result of women's increased economic autonomy, either in domestic production or wage labor. Rising labor force participation, particularly on the part of middle-class women, raised their consciousness regarding their dependent status and elevated their desire to acquire greater economic independence to bolster their demands for greater equality. These middle-class women were among the first feminists who openly championed women's right to vote, to hold property, and to control their own sexuality.

Wage labor was not the only way women acquired greater economic autonomy or gender consciousness. Women's domestic production in peasant households or as artisans also comprises an important contribution to the household economy (Deere 1990; Nash 1993), but as this work was often unpaid and under male control, it did not challenge male authority as much as independent wage labor. In fact, women's efforts to gain greater control over their own pottery or weaving production in Chiapas have led to increasing marital tension, as men feel their patriarchal control is threatened (Nash 1993; Eber and Rosenbaum 1993). Benería and Roldán (1987) also document how subcontracted home work has led to increased women's authority in the household in direct proportion to the amount women contribute, but its impact on gender subordination is again diminished by women's confinement to the home and continued dependence on male breadwinners.

My analysis here will be limited to the impact of formal wage labor on women's economic autonomy and gender consciousness. Other factors also have contributed to producing women more able and willing to enter wage labor, such as increased educational levels and declining fertility rates. Clearly, wage labor is not the sole source of empowerment among women, nor does paid employment have the same impact on women of different cultures, races, and classes, even within advanced capitalist societies. Bonds among women based on race, ethnicity, neighborhood, and kinship also offer women collective forms of resistance to capitalist exploitation (Sacks 1989; Susser 1986; Stack 1974). However, as long as the normative ideal was based on separate spheres, with women confined to the home and men dominating the public sphere, women lacked legitimacy to press demands that were not extensions of their domestic role. The notion of separate spheres was heavily dependent upon the man's role as principal breadwinner, which gave the man control over family income and family labor and ensured women's economic dependence. This myth of the male breadwinner persists, despite the increasing importance of women's wages in the household. The origins of this myth must be sought in the changing sexual division of labor that accompanied the rise of industrial capitalism.

Changes in the Sexual Division of Labor

Defining a woman as an "unproductive housewife" was a result of the rise of a market economy and industrial capitalism in the nineteenth century (Folbre 1991). As production moved outside the home into the factory, women ceased to be seen as productive members of the household and became increasingly dependent on male wages earned outside the home. Women were relegated to the reproductive sphere of child-rearing, enshrined in the "cult of domesticity," despite the economic de-valuation of housework. The state institutionalized the concept of the unproductive housewife in the census and through family law, while so-cial security legislation such as workmen's compensation was designed primarily to protect white male industrial workers (Nelson 1990). Male unions strove for a family wage that would exclude women from the la-bor force and enable men to support their dependent wives and chil-dren (Hartman 1981). The family wage strengthened the control of the male head of household over his wife's labor by defining men as the principal wage earners. Single women worked, but their wages could not support a family and most left employment upon marriage. These changes were strongest in advanced industrial societies such as the United States and England, and even here the bourgeois ideal of the "idle housewife" did not hold for black and immigrant women and some of the white working class, who could not survive without a woman's wages.

The rewards of wage labor in the United States were governed by race, class, and gender hierarchies and maintained the supremacy of the male white elite. White elite men monopolized the top managerial, administrative, and professional jobs, while white elite women dominated the feminine professions and clerical work. In the early twentieth century, people of color remained overly concentrated in the preindustrial sectors of agriculture and domestic service, which were mainly the spheres of black women. Domestic service was the single most important occupation for women in 1900. In 1920, black women had the highest gainful employment rate of any ethnic group in the United States (38.9 percent), twice the rate for white American women (Amott and Matthaei 1991: 299). Married women faced a "marriage bar" in teaching and clerical work, while employers, labor unions, and professional associations barred people of color and women from the more lucrative jobs in crafts and the professions. Since women often left jobs upon marriage, they were given dead-end jobs requiring fewer skills and seldom acquired a college education. These sectoral differences were reflected in earnings differences, where men earned more than women and whites earned more than blacks and other ethnic groups. Occupational segregation and wage differentials still persist, but with the growth of wage labor, the boundaries have blurred and there are now considerable differences within each ethnic group and among women.

As increasing numbers of women, particularly married white middle-class women, began to enter the labor force in advanced capitalist societies during and after World War II, the concept of housewife began to change to that of supplementary wage earner. Fewer than 15 percent of all married women and 30 percent of black women with wage-earning husbands were regularly employed by the 1930s (Kessler-Harris 1990: 29). Women's share of the U.S. labor force increased from 18 percent in 1900 to 45 percent in 1988, with much of the growth among married women and mothers (Amott and Matthaei 1991: 307). Yet wage differentials and occupational segregation reinforced the view that men were still the primary breadwinners and justified women's attachment to their families. In the United States, state benefits to women such as social security or Aid to Families with Dependent Children (AFDC) were directly linked to their maternal or parental status and designed to substitute for the wage of the absent father, thereby extending the notion of female dependence from the male breadwinner to the state (Acker 1988). Many of these maternalist policies were promoted by white middle-class feminists of the Progressive Era concerned with protecting women's domestic role and neglected working mothers, both black and white, who had to seek employment. However, as greater numbers of middle-class women entered college and white-collar and professional jobs, the class composition of the female labor force changed and the importance and legitimacy of women's employment were enhanced.

The "demise of domesticity" in the United States did not begin until the 1960s with ever-increasing numbers of married women in paid employment (Kessler-Harris and Sacks 1987). The change from working daughters to working mothers (Lamphere 1986) was important, because the employment of mothers directly challenged the traditional sexual division of labor in the family. Many married women had to work, reflected in the increase in households maintained by women to 25 percent in 1990.[2] Among African-Americans or Puerto Ricans living in the United States the percentage is much higher (Amott 1993: 94). The nuclear family has never been as prevalent among these racial/ethnic groups and declined sharply after 1960 as a result of deindustrialization and a decline in male employment (Wilson 1987). In 1990, only 39 percent of black families with children were headed by a married couple (Billingsley 1992: 36). In addition, the economic crisis starting in the mid-1970s brought about higher unemployment and a decline in male wages across racial groups, which forced women to contribute more heavily to the household, and married women became more than supplementary wage earners. Male blue-collar workers (as well as women in labor-intensive jobs such as the garment industry) suffered a sharp decline in employment and earnings as a result of industrial restructuring and the relocation of production abroad (Nash 1989; Lamphere 1987; Lamphere et al. 1993). There was also an increasing demand for educated women in office work and the professions, while the rise in consumerism and women's desire for more personal economic security and autonomy increased their motivation to work (Hartman 1987). Married women remained employed rather than leaving at childbirth as they had done previously. This enabled children to prolong their education and to qualify for expanding white-collar and professional jobs. As children no longer contributed to the household economy, there was growing pressure on mothers to remain in the labor force, to supplement their husbands' wages or to support children on their own (Safa 1983). The increasing employment of married women also contributed to decreasing fertility, as a woman's reproductive labor shifted from an emphasis on large families to a smaller number of educated children capable of entering an increasingly skilled labor force.

Gradually in the United States, the concept of the family wage has been replaced with that of the two wage-earner family, as 65 percent of mothers in dual parent families were in the workforce in 1990 (Alt-WID 1992: 10). Most mothers no longer withdraw from the workforce to raise small children and instead see themselves as permanently employed. The possibility of earning their own, independent wage represents a basis for resisting gender and generational subordination within the family, giving women more autonomy and the ability to dissolve an unhappy marriage and head their own household. Divorce rates have risen, contributing to the growing percentage of female heads of households and reinforcing the importance of women's wages in the household. Employed women have become more active in unions, increasing their membership from 25 percent in 1980 to 41 percent a decade later (Amott and Matthaei 1991: 309), and have begun to press for wider family-oriented benefits from the state and employers such as paid maternity leave and child care. Although women's wages in the United States have improved relative to men's wages, women in 1988 still earned on average 66 cents for every dollar earned by men (Alt-WID 1992). As both women and men become recognized as providers, a woman's wage is now increasingly seen as job-based rather than need-based as previously.

The 1963 U.S. law guaranteeing equal pay for equal work embodies this shift, for as long as women were seen as dependents or supplementary wage earners, their wages were based on need and not on the jobs they performed (Kessler-Harris 1990). Women were expected to be self-supporting or to contribute to the family income, but not to maintain a family as men did. Earlier need-based concepts of women's wages rested on the ideology of women's separate sphere, which idealized the domestic sphere at the same time that it restricted women's presence in the public sphere. Underlying the notion of separate spheres was a clear division between the public male world of work and the private female world of the home, which was being increasingly eroded with the increasing number of women in the labor force. Equal pay for equal work acknowledged this change and embodied a very different notion of gender roles based on individual rights rather than family responsibilities (Kessler-Harris 1990). Though its effects were diluted by continued occupational segregation, it moved away from an identity based on gender differences to one based on gender equality.

In large part, women's struggle against gender subordination in advanced industrial societies has now shifted from the home to the workplace and increasingly the state. The increasing importance of women as wage earners has facilitated this transition. In part, a shift in focus has been made necessary by the attack during the 1980s on the welfare state and social services and by restrictions on abortions and family planning in countries such as the United States and England. Many of these attacks centered on the growing number of female-headed households, who represented 54 percent of all poor families in the United States in 1990 (Buvinic and Gupta 1994: 23). This increase has been found to be strongly associated with increases in the labor force participation of white women and the rising unemployment of black men, which in turn is linked to deindustrialization (Garfinkel and McLanahan 1986). The growing crisis over the redistributive functions of government in advanced capitalist societies and the familism of the right-to-life movement can be seen as a way of reasserting private patriarchy, as the state withdraws from its responsibilities for social reproduction and shifts this back to the individual family. This is the same philosophy embodied in the structural adjustment programs of the IMF imposed on many Latin American and other developing countries. However, cuts in social services and transfer payments drive more women into the labor force, while the number of blue-collar and white-collar jobs continues to shrink, so that female as well as male unemployment figures continue to grow. Women who have become permanent members of the labor force can no longer retreat into the category of housewife in order to disguise their unemployment.

In sum, patriarchy underwent two major modifications in Western industrial societies with the development of industrial capitalism: Primary control over women's labor shifted from individual male heads of household to capital and the state, as the household declined in economic and political importance; and the sexual division of labor in the family changed as women became increasingly important wage earners and economic providers. These changes were marked by an increase in the percentage of women employed, particularly married women, and in the importance of their contribution to the household economy.

An ideological shift accompanied these structural changes. As women began to move into the workforce in greater numbers, the notion of women's separate spheres was gradually replaced by the notion of individùal rights based on equality between men and women. Separate spheres is based on complementarity between men and women, on the assumption that each can excel in their own sphere, women in the home, and men in the public world of work and politics. It extols motherhood and sees women's public roles as basically extensions of their domestic roles. The decreasing importance placed by society on the family and housework undermined their value for women, while increasing numbers of women were contributing to the household economy or were female heads of household supporting households on their own. Women demanded a greater presence in the public sphere and began to claim individual rights based on equality with men and not simply on the basis of protecting women's separate domestic sphere. This marked a fundamental change in women's conceptualization of gender roles and gender subordination (Kessler-Harris 1990). With the massive incorporation of women into the labor force, gender subordination was no longer defined solely on the basis of male domination in the home, but on the limitations to gender equality in the workplace and in the state. Women looked increasingly to the state to achieve greater gender equality, thus reinforcing the shift from private to public patriarchy.

Changing Forms of Patriarchy in the Caribbean: The Intersection of Race, Class, and Gender

Can this theoretical framework documenting historical changes in the relationship between women's wage labor and gender subordination in advanced industrial countries be applied as well to developing countries differing in historical and cultural formation, in racial and ethnic composition, and in levels of development? Has the ideological shift away from separate spheres into equal individual rights for men and women occurred as well in these developing countries? Has the increase in women's labor force participation redefined their role so that they are no longer seen as supplementary wage earners, but major contributors to the household economy?

Obviously, there are dangers here in assuming that developing countries will follow the same changes in gender roles described for advanced industrial societies like the United States. I shall not attempt to conduct a global analysis of the impact of wage labor on women's status, but shall focus my discussion on Latin America and the Hispanic Carib-

bean with special reference to Cuba and Puerto Rico, where the historical documentation on women's labor force participation is more complete than in the Dominican Republic. With the exception of some
indigenous cultures, Latin America is characterized by a bilateral kinship system with an absence of corporate kin groups, but male control
of women's labor and sexuality is maintained through an emphasis on
family honor and female virginity fostered by Catholicism. Many of the
ideologies discussed above such as the cult of domesticity and the emphasis on men as providers and protectors are even stronger in Latin
America and are expressed in the basic distinction between the *casa* or
home, the domain of women, and the *calle,* or street, the domain of
men. The boundaries between the public and private spheres have not
been eroded to the extent they have been in the United States, but patriarchal norms vary by class and race as well as over time. Control over
women's labor and sexuality is strongest among the white elite, where
economic power and the patrilineal household provide a stronger base
for patriarchy than among the black/mulatto and indigenous/mestizo
working classes. Because of colonial domination of large indigenous
and slave populations, race is even more important in many areas of
Latin America and the Caribbean than in the United States, where non-
whites are in the minority. Although race and class often coincide, with
dark-skinned people at the lower end of the socio-economic scale, racial
boundaries are blurred by a racial continuum brought about by extensive interracial unions and by the primacy of class distinctions over
strictly physical attributes.

Nash (1978) has shown that women in precolonial kin-based Mayan
society enjoyed economic and legal equality with men, but Aztec con-
quest kept women out of the new predatory economy of war and tribute
and intensified the sexual division of labor. Spanish colonialism intensified patriarchal control over women's labor and sexuality, especially of
elite white women who were largely confined to the home. Under Spanish colonial law, *patria potestad* or paternal authority gave a husband
exclusive control over his children and most of his wife's legal transac-
tions, property, earnings, and sexuality (Arrom 1985: 65–70). The Catho-
lic Church reinforced civil authority and male patriarchy, through its
moral insistence on female virginity and male superiority, which sanctioned double standards of sexuality for the sexes. Christian patriarchal-
ism defined the notion of authority for both the family and the state, and
though rooted in the family, the state or king later became the model
and source of legitimation for the patriarchal authority of the family, indicating the close ties between private and public patriarchy (Boyer
1989: 254). Family honor was based on the *casa/calle* distinction, which

created a sharp division between the private world of the family and the public sphere. It also ensured women's economic dependency on men by restricting their activities to the home. However, there were clear class and racial/ethnic differences between elite white or mestizo women and poor indigenous or black women, who assumed greater economic responsibility for the family and never established the same patterns of male dependency. For example, in Mexico City during the early nineteenth century, though women constituted almost one-third of the labor force, it was largely the poorest women who worked—rural migrants, Indian women—and the majority were single women who were employed as domestic servants (Arrom 1985: 157–158). In all *castas* or racial groups, single women and widows worked more than married women, who were clearly expected to "subsist on the earnings of their male head," as a petition by women tobacco factory workers noted (Arrom 1985: 200).

The *casa/calle* distinction in the Hispanic Caribbean never applied to African slaves, who were brought over in massive numbers to work on sugar plantations, particularly in the early nineteenth century. This was particularly true in Cuba, where the number of slaves and the scale of sugar production far exceeded that of Puerto Rico and the Dominican Republic, so that blacks and mulattoes exceeded half the population until the interruption of the slave trade in the early 1860s (de la Fuente 1995: 9). Among slaves, women and men worked at the same tasks in the field, but women were also likely to be retained for domestic duties, while only men rose to supervisory positions in sugar production (Moreno Fraginals 1976). Women depended on their own labor to provide for themselves and their children and could expect little help from men, who were often sold off separately regardless of their family ties. Thus, black slave women did not develop a tradition of dependency on men as did women of the white elite.

One of the most common ways for women and their children to escape from slavery was through a sexual liaison with a white male, who could buy or grant their freedom. Interracial unions and a liberal policy of manumission gave rise to a large group of free colored people in the Hispanic Caribbean, who constituted a socially intermediate group that contributed significantly to the process of racial integration. The free colored group was substantially larger in Puerto Rico than in Cuba, where the state feared the large proportion of blacks posed a threat to political stability (especially after the Haitian revolution). Cuba restricted interracial marriages, requiring not only parental consent but the approval of civil authorities, a sign that patriarchal control was already passing from the hands of individual men to the state. However, regulations against interracial marriages were lifted in 1881, one year after abolition, in recognition of the growing population of free colored people and the need for racial integration in the movement for Cuban autonomy from Spain (Martínez-Alier 1974). The need of the nation for racial integration took precedence over the defense of family honor and purity.

Many interracial liaisons took place outside of legal marriage through consensual unions, which were always more prevalent among the Afro-Cuban population than among whites, and also contributed to a high rate of marital dissolution (de la Fuente 1995: Table 6). Consensual unions weakened dependence on a male breadwinner, because women often carried greater economic responsibility for their children than legally married women, particularly if they had children from several unions. This helps explain why, from 1899 to 1920, Cuban labor force participation rates were three to five times higher among Afro-Cuban women than among white women, while among men, the percentages were almost equal (de la Fuente 1995: Table 13). In 1899, nearly three-quarters of all female wage earners were Afro-Cuban, although they composed only one-third of the population. As in the United States, most were found in domestic service, which continued to be the major occupation for women until the revolution (Pérez 1988: 206). The 1930 depression severely reduced participation rates among Afro-Cuban women, after which the differences between them and white women were not as great.

Lower incomes among Afro-Cubans also account for women's higher labor force participation and were manifest in wage differentials by race that spanned the entire class structure from low-paid and largely black activities as domestic service to well-paid jobs in banking and the public sector. In fact, the higher the occupational category, the greater the differential, while among peasants, the poorest group, there was little difference in income (de la Fuente 1995). Discrimination against Afro-Cubans was also shown by lower literacy and educational levels, by higher mortality, and by underrepresentation in the liberal professions, which required a university education (de la Fuente 1995). In general, though Afro-Cubans demonstrated considerable upward mobility in the prerevolutionary period, deep racial cleavages remained, which were only reduced after the Cuban revolution in 1959.

U.S. occupation of Cuba in 1898 spurred the development of the sugar plantation economy but also promoted social reforms such as free public education and the separation of church and state. For example, as early as 1901, women gained access to free public education and by 1919, 63 percent of the population was literate, with women attaining higher levels of literacy than men in both the Afro-Cuban and white population (de la Fuente 1995: Table 7). Educated, middle-class women were at the forefront of a feminist movement that strove for women's rights and contributed to significant legal reforms in areas such as women's property rights, the right to divorce (granted in 1918), and the right to vote (Stoner 1991). The 1940 Cuban constitution was the most progressive in the Western Hemisphere and granted women the right to vote and hold office and incorporated an equal rights article recognizing the equality of the sexes (Stoner 1991). However, most of these reforms were of greatest benefit to the privileged women who promoted them, without attacking directly the deep racial and class stratification of Cuban society. They facilitated the entrance of elite Cuban women into certain spheres of the public domain, such as education and welfare, thus preserving class and racial distinctions as well as confining women to certain feminine occupations that were seen as extensions of their domestic role. Even the institution of a maternity code for working women symbolized feminists' concern for motherhood, for which they now sought the protection of the state rather than relying exclusively on individual men. The reform of Cuban family law is thus an excellent example of how the feminist movement and concern for women's rights helped to shift patriarchy from the private to the public domain, which reduced the power of individual men but made the state the new protector of women. This paved the way for the socialist state to champion women's rights after the Cuban revolution in 1959.

Despite the feminist movement and changes in family law, women's share of the total labor force increased from only 10 percent in 1899 to 12 percent in 1953 (Pérez 1988: 206, 305) and even in 1959 had only reached 13 percent, the lowest in Latin America (Stoner 1991: 168). This reflected the stigma against female wage labor and the sharp racial and class differences among women, which were manifest in distinct occupational patterns. The majority of Afro-Cuban women were confined to domestic service and manufacturing, particularly as stemmers in the tobacco industry, which in the first half of the twentieth century employed growing numbers of Afro-Cuban and white women (Stubbs 1985). Many servants ended up in prostitution which, though unrecorded, was the fourth largest source of female income in Cuba, also recruiting many poor, illiterate young white women. Afro-Cuban women also outnumbered white women in agriculture, although women working as unpaid family members on small farms may have gone largely unrecorded.[3] However, almost one-third of all college-educated Cubans were women, and by the early 1950s, women accounted for more than 55 percent of professional and technical occupations, mostly as teachers, particularly at the secondary and primary levels (Pérez 1988: 306). Afro-Cuban professional women were also most heavily represented in the teaching profession, in which married women of all races were discriminated against. Most of the female teachers were single or widowed, and married women did not enter the labor force in substantial numbers until after 1970 (Reca et al. 1990: 66), maintaining the continued ideological separation of men and married women into the separate spheres of *casa/calle*.

Despite their important participation in the Cuban war for independence, Afro-Cubans were excluded from the mainstream political parties in the early twentieth century following U.S. occupation. Their formation of the Independent Party of Color was suppressed by the ruling party, leading to armed rebellion and the slaying of thousands of black people in the Little War of May 1912 (Pérez 1988: 222). Again the size of the Afro-Cuban population, augmented by Jamaican and Haitian immigration for work on sugar plantations in Oriente in the early twentieth century, made racial integration more difficult. In 1953, Afro-Cubans made up 27 percent of the total population and constituted approximately the same percentage of the labor force, but principally occupied the lower end of the socio-economic order. Though racial discrimination was legally outlawed in the 1940 constitution, racism was manifest in education, employment, wage levels, housing, health care, social clubs, hotels, and restaurants until the Cuban revolution made systematic efforts to eliminate these barriers (Pérez 1988: 306–307).

Racial divisions were more important in Cuba than in Puerto Rico, where before U.S. occupation in 1898, the plantation economy was not as developed and the slave population was much smaller. In 1873 at the time of abolition, slaves constituted only 5 percent of the total population (Amott and Matthaei 1991: 260). The free colored population of Puerto Rico outnumbered slaves and worked with whites on family-owned coffee haciendas, which constituted the primary economic enterprise in the nineteenth century. There was a high incidence of interracial marriages, often through consensual union, further blurring racial boundaries. Class boundaries between landed and landless rather than race became the chief line of social cleavage, and were typified by the paternalistic social order of the hacienda, in which the *hacendado* represented the father figure and the workers his children (Duany 1985). The racial and cultural synthesis produced by the hacienda was later replicated by the state in its attempt to incorporate all classes and races under the banner of nationalism, in *la gran familia puertorriqueña*. The synthesis was successful in blurring racial boundaries, to the extent that they are often ignored in studies of inequality, though racism persists in the continued perceived superiority of white skin and European culture (Safa 1986).

The proletarianization of Puerto Rican women took place earlier than in Cuba, perhaps due to more severe land fragmentation and the expulsion of peasants from subsistence production, especially after U.S. occupation in 1898. In 1899, only 9.9 percent of women were in the paid labor force and, as in Cuba, more than three-fourths were employed as domestic servants, laundresses, and seamstresses. By 1930, this figure had grown to 26 percent, higher than in subsequent decades, even after the start of Operation Bootstrap (Picó Vidal 1980: 203–205). This increase was due largely to the growth of the tobacco industry and home needlework enterprises, which included married women but generally confined them to the home. During the depression, high rates of male unemployment and low wages forced women to contribute to the household economy, but home needlework was paid as little as one cent per hour (Picó Vidal 1980). Needlework constituted the second most important export from Puerto Rico during the depression and war years, when sugar entered a prolonged slump. As a result, the number of married women employed doubled, increasing from 31.8 percent of the female labor force in 1920 to 39.4 percent in 1935, much earlier than in Cuba (Baerga 1993: 114). Many of our older respondents now working in the garment industry started in the home needlework industry, earning as little as $10 a week. Some of the women workers in the tobacco and needlework industry became militant trade unionists who participated in strikes and strove for better wages and working conditions with the support of the Free Labor Federation (FLT) and the Socialist Party, though few women ever occupied top leadership positions in either organization. While the Socialist Party defended universal suffrage for men and women and required female representation on its committees, the party and the FLT failed to back worker demands to include Puerto Rico in the minimum wage legislation passed under the Fair Labor Standards Act, which would have raised the wages of workers of both sexes (Silvestrini 1980: 63). The limited effectiveness of women workers in the public world of unions and politics contributed to the disillusionment of women workers with labor leaders and government officials, which continues to this day.

The level of proletarianization also varied among different island subcultures and was highest among landless sugar cane workers and urban workers and lowest in the tobacco- and coffee-growing communities, where control of family land and labor still gave men a greater basis of authority in the family (Steward 1956). Women could resist male dominance more easily in these more proletarianized communities, as evidenced by a higher level of consensual unions and more sources of income as well as control of the household's economic resources (Colón 1993).

In the early twentieth century, elite Puerto Rican women were also beginning to enter the labor force in greater numbers in the professions and white-collar work. As in Cuba, they were the principal proponents of women's suffrage, but with little support from working-class women, who focused on class issues. Women's suffrage was approved in 1929 after ten years of struggle by these elite women, but the literacy requirement was not abolished until 1936, again marking class and color distinctions (Picó Vidal 1980: 211). In Puerto Rico as in Cuba, racial and class differences divided the early women's movement and weakened their struggle for greater equality. The efforts of middle-class women were directed primarily at securing the vote in both Cuba and Puerto Rico, and literacy requirements denied this right to poor women initially. Concern over child welfare in Puerto Rico accelerated in the l930s and 1940s and emphasized women's maternal role through health, education, and social programs, while partially paid maternity leave was passed in 1942 (Colón 1993). Male dominance in the family was not questioned, but concern for male abandonment led to the provisions of safeguards for child maintenance for legally married women. This helped produce a drop in the percentage of consensual unions in Puerto Rico from 34 percent in 1899 to 4 percent in 1980, much lower than in Cuba (Vásquez Calzada 1988). However, a study conducted in 1982 suggests that the latter figure probably underestimates the actual number of couples living together, which appears to be increasing since the 1970s. Many of these are couples of higher socio-economic status, who do not define themselves as being in consensual unions. Traditional consensual unions are most common among the very young and older rural women and among those of lower socio-economic status, but there are no racial differentiations given. Consensual unions are very unstable, although they may be legalized over time, especially if there are children (Vásquez Calzada 1988).

In the Dominican Republic, the middle-class feminist movements of the 1930s and 1940s also secured the vote in 1942, with the support of the dictator Trujillo. Their reemergence under the conservative government of Balaguer in the 1960s revealed the same class and maternalist bias, and the feminist movement limited its activities to education and legal reforms (Mota 1980). In the 1970s a more widespread feminist movement began to develop with the establishment of feminist research

Puerto Rican women lining up to vote after the passage of women's suffrage in 1929. Note that most are white and well dressed. Courtesy of the Photographic Lab, University of Puerto Rico.

and action centers such as CIPAF, whose study on the free trade zones is the basis of the Dominican data used here.

The identification of wage work with blacks and lower-class status reinforced the patriarchal ideal of the confinement of women to the home in Puerto Rico, the Dominican Republic, and especially Cuba, particularly among the elite, who did not seek paid employment until professional and white-collar jobs commensurate with their status opened up. Most attempts by women to seek paid employment were either confined to the home, as in domestic service or home needlework, or seen as extensions of domestic roles, such as teaching and nursing. Even agricultural work came to be so associated with slavery and blacks that white peasant women ordinarily did not work in the fields, except during harvest time, and were seldom recruited as day laborers. Patriarchal norms were not as entrenched in urban working-class households, particularly among people of color, because low wages and unstable employment forced both partners to contribute to the household and because a higher proportion of consensual unions led to greater marital instability and more female-headed households.

Labor force participation rates and marital patterns continued to be racially differentiated even after the Cuban revolution. In the 1981 Cuban census, black women have higher labor force participation rates than white or mulatto women. The percentage of marriages and consensual unions among blacks and mulattoes is about equal, while among whites the percentage of marriages is much higher. Blacks also show a higher rate of marital dissolution, which has increased for all racial groups after the revolution. The percentage of consensual unions has actually increased after the revolution, particularly among whites (de la Fuente 1995: Table 6), while the percentage of legally married women has declined. In 1987, 28.7 percent of Cuban women in the reproductive ages of 15 to 49 were in consensual unions compared to 34.7 percent of legally married women (Catasús Cervera 1992: 7). This is surprising, given the increasing educational and occupational opportunities for women in Cuba after the revolution.

Cuba has also maintained a high degree of racial endogamy after the revolution, which is also surprising given the gains Afro-Cubans have made in terms of employment and education. The 1981 census reveals that 93 percent of white heads of household marry someone of the same race, while the corresponding figures for blacks are 70 percent and for mulattoes 68.7 percent (Reca et al. 1990: 50–51).

The matrifocal family that emerged from this process of class, gender, and racial subordination differs considerably from the more patriarchal forms of family structure among the white elite in the Hispanic Caribbean. The matrifocal family is based on the mother-child bond rather than the conjugal unit, and women are a central source of economic and social support, reducing dependence on a male breadwinner. Its origins have been traced to a variety of factors, including African retentions, slavery, a high level of male migration, and male marginalization due to the man's inability to carry out his role as male breadwinner (Smith 1956; Herskovits 1958; Frazier 1939; González 1970; Safa 1974). The conjugal tie is weakened by marked sex role segregation, strong consanguineal ties for both men and women, and consensual unions, which contribute to marital instability and a high percentage of female-headed households. However, female-headed households represent only one extreme of matrifocality, which can also be found in stable unions where the bond between a woman, her children, and her female kin is more important and enduring than the conjugal tie. Matrifocality is generally associated with the black and mulatto urban poor in the Caribbean, where male marginalization is most severe and where the man's authority is totally dependent on his earning capacity (Safa 1974). Among the peasantry, male control of land and family labor reinforces his authority, while among the middle class, the man's occupation is an important status indicator for the family. In addition, the middle class attaches greater importance to legal marriage and the legitimacy of children (R. T. Smith 1988). However, at all class levels, consanguineal kin groups are also important as a source of emotional and material support, particularly for women.

Matrifocality in the Caribbean thus weakens at the domestic level the pattern of male dominance prevalent among more patriarchal elite households and common in the public sphere. However, matrifocality is limited to the domestic domain and does not assure women of equality in the public sphere, which continues to be dominated by white or mulatto elite men. Even in the English-speaking Caribbean, where matrifocality is much stronger and female labor force participation rates are much higher, women have been unable to translate their importance at the domestic level into greater equality for women at the public level (Safa 1986).

Conclusion

The continued separation between the private and public spheres in the Hispanic Caribbean, or the distinction between *casa/calle*, helps explain why the impact of women's paid wage labor may be stronger in the home than at the workplace or in the polity. Women of all class levels have always had greater legitimacy and therefore greater bargaining power within the home than in the public sphere. Matrifocality actually encourages women's attachment to the family and their domestic role, because it enhances the importance of women in the household, while the strong bond between women, children, and their female kin makes domestic work less alienating than in isolated nuclear households such as those found in the U.S. middle class (Safa 1980). As we shall see, working-class women's paid employment is commonly justified in terms of their family's need rather than in terms of personal fulfillment. Though women have gained some visibility in the public sphere, it continues to be principally the domain of men.

This suggests that in Latin America and the Caribbean, gender differences continue to be emphasized over individual rights, with women seen primarily as housewives and mothers and men primarily as breadwinners. The norm of the male breadwinner is so strong that even among the working class, men usually have the role of providers and heads of household, which forms the basis of their authority in the household (Safa 1974). This reflects socio-economic factors such as the more recent and lower rate of incorporation of women, particularly married women, into the labor force in Latin America and the Caribbean as compared to the United States and other advanced industrialized societies. It also reflects cultural differences in the form of the family and of the state. In Latin America and the Caribbean, the family and extended kin ties remain more important both for economic and emotional support at all class levels, since there is less social and physical mobility than in more industrialized societies. Family structure also varies by class and race. Male dominance is strongest among the elite, where men wield considerable economic power and women have been traditionally most confined to the home. Among the poor and working class and particularly among blacks and mulattoes, women have always contributed to the household economy, whether through wages or domestic production, because low incomes and marital instability require it. Racial differences in employment and marital patterns are more pronounced in Cuba than in Puerto Rico, but unfortunately these are not pursued in this study because their importance in the predominantly white samples in both countries was not immediately obvious.

The redistributive state in Latin America and the Caribbean is also much less developed than in advanced industrial societies like the United States. The task of social reproduction is left largely to the family, which increases dependence on male wages and a male breadwinner. This also helps account for the family's continued importance in the region. With increasing industrialization and urbanization and the growth of a developmentalist state, some Latin American governments have begun to institute measures to support labor such as social security, public education and health, and minimum wage laws. As in the United States, most of these measures have been designed for a male labor force, while women are regarded as supplementary wage earners or housewives. But even these redistributive mechanisms have come under attack as a result of the economic crisis and structural adjustment policies, which have forced the state to withdraw many social services and place these responsibilities back on the family, which is already weakened by high unemployment, inflation, lower wages, and other factors. Grassroots social movements have arisen among poor women in Latin America since the 1980s to protest cuts in public services and to institute communal kitchens and other self-help forms of collective consumption. However, as in an earlier period in the United States, the demands made on the state are justified in terms of women's domestic role rather than in terms of gender equality (Safa 1990a). Even in Cuba, where under socialism the state has assumed the most complete responsibility for social reproduction, it is evident that women still focus their demands on the state within a domestic framework, emphasizing practical needs such as day care and housing over gender equality.

Still, women's gender consciousness and bargaining power in the household have increased as a result of the massive incorporation of women into the labor force in recent decades. Increasing employment has forced women to redefine their role within the home and to challenge the myth of the male breadwinner. The inability of men to earn an adequate living due to the economic crisis, restructuring, and other changes in the global economy means that they are no longer able to offer their families support and protection in return for obedience, as was the norm in an earlier period of private patriarchy. But the cultural norm of the male breadwinner has been absorbed in the workplace and the state, as I shall discuss in the following chapters.

Notes

1. Nash (1988) argues that we should distinguish patriarchy rooted in kinship relations, which implies reciprocal obligations of male support and protection in return for women's obedience, from these more modern forms of male hegemony, where control involves little or no responsibility. However, I continue to use the term patriarchy here, while distinguishing between different types.

2. Includes only female-headed households with no husband present.

3. The underrepresentation in the census of women in prostitution, agriculture, and other areas also helps explain the low percentage of women in the labor force. The many non-wage subsistence activities such as growing food, washing clothes, and sewing, through which women contribute income to the household economy in all three countries studied, are also not generally included in these formal wage labor participation rates. For an excellent discussion of the shift from non-wage to wage activities in Puerto Rican households during the early twentieth century, see Baerga (1992 and 1993).

3

Women Workers and the Rise and Decline of Puerto Rico's Operation Bootstrap

When I interviewed Myrna in 1986, she had been working for the same garment firm for 30 years. She began working at age 15, sewing gloves at home in the old needlework industry. Myrna originally made $10 a week working in the original plant in Mayaguez, which has since shut down, and she now commutes to work in a branch plant in a nearby town. She complains of the commute: "*Yo me tengo que levantar a las cinco de la mañana, para ya a las seis menos cuarto ir donde la muchacha que me lleva, entonces para Rincón. Yo no tengo carro, yo mientras pueda para Rincón no voy. Yo trabajé allá, trabajé allá dos años y sufrí mucho, porque usted sabe que el que no tiene carro, que no tiene para moverse, sufre.*" (I have to get up at five in the morning, in order to leave at a quarter to six for the girl who takes me to Rincón. I don't have a car, as long as I can I won't go to Rincón. I worked there, worked there two years, and suffered a lot, because you know that if you don't have a car, if you have no way to move, you suffer.) Rincón is the branch plant located furthest away from Mayaguez.

Although she has lived in Mayaguez all her life, where schools are more available than in the rural area, Myrna never went to school and cannot read or write. She was married at age 13 to her first partner for ten years, and they had three children, the first of whom was born when she was 15. They separated, and she later lived with another man, who helped her raise her children. Although he left her for another woman and she has lived alone for 18 years, she helped to take care of him when he became ill and died because "*él se portó muy bien conmigo, con los nenes. Porque no eran hijos de él, él me los ayudó a cuidar, mi segundo esposo.*" (He treated me very well, with the children. Because they were not his children, he helped me to take care of them, my second husband.) Still, at age 52, she has no plans to remarry, even though "*no me gusta, es malo estar uno solo. Pero pa' los hombres que se están dando hoy en día, es mejor estar uno solo."* (I don't like it, it's bad to be alone. But with the men around today, it's better to be alone.)

For the last 12 years Myrna has lived by herself, in an apartment in public housing, for which she pays $125 a month, equivalent to one week's salary. Her grown daughter currently lives with her but does not work, and helps her mother out with some of the money she receives from social security. The daughter plans to leave shortly for Ohio to visit her children. Myrna's two other children also live nearby with their families.

Myrna is very grateful to the company and management for keeping her employed all these years and helping her raise her children. *"Porque ahora una persona como yo, que no sé de letra, usted sabe que ahora usted no sabe de letra no lo cogen en ningún lado, pa' trabajar."* (Because now a person like myself, who doesn't know how to write, you know that now if you don't know how to write, they don't take you anywhere to work.) Myrna says there was more solidarity among the workers in the early years, but not now: *"Porque antes había compañerismo, ahora no, porque antes nosotras trabajábamos todas con ese amor y esa humildad, pero ahora no, ahora todo es demasiado. Y ahora no, como que todo el mundo tira para sí mismo, pero nosotras nos llevábamos como hermanas. Que si usted acababa primero le daba la mano al que acababa, al que estaba atrasado. Con un egoísmo que se trabaja ahora."* (Because before there was companionship, not now, because before we all worked with that love and humility, but not now, now everything is too much. And now, as if everyone is out for himself, but we got along like sisters. If you finished first, you helped out the other to finish, the one who was behind. Now they work with egoism.) Still Myrna says the company prefers younger women because they are fresher and work faster. (They are also more educated.) Nevertheless, when she had difficulty with one supervisor for not working fast enough and blamed it on a bad sewing machine, the manager took her side and chastised the supervisor for not checking the machine properly.

Myrna clearly is more loyal to the company than to the union, about which she has many complaints. She claims the union is a company union and was forced on the workers shortly after the plant opened: *"Dicen que la unión de nosotras está, es patronal. Porque esa unión usted sabe que viene de Estados Unidos, que esa unión cuando vino acá al Malecón, eso vino, todo el mundo se tuvo que meter a la unión. Porque el que no se metiera a la unión se tenía que ir de la compañía."* (They say that this union of ours is a company union. Because that union you know came from the United States, that the union when it came here to the Malecón [name of Mayaguez plant], it came, everyone had to join the union. Because if you didn't join, you had to leave the company.) Her complaints center on the medical plan, which does not provide adequate coverage for medicine, and especially the doctor, whom many of the workers think should be changed. Apparently he tries to save money by not sending the workers for additional consultation and fails to keep appointments, but the union has done nothing. Myrna claims many of their union benefits are actually provided by the company, such as the medical plan and paid vacations: "*Entonces para que nosotros queremos unión si to' sale de la compañía?*" (So what do we want the union for if everything comes from the company?) Myrna is also angry that the union is trying to collect money to repair the Statue of Liberty, with which, as a Puerto Rican, she clearly does not identify: "*La unión de nosotros aportó a la Estatua de la Libertad diez mil pesos, pa' sacárnoslo a nosotros. Ven ... vendernos unas cosas que nos vendieron allí, yo no compré na', yo dije que yo no iba a comprar na', entonces le dan un botoncito a uno, si uno no ha, ningún puertorriqueño mandó a que él diera diez mil pesos pa', a cuenta de nosotros.*" (Our union is giving ten thousand dollars to the Statue of Liberty, to take it out of us. Look, to sell us some things that they sell us there, I didn't buy anything, I said that I wouldn't buy anything. Then they give you this little button, no Puerto Rican asked him to give ten thousand dollars, as our responsibility.)

Still Myrna plans to continue working until she is 62 and can collect her retirement benefits of $100 a month, although she says even this has become harder to collect. She blames the plant slowdowns and closings on the relocation of production abroad, citing company factories in the Dominican Republic, Jamaica, Antigua, and even Spain. She knows they are all looking for cheap labor, referring to the miserable salary these workers receive: "*Usted sabe que allá le trabajan por cáscara de batata, dicen que lo que le pagan a las mujeres allá son y que cincuenta y pico de chavos, verdad? Creo que cincuenta y cinco chavos o algo.*" (You know that there they work for [sweet] potato peel, they say that what they pay the women there is a little over 50 cents, right? I think that it's 55 cents or something.) This is what Dominican women workers in the free trade zones were earning in 1986, and the Puerto Rican plant in which Myrna worked had a twin operation with a Dominican plant. Myrna fears that if the company closes in Puerto Rico, the workers will be left without anything, even their retirement. However, she claims the company cannot declare bankruptcy while it has so many plants abroad.

Myrna illustrates many of the problems older Puerto Rican garment workers face: job insecurity; a company union; lack of schooling; work, marriage, and childbirth at an early age; and marital breakdowns and little spouse support, which forced her to raise her children largely on her own. Though she lives in public housing, the rent is quite high, and she receives no help from her children, who have their own families or, like her daughter, have no steady employment. She is very conscious of many issues such as the movement of production abroad and the lack of adequate representation by the union, but is still very devoted to the company and management for keeping her employed all these years. Both the union and management have fostered this type of paternalism among their workers in order to maintain a docile, loyal labor force.

Myrna suggests that the union, the ILGWU, was brought in by management rather than in response to workers organizing. The ILGWU was one of the dominant unions in the rapid growth of AFL-CIO affiliates in Puerto Rico between 1954 and 1964, particularly among industrial workers. These unions established affiliates only after failing to prevent the movement of U.S. firms to Puerto Rico, and David Dubinsky, then longtime president of the ILGWU, was one of the most vocal opponents of relocation because of the threat it posed to union membership on the mainland (Cabán 1984: 163). However, the union later reached an accommodation with management as well as with the government of Puerto Rico, whereby it reinforced workers' discipline rather than producing worker solidarity. Now the union is facing industry relocation to overseas sites where it has even less leverage, which further reduces the incentive to pressure management to meet workers' demands.

Methodology

As the history of the ILGWU in Puerto Rico demonstrates, the garment industry has undergone extensive internationalization of production since the 1950s, first to Puerto Rico and then to cheaper wage areas like the Dominican Republic (Safa 1981). The garment company studied here illustrates this process. Though established initially in New Jersey, the company began to move production operations to West Virginia and then to Puerto Rico in the 1950s in order to avoid rising labor costs. As production moved elsewhere, the number of production workers in its headquarters plant declined, a process I documented in an earlier study conducted in the late 1970s (Safa 1987). Eventually, this New Jersey plant came to serve as only a shipping and administrative center for the entire firm's operations.

Through my prior research, I came to know management and the ILGWU and obtained their permission to study their Puerto Rican operations. With their assistance, I selected the three plants studied here, all located in the western part of the island. I was especially interested in this region, because it had been the center of the earlier home needlework industry, giving the area a long tradition in the needle trades, as Myrna's life history indicates. Mayaguez, the major city in this region, continues to be a center of garment production, with more apparel employment in 1982 than any other municipality, including San Juan (Priestland and Jones 1985: 19).

The data analyzed here consist of a survey of 157 garment workers conducted in 1980 by a research assistant,[1] along with interviews with plant managers and union officials, plus in-depth interviews with a subsample of 15 women that I conducted in 1986. The sample of 157 women was drawn from a total of 757 workers employed in three different branches of the company in the western region of Puerto Rico, although at the time the company had four additional plants operating on the island. The firm is a well-known company producing a quality brand of lingerie, which has survived longer in Puerto Rico than standard manufacturers producing cheaper products because it can afford to pay slightly higher wages. However, as Myrna notes, production is now declining as the firm moves to cheaper wage areas in other parts of the Caribbean and other overseas locations.

This sample does not claim to be representative of the female industrial labor force in Puerto Rico nor even of the garment industry. Most plants in Puerto Rico have fewer than 50 employees (Priestland and Jones 1985: 18), whereas in 1980, two of the three plants studied here numbered over 250 employees, while the third plant in Mayaguez had declined to 128 employees because it was in the process of being shut down. Smaller companies producing lower-quality goods and located in the San Juan metropolitan area undoubtedly would have demonstrated even greater instability and labor turnover. In addition, the data were collected on one company in one region, and we slightly over-sampled long-term employees. Because of our interest in long-term employment, the sample was chosen on the basis of length of time employed. We sampled 25 percent of women who in 1980 had been working for the company ten years or more (considered long-term employees) and 20 percent of those who had worked less (considered short-term employees). The Mayaguez factory was the first plant of this company established on the island in 1952 and had the largest number of long-term employees. The other two factories are located in nearby rural towns and were established in 1964 and 1965, respectively, partly in response to longer-term tax exemptions offered at that time to plants locating outside of major urban centers.

Approximately one-third of the 157 women in the sample were long-term employees, but upon analysis it appeared that length of employment was not in itself a crucial determinant of any of the important variables in this study. In fact, length of employment is highly correlated with other demographic variables such as age and rural-urban residence, so that short-term employees tend to be predominantly young rural women, while long-term employees tend to be predominantly older urban women, like Myrna. Two-thirds of our sample are married women, who tend to be fairly evenly distributed among the three plants and among long-term and short-term employees. Female heads of household, which includes divorced and separated women and widows, are concentrated among older long-term employees, while with one exception, all single women under 30 are short-term employees. These demographic differences among women were clearly more important than the plant in which they worked in terms of their effect on female employment, and this led us to use the household rather than the factory itself as the unit of analysis.

Though it does not claim to be representative, this sample corresponds fairly closely in terms of age and marital status to the general profile of female industrial workers in Puerto Rico, who tend to be married, with children, and between 26 and 35 years of age (Acevedo 1993). In each of these respects, Puerto Rican women industrial workers differ from the global norm for multinationals, which tends toward young, single women without children (ILO 1985: 31–34). These differences reflect both the long-term history of the garment industry in Puerto Rico in comparison to the newer export-processing zones and alternative job opportunities for younger, better-educated women in the growing service and white-collar sectors. However, for illiterate older women like Myrna, there are no job alternatives, which partially explains her loyalty to the company.

The sample also provides us with a full life cycle, from young, single women still living with their parent(s), to middle-aged women married and living with their husbands and usually children, to women older than 45, both married and female heads of household. These stages of the life cycle appear to be major determinants of the role women play in the social reproduction of these working-class households, on at least two levels. First, as we shall see, life cycle is a principal factor in labor recruitment strategies, with management, even in the garment industry, generally preferring younger, single women, as Myrna noted. Secondly, the life cycle affects the way in which women regard their earnings and the contributions they make toward the household economy. The importance of their contribution must be measured against the contributions of other household members as well as against other sources of income, such as transfer payments, which also vary over the life cycle.

Puerto Rico presents several advantages for studying the impact of industrial employment on women workers. Because of its long history of export-led industrialization, it is possible to view both the rise and decline of the garment industry through the eyes of older women workers like Myrna, who has spent most of her life working for the same firm. I myself lived in Puerto Rico from 1954 to 1956, and again from 1959 to 1960, when I conducted a study for the Puerto Rican Urban Planning and Housing Authority (Corporación de Renovación Urbana y Vivienda). This study on the relocation of shantytown residents into public housing served as the basis for my doctoral dissertation in anthropology at Columbia University. Though I have not lived in Puerto Rico since 1960, I have returned frequently and did a restudy of these urban poor families in 1969, and the entire study was subsequently published as a monograph (Safa 1974). This long-term perspective has given me a personal view of the industrialization process in Puerto Rico, which I have drawn upon in this current study. Profound changes have taken place in Puerto Rico during this 30-year period, due largely to the growth of industrialization, urbanization, and migration, and are reflected not only at the macro level, but also at the household level, particularly regarding the role of women. Though we do not have a control group of non-working women with which to compare our respondents, I can personally attest to the empowering effects that long-term employment has had on women. Compared to 30 years ago, Puerto Rico's working women are more assertive and less subservient to male dominance, but also carry greater economic responsibilities as they have become major contributors to the household economy.

Wages and Working Conditions

The garment industry played a unique role in the history of Puerto Rican economic development. For 20 years, from the mid-1950s to the mid-1970s, the garment industry supplied from one-quarter to one-third of all manufacturing jobs on the island and is still the largest single employer in the manufacturing sector. However, between 1973 and 1983, garment employment in Puerto Rico fell 26 percent, paralleling similar declines in garment employment in the United States (Priestland and Jones 1985: 3, 6). In both cases, most of the job loss is due to imports, which continue to plague the domestic garment industry today.

The decline in the garment industry in Puerto Rico involves every segment of the industry in different ways. Faced by increasing international competition, management augments the decline by shifting more of its production abroad to cut costs. The union faces a declining and increas-

A Puerto Rican garment worker sewing gloves in the 1950s, the early days of the garment industry in Puerto Rico. Courtesy of the General Archives of Puerto Rico, Commonwealth of Puerto Rico. DOCUMENTARY SOURCE: Department of Public Education, photographed by Jack Delano.

ingly disgruntled membership while trying not to antagonize management in order to persuade the industry to remain in Puerto Rico. And workers fear for their jobs as they see plants closing and production slowing down to cope with declining demand. The result is a deterioration in working conditions in the Puerto Rican garment industry and increasing unemployment and reliance on transfer payments for survival. This has a particular effect on older workers like Myrna who have spent 20 or 30 years in the garment industry and feel they are now too old to find a job in another sector.

Concern with job stability is particularly acute in the Mayaguez plant, where most of the workers are older and where production began to decline with the opening of the rural plants in the mid-1960s. The number of production workers in Mayaguez declined from a peak of 300 to 128 when we chose our sample in 1980 and fell to 36 a year later. Eventually production ceased completely, although the plant continued to be used as a warehouse and office for the district manager. The building was old and subject to flooding and had also lost its tax exemption. Because of the union, workers were given the option of transferring to one of the newer factories in the rural towns, which accounts for many of the older women in these plants in our sample. These older women are not happy about having to travel several miles to work, which means they must spend more time and money on transportation. But to receive social security and a union pension of $100 a month, workers must be at least 62 years of age and must have worked a minimum of ten years. Evarista now commutes to one of the rural plants from her home in Mayaguez, although she is 59 years old and has worked for the company since 1958. She echoes the sentiments of many older workers, who hope they can hang on until retirement age, noting: "*Estoy loca por tener ya los sesenta y dos pa', para poderme retirar, porque en realidad no me encuentro tan poco allá bien de salud.*" (I am anxious to reach 62 to be able to retire, because really I am not in the best of health.) Her take-home pay is reduced through union fees, social security, and other standard deductions as well as payments she continues to make on a modest house bought in 1968. As a result, there are weeks when her net pay is less than $10 a week, because she has not worked more than a couple of days. But she manages with the aid of unemployment insurance, food coupons, and occasional assistance from her children, all of whom are high school graduates.

As Evarista indicates, even the newer, rural plants are subject to production cutbacks due to lack of demand, during which the plant may reduce employment to a few days a week. Production cutbacks have affected 85 percent of the women in our sample (higher in Mayaguez), and this signifies a substantial loss in earnings, since women are paid only for the hours worked. Women may apply for unemployment compensation for the days not worked, but payment is often delayed for weeks or even months. Management has moved production to these rural plants for several reasons. Plants in rural areas enjoy a longer-term tax exemption and as these expire, newer plants are built to requalify. Despite recent cutbacks in production in both of these rural plants, new buildings have been constructed alongside each one and new workers hired, although some workers were transferred. Workers in the rural plants are also younger and better-educated than in the older Mayaguez plant, where over half of our sample are over 45, and few of these older women have gone beyond eighth grade (Table 3.1). In comparison, all but four of the women under 30 in our sample work in the rural plants and nearly two-thirds of these younger women have at least completed high school. These generational differences also reflect the great educational advances made in Puerto Rico since 1950. The garment industry can afford to be more selective in these rural towns, which offer women fewer alternative sources of employment than the city. One of the towns has a General Electric plant, and many of the younger women thought they

TABLE 3.1

Educational Level by Age in the Puerto Rican Sample

Age	Grade 8 or Less		Grade 9-11		High School or Vocational Graduate		University Studies	
	No.	Percentage	No.	Percentage	No.	Percentage	No.	Percentage
Under 30	10	17.2	16	43.2	37	67.3	3	75.0
30-44	19	32.8	16	43.2	16	29.1	--	--
45 and over	29	50.0	5	13.6	2	3.6	1	25.0
Total	58	100.0	37	100.0	55	100.0	4	100.0

Source: Data compiled by Helen I. Safa.

could find employment there if necessary, but the older women felt they were not qualified because of their age and lower educational levels.

The predominance of older married women in our sample partly reflects the decline of the garment industry in Puerto Rico and its difficulty in attracting young, single women who prefer better-paying factory or white-collar jobs.[2] Some managers say they prefer married women because their family obligations make them more responsible, but most managers prefer to hire young, single women because they are supposed to be more efficient, to have lower rates of absenteeism, and cost less in terms of maternity benefits. Three-fourths of the women under 30 in our sample have been hired in the last five years, and for most of them this is their first job. Managers claim that younger women complain less and produce more, because they are interested only in earning money and have not developed "bad habits." Some managers said they prefer to train new workers rather than hire those with prior experience because "*uno las moldea, a la forma de* [*la firma*]" (one molds new women in the form of [the firm]). However, all workers must have some knowledge of running industrial sewing machines, because the firm teaches them only specific operations. Women may learn through high school or special government training programs. New workers are given a sewing test and also must pass a trial period to see if they can meet the heavy production quotas.

Recruitment is often through word of mouth, with the manager announcing vacancies on the speaker, while some younger women are also recruited through the Department of Labor or through the vocational school. This helps to explain why over 55 percent of the women in our sample have relatives working in the same factory, a figure that is even higher among younger women working in the rural towns. They are often sisters or cousins who live in the same neighborhood and frequently travel to work together in someone's car, because there is no

public transportation, only *públicos,* which are like taxis covering speci-
fied routes.

Most of the women in our sample in 1980 earned a net weekly wage
between $120 and $129, a figure that is lower than the 1980 average
weekly earnings for manufacturing in Puerto Rico of $154.98 (Economic
Development Administration 1989: Table 4, p. 7). Production work in the
garment industry is generally on a piecework basis, which workers prefer since they can increase their earnings through greater productivity.
In fact, one of our younger respondents claimed she was earning as
much as some of her friends in secretarial jobs. However, the garment
industry is still the lowest-paid industrial sector in Puerto Rico, with average hourly earnings in 1980 of $3.40 (Economic Development Admin-
istration 1989: 8). This is not enough to support a family and reflects the
common misconception, cited in a government study of the garment industry, that "women's earnings supplement the family income" (Priestland and Jones 1985: 40). There is no increase in earnings with seniority.
On the contrary, some older workers say younger women are given preference during production cutbacks because they are considered more
productive and learn new operations more easily. There is also little possibility of mobility, although a few women have become supervisors, like
Awilda, who has worked for the firm since 1967. Supervisors have a fixed
salary and a guaranteed work week and are not members of the union.
However, no supervisors have risen to management positions, all of
which are occupied by men. Most managers have spent many years
working with the company and have developed a strong paternalistic
relationship with their employees, especially those who have also
worked there a long time. For example, when one of the managers in
Mayaguez was transferred to a rural plant in 1970, María Isabel went
with him "*porque me gusta trabajar con Reyes*" (because I like to work
with Reyes).

Many of the older workers like Myrna or María Isabel have established a strong identification with the company, which is reinforced by
the high percentage of long-term employees. María Isabel was 19 when
she began working for the company in 1952, and though she is a union
delegate, she is very loyal: "*Tengo toda una vida trabajando en el mismo
sitio y, pues le tengo un amor a la fábrica.*" (I have a whole life working in
the same place, and well, I love the factory.) María Isabel, who is now 59,
feels she owes much of the progress she has made to the company, noting: "*Mire, yo compré el carrito, yo arreglé mi casita desde que estoy
trabajando. Yo no me quejo de la compañía, porque eso, lo que yo tengo,
lo poquito que yo tengo me lo ha dado la compañía por medio de mi
trabajo.*" (Look, I bought my car, I fixed up my house since I am working,

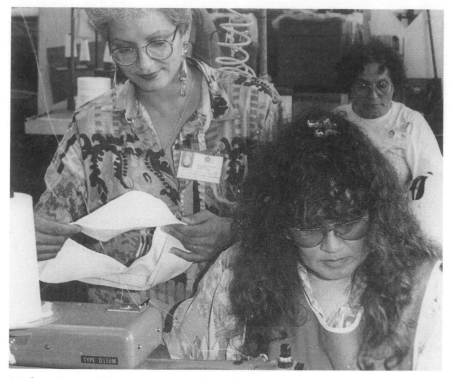

Modern Puerto Rican garment workers with their supervisor. Courtesy of Office of Communications, Industrial Development Company, Commonwealth of Puerto Rico.

I don't complain about the company, because what I have, the little I have, the company has given me through my work.) Undoubtedly, this strong identification with the company, especially among long-term employees, has contributed to the lack of worker solidarity in the company and is fostered by paternalism.

In our sample, nearly 90 percent think factory jobs are good for women, and most are satisfied with their work and plan to continue working indefinitely. Over half of our sample have not missed any work during the past year, while those who have cited illness and pregnancy as the most important reasons. In addition, 85 percent say they would look for another job if they lost their present one, indicating a strong work commitment. As the husband of one middle-aged worker with two young children noted: "*Tiene uno que seguir trabajando, porque si no, hay como diez que están fuera esperando coger.*" (One has to keep working because if not, there are like ten waiting outside to take [your job].)

Nevertheless, the district manager claims absenteeism has risen from 2 percent to 4 percent before 1970 to 12 and 14 percent in 1980. He says: "*No hay ese orgullo de trabajar que había antes.*" (There is not the pride in work there was before.) Managers claim that transfer programs such as unemployment insurance and food stamps have undermined the work ethic in Puerto Rico, by making it possible for families to survive without employment. However, as we noted earlier, these transfer programs also subsidize low-wage industries such as garment firms by reducing a family's dependence on wages for an income. Workers who are employed less than 30 hours a week because of production slowdowns are entitled to request unemployment insurance, though this may take weeks to collect. This is a great asset to the garment industry, where employment is highly seasonal, and helps to maintain a cheap labor market.

Only 19 percent of our sample receive food stamps, and these are generally female heads of household or large, rural families in which the daughter is often the sole wage earner. For example, Teresa lives with her parents, several siblings, and a young nephew, but she is the only one with full-time work in the family. Her father in his fifties has not worked for ten years, and her brother studied accounting in Mayaguez for two years, but has been unable to find steady employment. He has custody of his four-year-old son, whom the family is raising. Teresa does the weekly shopping of about $75 with her salary and keeps about $45 for her own expenses. Her household shares the cost of water and electricity with her sister and other relatives who live next door, and they often cook together. Teresa's family does not have to pay housing in their self-built house on a *parcela*[3] given them by the government, and they also receive *cupones* to buy food but no social security or unemployment insurance. Teresa has three sisters working in the same factory, one as a secretary who recruited the rest, but they are married and live apart.

Teresa's family illustrates the problem of male unemployment in the area, which has caused many men to withdraw from the labor force or to migrate. Ninety percent of our sample say it is easier for a woman to find a job than for a man, which helps explain why these women can no longer look to men as primary wage earners. Two-thirds of the husbands of the women in our sample have been unemployed at some time since they started working, but only a few were unemployed at the time of our study in 1980. Over half earn salaries between $100 and $175 weekly, working in a factory or service jobs, for the government, or in their own business (usually as *público* drivers). Older men may retire to live on social security or veteran's benefits. Unemployment is most acute among younger men like Teresa's brother, unable to find a job even with a college education. In 1986, when these in-depth interviews were conducted, the rate of unemployment among youth aged 16 to 19 was 54.6 percent, over twice the national average, and nearly half the migrants between 1970 and 1980 were between the ages of 16 and 24, of whom about one-third were students. Migration in 1986 reached 46,619 persons, its highest peak since 1957, and included a higher percentage of professionals and other white-collar workers (Puerto Rico Planning Board 1987: 35–42). This represents a serious drain on the Puerto Rican economy and demonstrates the gravity of unemployment, especially among men.

High unemployment led to heavy out-migration from the western region of Puerto Rico since the 1950s, particularly among men because of the decline in male agricultural employment (Monk 1981: 41). In our entire sample, 62 percent of the women have husbands who have lived in the United States, and 46 percent have brothers who are currently living there, but the percentage of sisters and women themselves who have migrated is considerably less. Some of our respondents are return migrants who have lived in the United States for periods of several years and who have returned because of difficulties in finding employment there or for family reasons. For example, the Flores family returned in 1974 after living in New York for 25 years because they feared the effect of crime and drugs on their teenage children. All four of their children live at home and the three oldest have gone to the university. They built a beautifully furnished three-bedroom house on a *parcela* that they bought for $12,000, with savings they brought from New York. As a unionized blue-collar worker, Mr. Flores earned $600 a week in New York, and his wife did not work after they were married. However, now that his weekly salary is only $250 and their children are still in school and the cost of living keeps rising, Mrs. Flores is also working. She still has two sisters living in New York who visit her yearly, and one plans to return to retire in Puerto Rico.

Opinions differ among management and the union as to the reasons for high unemployment in Puerto Rico and for production cutbacks in the garment industry specifically. Management tends to put the primary responsibility for unemployment on the "laziness" of workers who can now turn to food stamps and other transfer programs as alternative sources of income and are no longer willing to do hard, manual work like cutting cane and fixing roads. They do not deny the flight of industry to cheaper wage areas but blame it on the high cost of labor in Puerto Rico and declining demand in the United States. However, the male regional director of the ILGWU in Puerto Rico maintained that wages could not be reduced to compete with the ridiculously low levels paid in a country like the Dominican Republic (about 50 cents an hour in the early 1980s) because of the high cost of living in the island. He thinks this high cost of living in Puerto Rico makes programs like food stamps "vital," because they subsidize the low wages the garment manufacturers pay. Still he is pessimistic about the future of the garment industry in Puerto Rico, which has seen its membership decline from a peak of 15,000 in 1972/1974 to 13,000 in 1980 (and probably lower now).[4] He claims the garment industry has always sought out the cheapest possible wage workers, and that the only solution to declining employment in the garment industry is higher tariffs on imports, since quotas are not enough. This protectionist position opposing imports is the position the ILGWU has tried unsuccessfully to defend in the U.S. Congress, sometimes with the support of textile and apparel manufacturers who have also been hurt by rising imports.

But if production in Puerto Rico is declining, why does the company continue to hire new workers? Forty percent of the workers in our sample were hired by this company between 1975 and 1980, almost all in the newer rural plants. Eighty percent of these workers were under 30, so perhaps new hiring reflects management's preference for younger, better-educated women, although because of union regulations, older women were also offered the option to transfer to one of the newer plants when the Mayaguez plant closed. New, younger workers also mean more dues for the union, while older workers represent a drain on pension funds, which are already running out of money. The union should have foreseen that the hiring of new workers would signify greater job instability for long-term employees, but it seems the union is afraid to make any heavy demands on management for fear the companies will leave. All of the managers said they had good relationships with the union, one adding "*Nos ayudamos mutuamente hasta donde esté a nuestro alcance y hasta donde esté al alcance de la unión.*" (We help each other, up to our limit and up to the union's limit.) Union objectives are set in the United States and not necessarily designed to defend or represent Puerto Rican workers, as Myrna's anger over the collection of money for the Statue of Liberty demonstrates. The regional director of the union was a North American, who came to Puerto Rico in 1965 and only retired in 1990.[5] As Myrna indicated, workers were never consulted about the initial formation of the union. Apparently it was the company and not the workers that asked the union to organize.

Puerto Rican garment workers accuse the ILGWU of being a company union (*unión patronal*) that does not defend their interests. Most workers feel that the union has brought about improvements, particularly in terms of fringe benefits such as medical insurance, paid vacations (two weeks a year), and the retirement pension. Some also argue that the union prevents workers from being laid off arbitrarily and has seen that the workload is distributed among workers during production cutbacks. However, because of their experience with the Mayaguez plant closing and frequent cutbacks, the most important concern of these garment workers is job stability, and on this issue, as in the United States, the union has been quite ineffective. Workers like Myrna are aware that production is being shipped to cheaper wage areas in the Caribbean and elsewhere, particularly since a twin plant with the Dominican Republic was opened in conjunction with one of the rural plants. In fact, workers claim that gradually almost the entire operation is being done in the Dominican Republic, so that only the cutting, labeling, and ticketing are carried out in Puerto Rico, in order to avoid import quotas in the United States.

Workers like Myrna were also very unhappy with the medical plan offered through the union. The doctor in charge in the Mayaguez region did not have office hours on Saturday (forcing them to take off a day from work for a medical visit), and some felt he was trying to save money by not offering them adequate medical care or by not referring them to other physicians. Many women preferred to use their own private physician, despite the cost. In 1986 a major protest broke out when the union wanted to raise the deductions for family coverage, citing the increasing cost of health care. Workers complained this increase would absorb half of their annual wage increase. It seems that many workers were unaware that basic medical coverage was paid by the company rather than the union and resented any increased deductions. The union is also facing financial pressure brought on by declining membership and has had to cut staff and increase dues. One of our younger respondents complained: "*Nos aumentan cada rato la cuota que tenemos que pagar de unión ... y los beneficios o se quedan igual o se bajan.*" (They are always raising the dues we have to pay the union ... but the benefits remain the same or are reduced.)

Child care is another need expressed by 85 percent of our respondents, and two-thirds said they would be willing to pay for it, though many women in our sample were beyond child-bearing age. Management and the union also recognize child care is a problem and a frequent cause of absenteeism, but the regional director of the union thinks that management should solve the problem, while management looks to the government for help. There is a public nursery school in one of the rural towns, but it is filled to capacity with a waiting list.

Decreasing support for the ILGWU in Puerto Rico has made union organizing more difficult. The fringe benefits offered by the union such as medical insurance or union pensions are facing increasing financial pressure, and these have difficulty competing with the array of benefits the government already offers workers. The regional director thinks the union's greatest accomplishment in Puerto Rico was getting the minimum wage raised to federal levels, which was done by the government but with union support.[6] He also thinks women are more difficult to organize than men, because they feel union organizing may cause the factory to close, and "women probably have more concern about the welfare of the family." Such attitudes reflect a paternalism toward women workers among the union hierarchy, which, like management, is almost entirely male.

Another reason the ILGWU may have difficulty organizing is the lack of rank-and-file participation in union decisions or negotiations. Many of our respondents say they do not attend union meetings, and only two have been union officers. They say meetings are called only to receive decisions made by union officials. The union functions mainly through committees and elected delegates, who work with the "business agent" appointed by the union. At the time of our study, this agent was a former garment worker at the same firm, who had been elected president of her local, lived in the area, and had been a member of the union since 1956. She tried her best to solve problems regarding medical insurance and child care, but the union made no attempt to instill a sense of collective action among its workers. On the contrary, one of its major concerns has been to quell any labor unrest. When workers in another branch plant threatened a one-day work stoppage to protest the increase in medical insurance, the regional director of the ILGWU in Puerto Rico visited the plants in the Mayaguez area to prevent the protest from spreading there.

Despite their criticism of the union and of certain management practices, the Puerto Rican women workers interviewed here are not aggressive in defending their rights. As a union delegate noted, workers complain, but "*entonces cuando les toca hablar, nadie quiere hablar*" (when they are supposed to speak, nobody wants to speak). Older women are more likely to question the authority of the union or management and to argue for their rights than younger women, who prefer to seek jobs outside the garment industry. As one of the older women workers whose daughter also works for the same firm remarked: "*Yo digo que para mi opinión las personas más mayores se preocupan más por el trabajo que las mismas jóvenes. Porque las jóvenes como ... a veces no tienen obligaciones y esas cosas y los maridos, serán que trabajan y le dan ...*" (I say that in my opinion older persons are more worried about work than the young. Because the young well ... sometimes they don't have obligations and such and maybe husbands work and give them [money].)

Older women have more at stake, since often their entire livelihood depends on their wages and they are unlikely to find other employment. However, they too fear high unemployment, the rising cost of living, and the flight of industry to cheaper wage areas elsewhere. In addition, they are held in check by a company union that fears any labor unrest will only hasten the flight of industry and lead to further decline in the apparel industry. The union shares with management and the government a paternalistic attitude toward women workers that mitigates worker solidarity or class consciousness. Workers are urged to seek individual solutions to their problems, through the union delegate, the manager, or a political party or government representative rather than through collective action. Paternalism is reinforced through gender hierarchies, since almost all production workers are women, while union leadership and management are all men, and the new union delegate is also male and quite inattentive to the needs of women workers. A few men are also employed in production as mechanics (who are much better paid) and in packing and shipping.

Many of the problems the ILGWU faces in Puerto Rico can also be found in the United States, suggesting that they can be traced to the historical roots of the ideology and structure of the union. Waldinger's (1985) study of the early years of the ILGWU from 1900 to 1930 in New York points out that the union gained strength and worked best with the establishment of larger, more stable firms such as the one studied here, which stood to gain from the union's standardization of wage rates and employment conditions. The ILGWU was weakened in the 1920s as changes in industrial structure and product demand favored smaller, informally organized firms, to whom some of the larger firms subcontracted. This is similar to changes now occurring in the United States and Puerto Rico as a result of increasing international competition and the movement of production abroad starting in the 1960s. At the same time, the male-dominated character of the ILGWU has long hampered the integration of female leaders, despite their overwhelming predominance among the membership. In 1978, though 80 percent of the membership of the ILGWU was female, there were only two women officers and board members (Milkman 1985: 306).[7] In Puerto Rico, the union suffers the added disadvantage (or advantage, depending on one's political perspective) of being seen as an extension of U.S. hegemony over the island. As in the United States, the union is seen as a way of containing class conflict rather than as a vehicle of class mobilization.

Union members of the CGT (Confederación General de Trabajadores, or General Confederation of Labor) on parade for the Fourth of July. Courtesy of the General Archives of Puerto Rico, Commonwealth of Puerto Rico. DOCUMENTARY SOURCE: Department of Public Education, photographed by Jack Delano.

Thus, many factors contribute to the lack of worker solidarity among women garment workers in Puerto Rico, which relate to both their class and gender. Both union and management are male-dominated and cultivate a paternalistic relationship with women workers, many of whom have spent a lifetime with the company. The ILGWU does little to foster rank-and-file female participation or leadership and is afraid of antagonizing management because of increasing international competition and plant shutdowns. Women workers themselves are threatened by the loss of jobs, growing unemployment, and the rising cost of living, and, as we shall see, are still governed by patriarchal norms emphasizing women's role as wife and mother (Waldinger 1985: 92). However, women are beginning to recognize their increasing importance as wage earners, while unions, management, and the state still regard them as supplementary workers who lack the same legitimacy as men. This increases the vulnerability of Puerto Rican garment workers in a declining labor market.

The Household, Life Cycle, and Authority Patterns

One key determinant of the impact of paid employment on women's status is the degree to which households are dependent on their earnings. While management, unions, and the state continue to regard women as supplementary wage earners, most of the women in our sample are making a major contribution to the household economy. Nearly three-fourths of the women in our sample claim their families could not survive without their working. In no case in our sample does the woman's salary represent less than 40 percent of total family income, and it is usually higher among married women and female heads of household. The contribution women make varies considerably by marital status and household composition, which affect the number of wage earners in the household and total household income.

The highest household incomes are found among single women, where over 40 percent of the households have annual incomes over $14,000[8] (Table 3.2). All but two of the single women in our Puerto Rican sample are under 30 years of age and are generally members of large rural households, where there are usually two and often three to five persons working. The strong correlation between number of persons working in the household and total family income is shown in Table 3.3, where 60 percent of those with the lowest income of $5,000 to $7,999 depend on a single wage earner, whereas those with two or more wage earners do significantly better. Though daughters often contribute less than married women or female heads of household to household income, the pooled income from various wage earners enables a family to do quite well. However, the relatively high incomes of these households represent a particular stage in the family's life cycle, when they have a maximum number of wage earners contributing to the family income. This larger income will be lost as children marry and set up households of their own. No households reported regular income from children no longer living at home.

In Leonidas's family, for example, previously several siblings contributed to the household income and together built a nice house in which the family now lives. But all of the older siblings except Leonidas are now married and living apart, and she is currently the only one working in

TABLE 3.2

Marital Status by Total Annual Family Income in the Puerto Rican Sample

Annual Family Income	*Married*		*Female Heads*		*Single*	
	No.	Percentage	No.	Percentage	No.	Percentage
$5,000 to 7,999	8	7.6	13	52.0	4	14.8
$8,000 to 9,999	11	10.5	4	16.0	6	22.2
$10,000 to 11,999	27	25.7	1	4.0	4	14.8
$12,000 to 13,999	33	31.4	4	16.0	2	7.4
$14,000 and over	26	24.8	3	12.0	11	40.7
Total	105	100.0	25	100.0	27	100.0

Source: Data compiled by Helen I. Safa.

the household. Four younger siblings are still at home and studying, while her father is ill and has not worked for years, and "earns" (*gana*) social security. Still Leonidas clearly regards her father as head of the household, although she is already 34 and has been working since she was 18. A daughter often continues to defer to her father, even if he is not working, especially if he owns the house in which the family lives. As one of ten children, Leonidas left school in the second year of high school to start working, but four of her siblings went on to the university and one is now a teacher, so that she helped finance their education as well. Now that she is the sole wage earner, the family also receives *cupones* of $200 a month for food. Thus, the employment of single women is less disruptive of traditional authority patterns, since, as a daughter, a woman worker does not directly challenge the male role of economic provider in the same way a wife may (Lamphere 1986: 127).

These large rural Puerto Rican households tend to maintain strong patriarchal traditions and to follow a strict sexual division of labor, which is supported by the extended family setting. Men are not expected to participate in housework or child care as long as there are other women around to carry out these chores. In Irma's household, for example, the father only does the shopping and pays the bills, while she, her mother, and sisters share the rest of the household chores. Her father is retired and receives social security, while both she and her sister (as well as several cousins) work in the same factory. Irma gives her parents $20 to $40 a week from her salary but is also paying off a loan with which they constructed a large, modern new house four years ago. Irma's mother takes care of the four-year-old daughter of her married sister, who lives nearby and works in another factory. Mothers often help working daughters with child care and household responsibilities, even if

TABLE 3.3

Total Annual Family Income by Number of Persons Working in the Puerto Rican Sample

Number of Persons Working	$5,000-7,999		$8,000-9,999		Annual Family Income $10,000-11,999		$12,000-13,999		$14,000 and over	
	No.	Percentage	No.	Percentage	No.	Percentage	No.	Percentage	No.	Percentage
Only 1	15	60.0	6	28.6	4	12.5	1	2.6	3	7.5
2 persons	6	24.0	13	61.9	25	78.1	31	79.5	27	67.5
3 or more	4	16.0	2	9.5	3	9.4	7	17.9	10	25.0
Total	25	100.0	21	100.0	32	100.0	39	100.0	40	100.0

Source: Data compiled by Helen I. Safa.

they are no longer living at home. While this pattern relieves working mothers of some of their domestic responsibility, it also reduces pressure on men and makes young women feel less conscious of the need to challenge traditional gender ideology.

Like Irma's family, these rural Puerto Rican households are part of a tightly knit network of kin and neighbors, who help each other out in child care, house building, shopping, and other activities. Over 80 percent of the entire sample and 95 percent of the younger women in our sample have relatives living nearby, most of whom they see daily. Over 55 percent of the women have relatives working in the same factory, and they often travel to work together. Thus, while young women have a strong sense of sharing and solidarity, it is not so much with fellow workers as with female kin and neighbors, who constitute for these women their most important reference group.

There is little evidence of class or gender consciousness among these young, single Puerto Rican women. They have not been working very long and are generally satisfied with their jobs. Irma, for example, complains of the union, but says that other factories in the area are also laying off people or closing down and that even in New York there is high unemployment. She also says the union prevents arbitrary dismissals: "*Por esa parte pues yo creo que la unión defiende. Porque en esas mismas otras fábricas que yo conozco que no hay unión, pues no importa la cantidad de tiempo que tenga la persona trabajando si hay que despedir una ciertos empleados, pues despiden. Y por lo menos en cuanto a eso pues la unión respalda mucho al empleado.*" (In that sense I think the union defends us. Because in those other factories that I know there is no union, and it doesn't matter how long the person has been working, if it is necessary to discharge some employees, they discharge them. And at least in this case the union supports the employee very much.) It is true that none of our Puerto Rican respondents complained of arbitrary dismissals in the factory, as we shall see occurs often in the Dominican Republic.

Though they are aware of problems on the job and in the larger society, such as inflation and the movement of industry to other areas, young women do not identify with these issues. They are concerned with getting ahead, finding a husband, and having a family, all matters that do not challenge the existing gender ideology or system of class inequality. Irma, for example, started to study in a secretarial school but had to drop out to help support her family. She has thought of returning to school to study nursing or secretarial work but says she earns more than most of her friends in these jobs. Most young women like Irma plan to continue working after marriage and are already saving to buy or

A Puerto Rican rural wooden house typical of the 1950s. Note that all of the men are outside, while the women and children remain indoors, typifying the public/private split in gender roles. Courtesy of the General Archives of Puerto Rico, Commonwealth of Puerto Rico. DOCUMENTARY SOURCE: Department of Public Education, photographed by Edwin Rosskam.

build their own homes (still a tradition in the rural area). Here we see how patriarchal norms emphasizing a woman's domestic role weaken their identification as workers.

Older Puerto Rican women workers like Myrna are less optimistic about the future and tend to be more isolated and alienated. This is particularly true of female-headed households, over half of whom live in smaller households of one to three persons. They are also more likely to live in the city and have fewer kin living nearby. They tend to socialize less frequently, even with neighbors or fellow workers with whom they may have been working for many years. Evarista, for example, feels quite lonely after her mother died a year ago and brought her grandson to live with her, while his divorced mother and another daughter live nearby in Mayaguez. She is now 59 years old and was divorced nearly 30 years ago. She brought up five children on her own, although she received some public welfare when they were very young. She says it was difficult, but she managed with the aid of her sister and her mother, who watched the children while she worked. All but one divorced daughter are now married and living apart. Over half of the female-headed households in our sample are headed by a woman who is over 45, and most of the children are grown and living apart. This later stage of the life cycle also explains the small family size. When the women heading these households were young, their mothers often helped out, living with them and caring for the children while they worked. In several cases like that of Evarista, mothers continued to live with their daughters until they died. Mother-daughter relationships reveal the strong bond between female kin in Puerto Rican working-class families, which reinforces matrifocality and the marginality of men.

Despite the struggle she had bringing up five children on her own, Evarista says it is better not to be dependent on a man. "*Porque que yo coja un hombre y que yo tenga que, que mantener ese hombre, pasar malos ratos y maltrato, pues me quedo sola veinte mil veces. Me encuentro mejor sola porque así sola yo tiro pa' donde quiera y no tengo que estarle pidiendo.*" (Because if I take a man and have to maintain that man, suffer bad times and bad treatment, well then I stay alone twenty thousand times. I feel better alone because alone I go where I want and don't have to be asking him.) Evarista expresses clearly the greater autonomy that older working women achieve and the resistance of female heads of household to remarrying.

Most of the female heads of household in our sample are divorced or separated from their former husbands (only four are widows), and like Evarista, two-thirds would prefer not to remarry. They see men as restricting their freedom rather than assisting them with the responsibility of raising a family. It is difficult to know whether men have become more irresponsible, as some women suggest, or whether women's expectations of men have increased and they are no longer willing to accept male abuse and domination, as my previous study suggested (Safa 1974: 91–92).

Both Evarista's and Myrna's husbands left them for other women. This seems to be the most common cause of marital breakdown, along with other personal problems such as male alcoholism, rather than financial problems. It is interesting that none of the divorced or separated women in our sample blamed the breakdown of their marriage on their working outside the home (Muñoz Vásquez and Fernández-Banzó 1988: 164). Most men were employed at the time of the breakdown, suggesting that unemployment and the inability of the man to carry out his role as economic provider were also not a major problem. It would appear that paid employment, while not precipitating marital breakdown, at least enables the woman to leave an unsatisfactory marriage by providing her with an alternative source of income.

For over half the female heads of household in our sample, they are the sole wage earner though some share expenses with an older child or other relative. As a result, many contribute their entire salaries to the household. The reduced number of wage earners helps explain why over half of these female-headed households have the lowest incomes of $5,000 to $8,000 annually (Table 3.2) and partially accounts for the high percentage nationally that falls below the poverty line, even if the women are working. In 1980, when this study was conducted, 32 percent of all Puerto Rican female heads of household were employed (higher than the national average), but 72 percent of these households were below the poverty line (Colón n.d.: Table 1).

Older women living alone or with an older child or sister can manage on these low incomes, especially if they own their own homes and are not paying rent or a mortgage. But women with young children to support must seek additional sources of support. Half of the female-headed households in our sample receive some assistance from federal transfer programs such as social security, public welfare, or most importantly food stamps, reflecting their low incomes. None of the divorced or separated women currently reports receiving regular support from their former husbands, although a few did when the marriage first broke up. Patria, for example, supports two children on her salary, but she manages because she lives in her parents' house and does not have to pay rent or a mortgage. Initially, her previous husband, from whom she is now divorced, sent her $50 a week for the children, but now she depends entirely on her own salary. She returned to Puerto Rico eight years ago from New York, where he still lives, leaving her husband because he was an *"enamorao"* (womanizer). Patria feels hurt that her husband has never come to see the children, both of whom are now teenage students preparing for college. Although Patria is 41 she considers her father the head of the household, because *"el dueño del edificio es el que manda"* (the owner of the house gives the orders). This also confirms the authority of parents over children, particularly when they own the house, as we mentioned earlier. Her parents are dependent on social security, so she shares in household expenses such as food and utilities as well as paying for her personal expenses like her car and the children's education.

Though Patria regrets her divorce, she thinks she is better off working, because she has more freedom and is not economically dependent on her husband. She comments on how marital relationships have changed, now that both husband and wife are working: *"Porque una persona que trabaja tiene sus derechos ... Ahora se ve obligado que ella mande, porque ella aporta ... Entonces ahora son los dos, antes era uno ... Pues por ese lado la mujer ha tenido ventaja."* (Because a person who

TABLE 3.4

Age of Married Women by Who Makes Household Decisions
in the Puerto Rican Sample

	Who Makes Household Decisions							
	Respondent		Spouse		Joint Decisions		Total	
Age	No.	Percentage	No.	Percentage	No.	Percentage	No.	Percentage
Under 30	2	5.0	14	35.0	24	60.0	40	100.0
30 - 44	5	12.2	12	29.3	24	58.5	41	100.0
45 and over	5	20.8	7	29.2	12	50.0	24	100.0
Total	12	11.4	33	31.4	60	57.2	105	100.0

Source: Data compiled by Helen I. Safa.

works has rights ... Now he [the husband] is obliged to let her give orders, because she is contributing ... Now it is both of them, before it was one ... Well in that sense the woman is better off.) Clearly, paid employment has given women a sense of independence that they did not enjoy as housewives and has probably led them to expect more from men as well.

The majority of married women in our sample maintain that they share household decisions with their husbands, though there is some variation by age (Table 3.4). This is a significant change from the patriarchal patterns prevalent earlier in most Puerto Rican working-class households. In my 1959 study of a shantytown in San Juan, husbands often refused to let their wives work or even leave the house alone to visit relatives, and the men made the major decisions regarding household purchases or the children's education (Safa 1974: 41–45). Men also represented the family to the outside world, whereas most women today act as their own spokespersons. Since both are working, earnings are usually pooled for household expenses and husbands no longer have exclusive budgetary control, as was common when the man was the sole breadwinner. Married women generally contribute 40 to 60 percent of the household income, which in over half our sample of married women falls between $12,000 and over $14,000 annually (Table 3.2). These higher-income households are generally those in which men have a steady, well-paid job, like Monserrate, whose husband makes $250 a week as an industrial mechanic. Her husband prefers that she not work, and while they lived in New York and the children were young, she stayed home. But after their return to Puerto Rico, she went to work at age 40 in the garment factory to help pay for the children's education and the high cost of living.

Most of the Puerto Rican husbands of our respondents now accept their wives working and no longer consider it a threat to their authority, because they realize it is impossible to live on a single wage. In some cases, the wife is the principal breadwinner, because the husband is incapacitated, retired, or does not have a steady job. Generosa's husband, for example, lived in the United States for 20 years and fought in the U.S. Army in World War II. The family returned to Puerto Rico 15 years ago and bought a small rural home, which they enlarged gradually with the aid of a loan from the Farmers' Home Administration. Generosa also worked in factories in New York, where she lived for ten years and met and married her husband. At 54, she is now the principal wage earner and plans to work until retirement at age 62. Her husband is ill and receives a disability payment of $275 a month through his military service. Their income is a little better now that her son, a college graduate, is working, but he is planning to leave shortly for the United States, while two older children are married and living apart. Generosa says they share expenses and household tasks, but she makes the major decisions since her husband is ill.

Jovita also says she makes the decisions in her house because her 62-year-old husband is incapacitated and has not worked in about four years. He worked for 30 years as a *público* driver but never paid social security, so now he has no income at all except for fishing. He doesn't like her working, but has to accept it because there is no alternative: "*Tiene que gustarle porque si no quién, verdad?*" (He has to like it because if not who, right?)

Jovita is 54 and has worked for 33 years for the company, although she was transferred from Mayaguez to one of the rural plants about five years ago. Her married daughter also worked for the same company, and both she and her husband formerly contributed to the household income. But now her daughter's husband joined the army, so the daughter quit to take care of her two small children and hopes to join him in the United States soon. After working so many years, Jovita would also like to quit, but hopes to hang on until retirement.

María Teresa has been working for the company for 27 years, and at 59 is now approaching retirement. Her second husband is 16 years younger than she, and as a construction worker, does not have a steady income. They have been married for 20 years, and he helped her to raise her two younger children by a previous marriage, both of whom are now married and living apart. But though he is younger, she cannot count on him for financial support. On the contrary, he expects her to work and María Teresa says he is annoyed when she doesn't work, noting: "*El no se molesta na', porque a veces yo falto un día al trabajo por cualquier cosa o algo, alguna diligencia o algo, y me dice 'Yo no sé porque tú faltas al trabajo pa' esa zanganá.'"* (It [her working] doesn't bother him at all, because if I miss a day of work for whatever reason, some errand or whatever, he tells me "I don't see why you miss work for that nonsense.") Other women also commented on how some men are now taking advantage of the fact that women have become the principal or sole contributor to the household, and like María Teresa's younger husband, relying on women for support.

However, while authority patterns are changing, the sexual division of labor has remained relatively intact, with women doing most of the household chores. María Teresa remarks: *"En los quehaceres de la casa, usted sabe que los hombres son vagos para los oficios, los oficios de la casa. … Me hace falta, pero pa' tener que pelear con él, pues mejor yo me quedo callada y nos llevamos así, bien, así. El dice que los oficios de la casa es de la mujer."* (In terms of household tasks, you know that men are lazy for those jobs, home jobs. … I need help, but to have to fight with him, well, it's better to keep quiet and we get along all right that way. He says that household tasks are for women.) Few of the married women in our sample pressured husbands to do more than the shopping and paying the bills, even when the men were no longer working. This is changing somewhat among younger married women, where a greater percentage of husbands help out, reflecting generational changes in gender roles. However, even among the children of our respondents, it is the daughters who most frequently help their mothers with household chores.

For most of the Puerto Rican working women in our sample, then, paid employment signifies a "double day." Younger single women are often relieved of household chores by their mothers, but married women and female heads of household have taken on heavy financial as well as household responsibilities. In return, most are demanding a greater share in decision making and budgetary control, while almost all married women say that both they and their husbands are the bosses in the household. We cannot assume that paid employment is the only factor bringing about this decided shift in authority patterns, especially since we do not have a control group of non-working women with whom to compare our sample. During the depression of the 1930s, Puerto Rican women working in the home needlework industry also made a major contribution to the household economy. However, as Baerga (1987: 102) notes, these women "saw their salaries as something additional in a period of severe economic crisis, as a complement to the supposed principal salary of the head of the household" (translation mine). With the move to permanent factory employment, women no longer see their salaries as complementary or supplementary but as fundamental to household survival.

Other studies of middle- and working-class families in Puerto Rico also indicate a shift toward more egalitarian authority patterns among married women in which husband and wife share in decision making and some household tasks (Muñoz Vásquez 1988: 114). Undoubtedly, additional factors noted in this chapter contributed to this shift, such as the large number of families who have lived in the United States, higher levels of education, and higher divorce rates as well as the virtual total transformation of Puerto Rico from an agrarian to an urban, industrial society. Another factor is the high level of unemployment and other changes in the occupational structure, which have for some time now weakened the economic role of the man but strengthened the importance of women as key contributors to the household economy. Transfer payments such as social security and food stamps have also provided women with alternate means of support, which reduces their reliance on male wages.

Politics, Class, and Mobility

While the working-class women in our sample have begun to challenge male authority in the home, they have made much less progress at the level of the state or the political process. In part this stems from a general disillusionment with politics, since governments change but there is little improvement in the overall situation of high unemployment and rising cost of living. As the middle-aged husband of Juanita, himself a government employee, noted: *"To' el gobierno que viene y el que sale, lo que quieren es to' pa' ellos y el pobre que, que uno se muera ... A nosotros nos aumentaron el trabajo, los chavos, no."* (Every government that comes and goes, what they want is everything for themselves, and the poor, one could die ... They increased our workload, but not our money.)

Eighty percent of the working women in our sample think that political parties in Puerto Rico have paid little attention to the needs of working women, and 60 percent think there is nothing they can do about it. Though there are state and federal laws protecting women against discrimination in employment as well as in other areas, the women in our sample apparently feel the state has not met their needs. These women want the government to provide more jobs and to control inflation, but in 1990, unemployment was still running at 14.2 percent of the total labor force (Table 1.3).

Despite their disillusionment with politics, these women are well informed about political figures. In the sample, almost all knew who their mayor and the governor of Puerto Rico were, and 80 percent named Carter as President of the United States in 1980, when the survey was conducted. Over two-thirds of the women in our sample voted in the 1976 election (the last major election before the survey), although the percentage fell below half among women under 30. Their vote was almost equally divided between the two major political parties, the Popular Democratic Party (PPD), which favors a continuation of the commonwealth status, and the New Progressive Party (PNP), which favors statehood. The PPD has apparently lost some of the support it enjoyed among the poor and working class; in the shantytown I studied in 1959, residents relied on the party (then in power for nearly 20 years) for the right to put up their homes on public land and for services ranging from water and electricity in exchange for their political allegiance and support (Safa 1974: 74). Today Puerto Ricans are even more dependent on the government for a range of services, but the PNP has gained electoral support. The PPD lost its unchallenged dominance in 1968, when the first PNP governor was elected.

Both the PNP and the PPD have argued that Puerto Rico is too small and poor to survive on its own, while economic and political dependence on the United States has grown. However, this has not diminished the sense of nationalism, which as in the earlier study is manifested among both PNP and PPD supporters. Statehood supporters think that Puerto Rico is too dependent on the United States to be independent and that the commonwealth status is obsolete. Monserrate's husband, who has lived in the United States for 25 years, is an ardent supporter of statehood, noting: "*Puerto Rico tiene que ser estado, no le dé más vuelta ... Entonces de lo único, a los más pobres lo único, la ventaja es la independencia, la estadidad. Cuando uno es un niño y el papá es grandote y está defendiendo a uno. Puerto Rico es muy pequeño como le dije para poder ser independiente, ve? Yo digo que si es independiente pues me voy para Miami.*" (Puerto Rico has to be a state, there is no alternative ... Then the only thing, for the poor the only thing, the advantage is independence, is statehood. When one is a child and the father is very big and is defending you. Puerto Rico is very small as I told you to be independent, see? I say if it is independent I am going to Miami.) The way in which he equates the relationship between the United States and Puerto Rico with father and son reveals the omnipotence with which many Puerto Ricans regard the United States, which he continuously refers to as "*la gran nación*" (the great nation). He also appears to equate independence with statehood. Many statehood supporters reject commonwealth status as a continuation of colonialism and feel Puerto Rico would enjoy more rights and autonomy as a state. Monserrate's husband claims that in the United States people are more conscious of their rights and protest to their congressmen, while Puerto Ricans are more apathetic. "*Aquí nadie se ocupa de nada, y ése es el problema que tenemos.*" (Here no one bothers about anything, and that is the problem we have.) The women in our sample are seldom so vocal about their political opinions, perhaps because they still think of politics as a male domain.

Because of their concern with unemployment and inflation, more than half of the women in our sample say it is not easy to advance in Puerto Rico, and nearly half say it is more difficult now than it was five years ago. Still 78 percent of our respondents think it was even more difficult for their parents, most of whom had less than an eighth-grade education. Many of their fathers worked as agricultural laborers, sometimes cutting cane, or in other manual labor jobs. Three-fourths of their mothers were reported to be housewives, but it would appear from our in-depth interviews that many sewed gloves at home, and this may not have been considered paid employment, which confirms our earlier observation regarding the difference between home and factory employment.

Generosa was part of the extensive home needlework industry prevalent in Puerto Rico in the 1920s and 1930s (Baerga 1993). She remembers the widespread poverty that existed in Puerto Rico when she was a child and left for the United States in 1951 at age 18: "*En aquel tiempo en Puerto Rico se vivía una pobreza enorme. En aquel tiempo sí, de aquel tiempo a éste, ha habido ... un cambio grande. Que en Puerto Rico antes las casas todas eran de madera. Y no había ni luz eléctrica más que en algunos sitios, no había agua.*" (At that time in Puerto Rico, there was enormous poverty. At that time yes, from that time to this, there has been ... a great change. Before in Puerto Rico all the houses were of wood. And there was no electric light except in a few places, there was no water.) Now all of our respondents have running water and electricity, and 60 percent own their own homes, which they have often built with their own labor, especially in the rural area. Investment in homes is one of the major forms of savings, particularly in the rural area. Most of the homes are well equipped, and almost all have washing machines and television sets, and 69 percent have stereos. Only about a quarter of our sample have telephones, which are still not available in some rural areas, but 80 percent have cars, which they use daily to get to work. However, many of these consumer items were bought on installment, which explains why 83 percent of our respondents have debts.[9] Most of these household debts are under $200 a month, which still represents a considerable drain on families where the modal annual income is $14,000. Sixty percent of the respondents in our sample have no cash

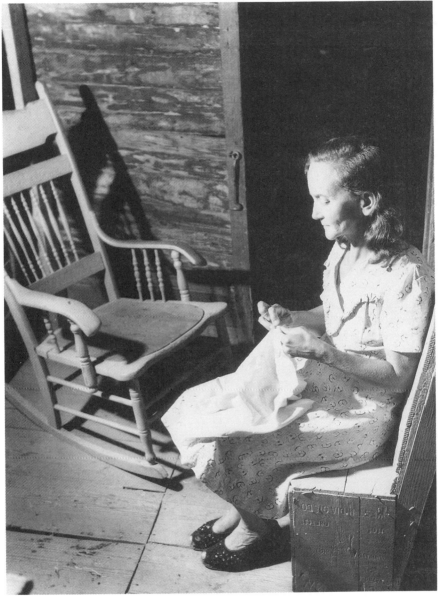

Home needlework was a typical form of employment in Puerto Rico in the 1920s and persisted up to the 1950s. Note that this needleworker is working by sunlight, probably because of the lack of electricity in rural areas before the 1950s. Courtesy of the General Archives of Puerto Rico, Commonwealth of Puerto Rico. DOCUMENTARY SOURCE: Department of Public Education, photographed by Jack Delano.

savings at all, although young women who are planning to marry often save to help buy a house or furnishings.

The nicest homes are often found among return migrants, who saved while in the United States to build and furnish a house in Puerto Rico. Their higher standard of living and competition for jobs have caused some resentment among less privileged neighbors, although Monserrate's husband says it has diminished with time, as more migrants have returned. He remarked: "*Había más antes cuando nosotros llegamos. Se nos tenía como una clase aparte, que éramos, tú sabes como algo aparte, pero lo cual es una gran mentira ... Yo para mí me siento tan americano como vamos a decir, como Eisenhower, como el apple pie y tan puertorriqueño como el coquí.*" (There was more [discrimination] when we arrived. They had us like a class apart, like we were, you know like something apart, but this is a big lie ... I personally feel as American as let's say, like Eisenhower, like apple pie, and as Puerto Rican as the *coquí*.)[10] Like many statehood supporters, he feels no contradiction between identifying as American and Puerto Rican at the same time.

Changes in class status are indicative of the progress most of our respondents feel they have made. Over half of our respondents identify as working class, while over half say their parents were poor. For our respondents, class status is based largely on annual family income and home ownership. About one-third of our sample identify as middle class, and three-fourths of them own their homes and two-thirds have annual incomes over $12,000. Class status also varies by life cycle, with 71 percent of young women identifying as working class, while a greater percentage of women over 30 identify as middle class (Table 3.5). These are generally married women whose husbands also earn a good salary (over $175 a week), so that they are likely to fall in the higher income brackets. Less than one-quarter of the female-headed households, who are generally poorer, identify as middle class.

Although three-fourths of our respondents feel they would have gone even further with more education, there does not seem to be a high correlation between educational level and class identification. Sixty percent of our respondents who identify as middle class have not finished high school, which is almost identical to respondents identifying as working class. However, 59 percent of the women with children in our sample think their children will be middle class, and here educational level does have a decided impact. Of the small number of children of our respondents who have completed their schooling (36 boys and 38 girls), half of these have gone on to college, and almost all of these college-educated youth are identified by their parents as middle class. A good number of these college-educated children are in white-collar professional jobs. Al-

TABLE 3.5

Class Identification by Age in the Puerto Rican Sample

Class	Under 30 Yrs.		30-44 Yrs.		45 and Over	
	No.	Percentage	No.	Percentage	No.	Percentage
Middle	12	17.4	20	39.2	19	51.4
Working	49	71.0	26	51.0	15	40.5
Poor	8	11.6	5	9.8	3	8.1
Total	69	100.0	51	100.0	37	100.0

Source: Data compiled by Helen I. Safa.

though some children have continued to work in factories, the great majority of women interviewed do not want their daughters or sons to have factory jobs.

Parents clearly have high aspirations for their children and have struggled hard to give their children a good education. However, parents complain that even children with a college education cannot find a job. Monserrate's son and daughter both studied at the Colegio de Mayaguez, a branch of the University of Puerto Rico, but her daughter is planning to leave for the United States after graduation because of the lack of employment. Monserrate complains: *"Los jóvenes se van porque ahora mismo todos los que se gradúan tienen que irse a buscar ... para allá trabajo porque aquí no se consigue."* (The young are leaving because right now all who graduate have to go to find ... work there because here you can't find any.) This coincides with the massive migration of young people in the 1980s noted earlier. Unemployment among youth aged 16–19 in 1990 was 36.4 percent and from 1981 to 1985 reached over 50 percent (Departamento del Trabajo y Recursos Humanos 1991: 32). The lack of employment possibilities, even for college graduates, helps explain why over a third of the women in our sample say it is harder for their children to advance than it was for them, although 60 percent claim it is easier. Even at the time of our earlier study, migration to the mainland represented an outlet for young people dissatisfied with life on the island, where the occupational possibilities even then failed to keep up with educational expansion (Safa 1974: 96).

Another important factor in explaining the possibilities for upward mobility in Puerto Rico is decreased fertility rates, which, as we noted earlier, fell drastically from 1950 to 1980 (Presser and Kishor 1991: 15). In our sample, nearly 65 percent of the women have three children or less, with a mean under two, while in the families in which they grew up, 85 percent had more than three children, sometimes reaching to ten or more.

It was common for earlier generations of Puerto Rican working-class families to have a large number of children and send them to work at an early age, as in Myrna's case described earlier. Almost 85 percent of the married women with children in our sample use some form of contraception, and about half of them have been sterilized, which was also the preferred form of birth control in the earlier study conducted in 1959. Smaller family size is undoubtedly linked to improved employment opportunities for women (Presser and Kishor 1991), since most of the women in our sample could not assume the responsibility for a large family and continue working. Though birth control, especially sterilization, was encouraged by state family planning services, especially in government-promoted plants (Pantojas-García 1990: 92), none of our respondents mentioned pressure in their decision to be sterilized.

Improved educational levels, lower fertility levels, and the independence of earning their own incomes have also made women more conscious of their rights as workers and more disposed toward gender equality. It is possible that exposure to the women's movement in the United States and in Puerto Rico has also influenced their attitudes. Ninety percent of our sample think a woman should earn the same as a man, and 80 percent think education is equally important for both sexes. Nevertheless, 44 percent of our sample continue to feel that women with children should not work outside the home, though daughters are less negative than wives or female heads of household, again reflecting generational differences. Many of the women say a mother's employment should depend on the age and number of the children, the availability of someone to take care of them, and on how badly the family needs the added income. Clearly, in the case of these women, the economic need to work prevailed over their continuing strong sense of responsibility as mothers.

Women are also conscious that their paid employment has contributed substantially to their own family's standard of living as well as to the social mobility of their children. The progress they and their children have made in terms of education, occupation, income levels, home ownership, and furnishings reflects in part the overall improvement in living standards in Puerto Rico since 1950, but the added income provided through female employment has also played a critical role. However, these women are beginning to express some doubts regarding the possibility of sustaining this progress in the face of continuing high unemployment and the rising cost of living. But they have yet to translate these concerns into greater political activism.

Conclusion

Clearly permanent paid employment has played an important role in increasing gender consciousness among Puerto Rican working-class women. It has contributed to their family's improved living standards and to their (sometimes misplaced) faith in education as a vehicle for upward mobility. It has enhanced their sense of self-worth to the point that they no longer depend on men as the sole or even primary bread-winners and are proud and confident of their contribution to the house-hold economy. And it has increased their awareness of issues such as unemployment, inflation, and even gender discrimination, though they remain quite apathetic in their response to these problems.

Puerto Rican women's failure to press their demands in the workplace stems primarily from the way in which they are incorporated into a de-clining industry in which labor has little leverage. As a result of interna-tional competition, the Puerto Rican garment industry, like that in the United States, has been plagued by plant shutdowns and production cutbacks that strengthen management's control over workers and un-dermine the collective bargaining power of the union and labor gener-ally. This is reinforced in the case examined here by older workers' strong identification with the company, for whom they have worked for many years. Workers are increasingly dissatisfied with a union identified with management and largely unresponsive to their demands, whether these concern child care, medical care, or especially job stability. At the same time, union practices have weakened rank-and-file participation and worker solidarity, reflecting the official role of unions as cooperative partners with management and the state in achieving economic devel-opment rather than as vehicles for class mobilization (Cabán Catan-zaro1984). Gender subordination is reinforced by the paternalistic treat-ment of women by male managers and male union leaders, who tend to dismiss women workers who complain, particularly older women, as "troublemakers."

Much of the same resignation and disillusionment is evident in the view women workers have of the political process. While these women have seen real improvement in their own lives and in Puerto Rican soci-ety as a whole during the period of Operation Bootstrap, their optimism is giving way to pessimism as they see progress becoming more difficult and fear that the future may not hold the same promises for their chil-dren that they once envisaged. Yet they feel that political parties, like la-bor unions, pay little attention to the needs of working women, and that politics remains a male domain in which women have little voice. At the same time, as public expenditures mount, there has been an erosion of state support for the costs of social reproduction—support that played such a crucial role in mitigating class conflict and underwriting low wages during the earlier stages of Operation Bootstrap. Low-income Puerto Ricans are paying more for public housing,[11] education, and medical care, but are still heavily dependent on transfer payments such as social security and food stamps. While this has lessened dependence on male wages, poor women are now increasingly dependent upon the state, thus substituting public patriarchy for the private patriarchy that existed previously.

The only arena in which Puerto Rican women feel they have some legitimacy is in the family. Partially as a result of paid employment, working-class women have gained a greater voice in household decisions and control over the budget, although they continue to do much of the housework. At the household level, women also have the support and assistance of the female kin group, while they lack comparable female support and solidarity in the workplace and in the political arena. The assistance of the female kin group and particularly the mother proves essential to the growing number of female-headed households who must struggle to support a family on their own. The marginal role of men in the family, even in their primary role as breadwinners, has tended to reinforce the traditional matrifocal nature of the Puerto Rican working-class family (Safa 1974) as well as to erode the last vestiges of deference to male authority in the household.

Thus, while male authority in the household has begun to weaken, it still remains largely unchallenged at the level of the workplace and in politics. Here I would argue that the fault lies more with the lack of support women workers receive from labor unions, the government, and political parties than with the women themselves. While the Puerto Rican female garment workers studied here have been quite acquiescent to the subordination they have suffered from these public institutions, they are also hampered by a paternalistic company union that makes no attempt to build worker solidarity and a government that fears the effect of labor unrest on foreign investment. Despite the long and extensive involvement of women workers in Puerto Rico's development process, they are not given the same legitimacy as workers as men are and continue to be regarded as subsidiary or supplementary breadwinners. Thus, the gender ideologies implanted in these institutions are as important as those generated in the home in maintaining women's subordination.

Notes

1. The research assistant was Carmen Pérez Herráns, then a Puerto Rican graduate student at Rutgers University, who completed her doctoral dissertation

on this research in 1989. She now teaches anthropology at the University of Puerto Rico. I supervised the survey design and analysis, and she conducted the interviews while living with the families of women workers.

2. Acevedo (1993: Tables 6 and 7) reports that in 1980, the average age of women in the garment industry was 34 compared to 30 for all high-tech industries, but over 65 percent of women in both industrial sectors were married.

3. The *parcela* program was instituted in the 1940s for the community resettlement of *agregados* who formerly lived on the land of rural landlords for whom they worked. The program was designed to eliminate this dependency and to provide rural laborers with greater social services to help counter the tendency toward urban migration. However, as this case illustrates, many *parceleros* are no longer doing agricultural work and have been absorbed into urban areas. In order to prevent speculation, *parceleros* were originally not given title to their land, but now this has changed, and *parcelas* are legally bought and sold (Pantojas-Garcia 1990).

4. At the national level, membership in the ILGWU has declined from 383,000 in 1955 to 210,000 in 1985, paralleling the decline in membership in other industrial unions such as steel (*New York Times,* October 27, 1985). As we noted in chapter 1, since 1980, the U.S. apparel industry has lost nearly 320,000 jobs, with probably half of them moving to Mexico, the Caribbean, and Central America (Justice 1993: 8).

5. The regional director, Clifford Depin, was very helpful to me in conducting this study but died shortly after his retirement.

6. The ILGWU and other U.S. affiliates initially tried to impose the same minimum wages in Puerto Rico as on the mainland to prevent relocation but were forced to accept gradual wage increases by industry. It was not until 1965 that Puerto Rican average hourly earnings in manufacturing approximated the U.S. minimum wage (Cabán Cantanzaro 1984: 164).

7. Milkman's (1990) article has an excellent discussion of the reason for the lack of women's leadership in the ILGWU and similar unions created in the 1910s.

8. In 1980, when this survey was conducted, the average family income in Puerto Rico was $14,762 (Economic Development Administration 1989: Table 1, p. 3).

9. Consumer debt in Puerto Rico as a whole rose from $237 million in 1963 to $3,276.4 million in 1983 (Dietz 1986: 261), showing that our sample is indicative of a more general trend.

10. A *coquí* is a small tree toad unique to Puerto Rico, which has come to symbolize much of national culture.

11. Public housing was privatized in 1992 through sale to tenants, and no new units are being built. This corresponds to the state's withdrawal of public support for the poor in the United States, which was intensified in Puerto Rico because of the huge federal debt.

4

The Dominican Republic:
Export Manufacturing
and the Economic Crisis

Hilda arrived in the free trade zone of La Romana in the Dominican Republic as a young woman with two daughters aged one and two. At 14, she had married a much older man, but he drank and mistreated her, so she left him and went to live with her sister in La Romana. Hilda started working almost immediately in the free trade zone in several factories, but has worked for about ten years in a blouse factory managed by a Cuban.

Hilda is very critical about the conditions in this factory. She says the manager is very strict and does not give them food or pay their transportation when they have to work overtime. Hilda was fired several years ago along with 60 other women for helping to organize a union in the factory. They received no support from the Ministry of Labor and Hilda was blacklisted from working in any other factories in La Romana. As the manager told them when they were fired: "*La que se meta en sindicato sabe que va a perder su empleo aquí y no va a trabajar más en Zona Franca, porque ustedes saben que el peje grande se come al peje chiquito.*" (Whoever gets involved in unions here knows she will lose her job and will no longer work in the free trade zone, because as you know the big fish eats the little fish.)

Despite her difficulties, Hilda managed to find work in other factories, although each time she found a job in La Romana, the manager had her fired. She went to work in the free trade zone in San Pedro de Macorís, about two hours by bus from La Romana, where transportation was very difficult but the manager was not concerned about her union activities. Although she was paid more there, she accepted when the Cuban manager asked her to return because she is a good operator, quick to learn, and hardworking. But she had to promise to cease involvement in union activity. Hilda says she prefers this factory, despite its bad reputation, because she has worked there so long and is able to do some business on the side like lending money at interest or playing *san*, a form of rotating credit association. Although playing *san* is not officially permitted, she can get away with it in this factory because she knows the personnel, and this business is an important addition to her salary. As Hilda says: "*Si yo viviera atenida a lo que me pagan en mi fábrica yo no pudiera sostener mi casa. Porque yo tengo cuatro niños ...*" (If I tried to live from what they pay me in the factory, I couldn't support my household. Because I have four children. ...) She has also put up a small store-front in her home where she sells soda, beer, and other items on weekends and in the evenings.

Since she arrived in La Romana, Hilda has had two additional children with a man with whom she lived for 14 years. But she has now been separated from him for four years. Although he did not want her to work initially, she convinced him out of economic necessity. Hilda says she feels much more secure working, especially since two of the children are not his. As Hilda notes, "*Las que no producen tienen que adaptarse a lo que el marido le da.*" (Those [women] who do not make money need to adapt to whatever the husband gives her.)

Hilda thinks it is very important for women to work, because life is very difficult and no family can live from one salary. She claims there are even young women who support men, who work while their partners are unemployed. She feels that many of these young women have a distorted vision of liberation that permits them to do the same as men. They say to men: "*Tú te vas, yo me voy, tú bebes yo bebo, tú llegas tarde, ah!, yo trabajo y yo gano, yo también, yo soy liberada y yo puedo hacer lo mismo con mi dinero.*" (You go, I go, you drink, I drink, you come late ah!, I work and I earn, I am also liberated and I can do the same with my money.) According to Hilda, these are the women who fill the discotheques on Friday evening. She claims many of them have left children with their grandmothers or other relatives in the country.

Hilda's second partner tried to return after he left her for another woman, and at one point threatened to force his way in and take his children. Hilda told him: "*No mijito, no, eso no es verdad, no. Tú te fuistes, tú te quedas. Y no es verdad que después que yo he vivido contigo 14 años yo voy a ponerme de amoríos. Ah, no cuando tú te casaste con otra, yo voy a entonces a vivir contigo como una amante, eso no es verdad.*" (No, my son, no, that is not true. You left, you stay. It is not true that after having lived with you for 14 years I am going to have an affair. Oh, no, when you married another one, I should then live with you like a lover, that is not true.) It is clear that Hilda is very independent and she says she has no interest in another man. Still she sends her 12-year-old son to stay with his father during the day at his radio and television repair shop so he will not get into trouble.

Hilda plans to continue working indefinitely in the free trade zone and says there are many improvements that could be made through a union, but the women are afraid. She notes the problems with transportation and with food and says that formerly there was a cheap lunchroom in the zone, but it was removed. She also notes the need for wage increases and says that many women are paid as little as DR$35 pesos a week because they are serving an apprenticeship that can last three months. Hilda claims there is a lot of turnover among these women, especially those doing simpler tasks like trimming and putting on buttons, because in this way the manager can save a lot of money.

Most of the Dominican women interviewed in the free trade zones complain about the wages and working conditions but feel powerless to do anything about them. Hilda is unusual both for her activism in the workplace and for her defiance of male dominance in the home. Her high level of consciousness appears to stem from her years of work experience and past involvement with leftist political parties, although she has only a fifth-grade education. As a 37-year-old female head of household with four children, she is also older than most of the women in our sample, who are largely young, recent entrants to the industrial labor force. Hilda must be a good worker, or her age and work experience would actually be held against her in the free trade zones, where most employers prefer a young, better-educated, docile labor force.

The youth and lack of job experience of most Dominican women workers in the free trade zones also reflect the recent boom in export manufacturing in the Dominican Republic compared to Puerto Rico, where the industrialization process started in the early 1950s and the garment industry is already in decline. As noted in chapter 1, several key factors help account for the Dominican Republic's rapid shift from sugar exports to export manufacturing as a development strategy in the 1980s: 1) stagnation in the price of traditional agricultural exports and the cut in U.S. sugar quotas from the Dominican Republic, which drastically reduced that country's principal source of foreign exchange; 2) special tariff incentives set by the United States for manufactured products assembled abroad; and 3) most importantly, the economic crisis, which through devaluation reduced labor costs in the Dominican Republic to the lowest in the Caribbean Basin. Dominican wages dropped from the equivalent of U.S.$1.33 an hour in 1984 to U.S.$.56 in 1990, while industrial exports grew in 1991 to U.S.$850 million, equivalent to 53 percent of all exports (Fundapec 1992: 32–34).

The Dominican state plays a major role in attracting foreign investment through tariff and tax incentives resembling those of Puerto Rico. Free trade zones are exempt from all taxes on profit for 8 to 20 years (depending on geographic location), and there are no duties on imports of raw material, machinery, or other inputs and no restrictions on profit repatriation (Abreu et al. 1989: 51–56). Though these investment incentives have been in effect since 1969, initial growth in export manufacturing was slow and only 87 firms employing 20,000 workers had been established by 1982 (Fundapec 1992: 31). All were located in the three original free trade zones studied here, namely La Romana, San Pedro de Macorís, and Santiago. La Romana and San Pedro de Macorís are both located in the southeastern region of the country, formerly dominated by sugar cane cultivation and cattle raising, while Santiago is the capital of the Cibao region in the center of the country, a region of diversified agriculture. La Romana is the oldest of the free trade zones in the Dominican Republic, established by the Gulf and Western Corporation in 1969, but San Pedro de Macorís was incorporated in 1973 by the government itself and operated by the Corporación de Fomento Industrial (Corporation for Industrial Development), a special agency of the Ministry of Industry. The zone in Santiago was established as a nonprofit venture in 1974 on the initiative of a group of local capitalists, in collaboration and with support from the Ministry of Industry. The Gulf and Western Corporation, which administered La Romana as a company town, had been a major force in the Dominican economy since the 1920s and owned about a third of the country's sugar cane acreage as well as a major sugar cane mill and a large tourist complex in the town. The introduction of the free trade zone and tourist complex was part of an attempt to diversify the economy and reduce unemployment in the area, a strategy now being employed in other areas where sugar production has been reduced. However, in 1984, Gulf and Western sold all of its holdings to a Cuban-American consortium controlled by the Fanjul brothers.

Methodology

The survey data analyzed here were part of a national survey of women workers in the modern industrial sector of the Dominican Republic conducted in 1981/1982 by CIPAF, a private feminist research center in that country. A total of 529 respondents were selected at random from women workers in domestic industries and in the three free trade zones then in operation, La Romana, San Pedro de Macorís, and Santiago. The analysis presented here is confined to the sample of 231 women workers in the three free trade zones, and the number in the sample from each zone is proportionate to the relative number of workers in each zone at that time. La Romana in 1981 had the highest representation with 98 workers in the sample, but by 1989, growth was much greater in the other two zones, which each had more than twice the number of employees as La Romana (Fundapec 1992: 36). Within each trade zone, the sample was also drawn proportionally to the number of workers in each industrial sector, with 66 of the 98 workers in La Romana in the garment industry. In the entire sample, 142 out of 231 workers, or 62 percent, were employed in the garment industry, making it quite comparable with our other sample of garment workers in Puerto Rico. This high percentage is also comparable with the 60 percent of all workers found in the garment industry in the free trade zones in the 1980s, illustrating the importance of the garment industry in Dominican export manufacturing (Dauhajre et al. 1989: 189). Other women in the sample were employed in the tobacco, leather, shoe, and food industries. In comparing the CIPAF sample with other studies conducted on workers and firms in the free trade zones, Dauhajre et al. (1989: 125) claim it is representative, though the sample was not drawn from industry files.

Magaly Pineda, director of CIPAF, allowed us to use these survey data, which formed the basis of several master of arts theses at the University of Florida carried out by Quintina Reyes, Milagros Ricourt, and Lorraine Catanzaro, from which I also benefited. In 1986, along with a Dominican research assistant, Francis Pou, I conducted in-depth interviews of 18 women, all drawn from the 66 female garment workers in La Romana in the 1981 CIPAF sample. We focused on garment workers because they would be more comparable with the sample in Puerto Rico, and on La Romana because of its interesting labor history as a company town dominated by a U.S. sugar corporation. Due to high turnover in jobs and residence, it was difficult to locate many of these women five years later, but we were able to obtain a sub-sample representative of various age groups and marital statuses. At any rate, our primary purpose in conducting these in-depth interviews was to test some of our hypotheses arising from the survey data and to see the changes that had taken place in the lives of these women during this critical period in the Dominican economy from 1981 to 1986.

The economic crisis that hit the Dominican Republic in 1982 accelerated the erosion of the man's role as primary breadwinner and increased the importance of the woman's contribution. Inflation, unemployment, and declining real wages resulted in a reduction in real income and increased the need for additional members of the household to join the labor force, particularly wives. The need for additional income is made more acute by the cut in government services mandated by IMF structural adjustment policies, which force families to spend more on medicine, health care, education, and other necessities. These cuts are particularly difficult for women, who are forced to absorb these added costs through their own labor in the home and in the workplace (Cornia et al. 1987; Deere et al. 1990). Women are clearly becoming major economic contributors to the household, but at the workplace and by the state they are still regarded as supplementary wage earners.

The Exploitation of Women's Wage Labor in the Workplace and by the State

Like export-processing workers in other parts of the world, most of the women workers in the Dominican free trade zones are young, recent entrants to the industrial labor force, which increases their vulnerability. Nearly three-fourths of the women in our sample are under 30 years of age and two-thirds have no previous job experience, while one-third have been working at their present jobs for less than one year. Over 78 percent of these women are migrants, and 60 percent have been living in the city for ten years or less. On the other hand, educational levels are quite high; over 40 percent have some secondary education compared to 15 percent of the general female population, indicating selective recruitment by employers in the free trade zones. Due to the high growth in educational levels between 1960 and 1981, the national educational levels of women are now equal to or even surpass men at the primary and secondary levels (Báez 1991: 4). In fact, a 1991 national-level survey of workers in the free trade zones indicates that women have higher educational levels than men, as they do nationally; in the free trade zones, 63 percent of women have completed secondary school compared to 47 percent of the men (Fundapec 1992: 128).

Young, single women have the highest educational levels in the sample, and many of them take courses after work at night or on weekends to learn English or secretarial skills in hopes of preparing for a better job. Higher educational levels also enable a woman to become more independent, as Dominga, a 20-year-old single woman claims: "*Si tú no tienes nada, pues nada vales. Y por eso yo he dedicado mi tiempo a estudiar. El día que yo me case, es lo que digo yo: 'Bueno, tú tienes la puerta para que salgas, mi'jo. Que yo dependo de mí, de mi trabajo.'*" (If you have nothing, then you are worth nothing. And for that reason I have dedicated my time to studying. The day that I marry, I can tell him, "Well, there's the door for you to leave, my son. I depend on myself, I depend on my work.")

In contrast to global patterns, which show a distinct preference for single women in export manufacturing, more than half of the women interviewed in the Dominican free trade zones are married,[1] while one-fourth are divorced or separated. This reflects both the early age of marital unions in the Dominican Republic and the increasing percentage of female-headed households, which constituted nearly one-fourth of all households in 1984 (Gómez 1990: 27). Two-thirds of our sample have children, but the number of children seldom exceeds four, which is comparable with the average fertility level in the Dominican Republic as a whole in 1980 (Duarte et al. 1989: 21). Some employers in the free trade zones in the Dominican Republic indicated a preference for women with children because they feel their need to work ensures greater job commitment (Joekes with Moayedi 1987: 59). However, to avoid the cost and burden of maternity leave, several employers also distribute birth control pills free of charge to their women workers, and a few require a pregnancy test or sterilization certificate before women are hired, illustrating the extent of control employers have over a woman's reproductive as well as productive roles.

Despite women's higher educational levels and increasing employment, they suffer several disadvantages in the labor market. Unemployment rates in the Dominican Republic are among the highest in all of Latin America and reached 29 percent in 1986, with underemployment estimated at about 40 percent. Unemployment rates are higher for women than for men, while wages are lower; in 1983, the average monthly wage for women was DR$165 compared to DR$291 for men (Báez 1991: 20). In the free trade zones as well, although women constitute the bulk of workers, they are employed primarily as unskilled production workers, receiving lower salaries than men, who are still preferred for more highly paid managerial, professional, or supervisory positions (Fundapec 1992: 118). Thus, even within the free trade zones with a largely female labor force, occupational segregation and wage differentials by gender are reasserted.

Although there have been several increases in the minimum wage to keep up with inflation, purchasing power has declined, and workers know that their salaries buy less now than previously. All workers in the Dominican free trade zones are paid the minimum wage, which in 1990 stood at $.56 an hour, one of the lowest in the Caribbean (Fundapec 1992: 34). Salaries are so low in the free trade zones that many workers try to earn extra income through a *san* or rotating credit association or a *rifa* (raffle) and sell objects ranging from food to jewelry, watches, and cosmetics to their fellow workers in the plant. Some managers prohibit these activities, but many workers still engage in them. Julia's husband was fired from his work in the free trade zone because of engaging in *rifas*. Now he earns money making and selling fried plantains in the

A Dominican garment plant with an all-women assembly line. Courtesy of *Rumbo* magazine, Santo Domingo, Dominican Republic.

neighborhood, and Julia says he is better off than before. She also has two brothers who live with them, neither of whom has a steady job. One collects and sells bottles and gives her money when he can, but neither helps with the housework or child care. Her younger, 18-year-old sister watches her children while Julia works. She has two children from a previous union and is expecting a third. She not only supports her siblings with her salary but helps out her elderly parents in the country as well. Julia wishes they would raise salaries so that she could help her brothers and parents more, because "*mis familias son pobres, yo tengo que ayudar a mi mamá también. A mi papá yo, casimente siempre tengo que mandarle dinero. Porque ellos lo que trabajan, o sea de lo que viven es de agricultura y poca y casimente no tienen de nada.*" (My families are poor, I have to help my mother also. And my father, I almost always have to send him money. Because they work, that is, they live from agriculture and have little or almost nothing.) Her parents occasionally send them some root vegetables (*víveres*) for home consumption.

In the survey sample, about three-fourths reported income from other sources than their salary, but this was chiefly from other household members who were working rather than from informal activities. However, it would appear from our in-depth interviews that the level of informal economic activity has increased because of the high cost of living brought on by devaluation and the economic crisis and because of the decline in wages and wage employment. More men than women are found in the informal sector, and in Santo Domingo in 1983, the informal sector employed more men than any other sector of the economy (Báez 1991: 19).

Despite several increases in the monthly minimum wage, the real wage declined 70 percent from January 1980 to July 1987, from a value of U.S.$98.43 to U.S.$67.20. During this same period, the weekly cost of a family food basket more than doubled (Ceara 1987), due to devaluation, the reduction in state price controls on staples such as rice and sugar, and increasing reliance on food imports. The result has been growing hunger and poorer health, as public health services deteriorated rapidly in the 1980s. Government expenditures on health and education have always been low in the Dominican Republic, which never fully assumed social welfare responsibilities for its citizens, but debt servicing commitments forced even greater cutbacks (Deere et al. 1990: 52–60). The burden of these economic hardships at the household level falls primarily on women, who attempt to maximize earnings while they minimize expenditures. Consumption patterns are changing, with increased reliance on cheap sources of food such as rice and root crops, while women's participation in both the formal and informal labor market is increasing.

The unstable and often inadequate income of men as they rely increasingly on the informal sector aggravates the need for female employment. Juana, for example, is 25 years old with two children from her first consensual union and at the time of our interview was on leave expecting her third child from her current partner. They live in one room with no private cooking or bathroom facilities, for which they pay $45 Dominican pesos a month. She also pays $20 Dominican pesos weekly to a girl to look after her youngest child, while her mother who lives in another neighborhood has the older six-year-old. Her husband drives a taxi (*público*) owned by his family but does not earn much because he has to buy gasoline and only receives a percentage of his intake, the rest of which goes to his father. Juana receives no financial assistance from the father of her children, who left town to work in another location, and she doesn't know his address. So with her weekly salary of $57 Dominican pesos and occasional bonuses for exceeding her production quota, she covers all basic costs including food, rent, and the baby-sitter as well as her own transportation, lunches, and other expenses.

Juana has worked for the same garment firm for eight years. Except for a six-month cleaning job, this was her first job at age 17 after arriving as a child with her family from a nearby town in the rural area. She thinks it is better to remain where she is than seek another job elsewhere, though she has many complaints. The company often requires employees to work overtime until 9:00 PM without notice, and if they cannot, they are fired, which is especially difficult for women with young children. They used to fire everyone every five years (perhaps to avoid the accumulation of seniority), and then they only paid about half of the required severance pay, but she claims the current manager has discontinued this practice. Juana has tried to earn a little extra playing *san*, but the company has a strict policy against any form of business activity in the plant. This company was also among the last to grant workers a government-mandated pay increase after devaluation. Juana wishes they would fire her so she could use her severance pay to set up her own business. With two (and now three) children to support, her husband's unstable income, and the high cost of living, she knows she has to continue working and plans to be sterilized after this child. Juana notes: "*De todas maneras yo tengo que trabajar, sea en la Zona o por ahí en una casa de familia, de todas maneras, porque es que yo, yo no puedo estar atenía al esposo mío. Porque lo que él gana no me da, para yo ayudar a mi familia y ayudarme en la casa.*" (Anyway, I have to work, either in the zone or in a private home [as a domestic], anyway, because I, I cannot be dependent on my husband. Because what he earns is not enough, to help my family and to help me here at home.)

As I noted earlier, Juana's situation is typical of what many women workers in the free trade zones face—low wages, poor working conditions, forced overtime, lack of child care, limited job alternatives, partners who offer no or limited assistance, and an increasingly high cost of living. Juana is conscious of these problems but sees no solutions. Like many of our informants, Juana and her partner are thinking of leaving, he for Puerto Rico and she for St. Maarten, where she has a friend working in the tourist industry, "*porque aquí lo que tú trabajas no da pa' la comida*" (because here what you earn doesn't even pay for food). Thus, discontent is expressed in turnover or eventual withdrawal, rather than through labor organizing, which Juana does not even want to talk about. It is clear that in the plant where she works, any union activity would be severely punished.

There are no legally recognized unions operating in the Dominican free trade zones, although they are not legally prohibited, and acknowledgment of workers' rights to association in free zones is included in the U.S. Generalized System of Preferences and mentioned as a criterion of eligibility under the CBI. The level of unionization in the country as a whole never represented more than 10 or 15 percent of the labor force, and unions cannot unite on issues because of fragmentation brought about by their ties to political parties (Espinal 1988). Workers are fired and blacklisted with other plants if any union activity is detected. As we have seen, Hilda was fired several years ago for trying to organize a union in the same factory where she and Juana work. Seventy percent of the women workers responding to this question in the CIPAF sample[2] indicated they were in favor of unionization, and Hilda thinks unions could bring about many improvements such as better wages, transportation, and cafeterias for workers, but that the majority of women are afraid: "*Porque sucede lo siguiente, la necesidad hace ley ... y uno no se quiere exponer a perder el pan de sus hijos.*" (Because what happens is the following, necessity makes law ... and one doesn't want to run the risk of losing the bread of one's children.)

Workers are conscious of their exploitation and of the need to organize but feel helpless to do anything about it. Workers can be dismissed for any reason and know that there are a lot of other women waiting for their jobs. Some feel that women are easier to intimidate than men. Dominga claims: "*El hombre es más fuerte que la mujer y cuando existen hombres, la cosa es mejor. Ellos le temen a los hombres. A las mujeres no, porque como las mujeres son tan sencillas, no podemos hacer nada.*" (The man is stronger than the women and when there are men, things are better. They are afraid of men. But not of women, because women are so simple, we can't do anything.) These patriarchal notions of male superiority are reinforced by gender hierarchies re-created in the workplace, with male managers in control of female workers, and weaken women's ability to undertake collective action.

The lack of support women receive from the Ministry of Labor is another factor designed to deter worker militancy. Women who have tried to take complaints of mistreatment or unjust dismissal to the Ministry of Labor have generally been rejected in favor of management. In the survey, 86 percent of the women in the free trade zones claim not to even know about this office, and only 12 percent have ever presented complaints. As Luz, a 26-year-old garment worker, stated: "*La Secretaría del Trabajo no se envuelve en defender a una de nosotras. O sea, ellos siempre se van a favor de los gerentes.*" (The Secretary of Labor does not defend one of us. That is, they are always in favor of the managers.)

Workers also complain about the quality of health care through the Instituto Dominicano de Seguro Social (IDSS), which is designed to cover all permanent employees through a fund to which employers, employees, and the state are supposed to contribute. However, in 1980 only 41 percent of the total labor force was actually covered (Ramírez et al. 1988: 102), and these are mostly workers in large, capital-intensive firms, most of whom are men. The government has also not made regular payments to the fund, resulting in a deterioration of health services. In the national-level study of free trade zone workers conducted in 1991, three-fourths were covered by IDSS (Fundapec 1992: 135). The women in our sample made full use of the maternity hospital of the IDSS and their 12 weeks of maternity leave but often go to private doctors for routine care, because of the poor quality of medical care and the long delays in treatment at IDSS facilities. The reductions in public health expenditure resulting from the economic crisis and structural adjustment have led to drastic shortages of medical personnel, medicine, surgical supplies, and vital equipment, and to increased rates of infant, child, and maternal mortality (Whiteford 1993: 222).

Why don't workers protest? Many factors contribute to the lack of worker solidarity in export manufacturing, including the youthfulness and constant turnover of workers, their recent entry into industrial employment, family responsibilities, high unemployment, and the lack of job alternatives. However, the principal obstacle to greater labor solidarity in the Dominican Republic is outright government repression. There have been several strikes in the free trade zones, principally over wage increases, and several attempts to set up labor unions, but all have been met by mass firings of the workers involved as well as blacklisting in other plants to intimidate other workers. However, a change in the Labor Code in 1992 permitted free trade zone workers to organize, and initially a large number of unions were created. Unfortunately, resistance by management combined with lack of government support and continued intimidation of women workers has led many of these unions to dissolve.

Dominican women still constitute a more vulnerable labor force than men. Nationally, their wage levels are lower than men and their unemployment levels are higher, creating an abundant but well-educated labor force. Even within the free trade zones the better-paid, more qualified jobs are given to men. Women workers lack representation in labor unions and political parties and receive no support from the state for their grievances. They are locked into dead-end, poorly paid jobs and have no opportunity to move into managerial or skilled positions. Thus, these public forms of patriarchy perpetuate the subordination of Dominican women workers.

Women's Resistance to Male Dominance in the Family

Dominican women workers in the free trade zones are relatively weak at the level of the workplace and the polity, where power must be exercised collectively to confront capital and the state, but these women have begun to assume more authority in the family. Their authority in the home is derived from their increased economic contribution to the household, which has taken on major significance in the light of declining male wages and the debilitating impact this has on a man's ability to be the sole breadwinner. In short, it is not simply a question of whether women are employed or not, but the importance of their contribution to the household economy, that gives women a basis of resistance to male dominance in the family.

Most women agree that paid employment has given them greater legitimacy to negotiate with their husbands, even if they still consider the husband to be the head of the household. In general, more egalitarian relationships seem to be found among couples who are both working, who are better educated, who have lived in the city longer, have not married very young, and are legally married rather than living in consensual union. For example, Julia was recently married in a civil ceremony at 24 years of age and is expecting her first child. Both she and her husband work in the zone, where she has worked for seven years, and she notes: "*Yo diría que eso me hace sentir más segura, porque ya yo misma manejo mi dinero y sé en que lo voy a gastar y lo que me corresponde.*" (I would say that [work] makes me feel more secure, because I manage my own money and I know what I will spend it on and what belongs to me.)

Women are clearly becoming major economic contributors to the household, and in our sample of Dominican women workers in export manufacturing, 38 percent consider themselves to be the principal provider. However, there is considerable variation in the importance of the woman's contribution to the household economy by marital status (Table 4.1), which affects household composition and the number of other contributors to the household economy. In our sample, only 20 percent of single women are the principal economic providers, because they are likely to share the support of the household with parents, siblings, or other relatives. Some single women live alone but most cannot afford more than a single room, because housing in La Romana is very expensive. Lydia, for example, has been working in the free trade zone for five years, after arriving at age 17 with her aunt and uncle from the rural area. Her relatives have since returned, and for two years she lived with another woman worker whom she met at the night secretarial school she attends. Now Lydia lives alone in a single room with no private bathroom or cooking facilities, but she has asked her sister from the country to join her. She doesn't tell anyone at work that she lives alone, because then men try to take advantage of her. Lydia claims that many young women living alone in La Romana have become pregnant: "*Un hombre porque cree que uno vive sola y decirle a uno 'yo voy a quedarme contigo,' eso es lo más que le dicen a uno y yo, para mí, lo detesto. Detesto los hombres que solamente quieren burlarse de uno.*" (A man thinks because you

TABLE 4.1

Women Workers in the Free Trade Zones of the Dominican Republic
by Marital Status and Principal Provider
Percentages

Principal Provider	Single	Married[a]	Widows, Divorced and Separated	Percentage in Total Sample
Woman Worker	19.6	26.3	74.2	37.7
Spouse	--	58.4	1.6	30.3
Parent(s)	35.3	.8	11.3	11.2
Other	45.1	14.5	12.9	20.8
Total %	100.0	100.0	100.0	100.0
N	51	118	62	231

[a] Includes consensual unions.
Source: Ricourt 1986:95.

live alone, all he has to do is say, "I am going to stay with you," that's all they say, and I, I detest that. I detest men who only want to make fun of you.)

Female heads of household carry the heaviest financial responsibility, and nearly three-fourths of these in our sample consider themselves the principal economic provider. Female heads of household constitute 26 percent of the women in our Dominican sample and are generally older than married or single women and have more children. While a few are widowed or divorced, most are separated from one or more consensual unions, which were often initiated before they were 20. It would appear that increased female employment has enabled some women to become less dependent on men and more prone to leave an unsatisfactory relationship. For example, Teresa is now 38 and lives alone, although she has had eight children in three consensual unions, starting at age 13. The younger children still live with their father, and she did not work while she lived with him. Her ability to leave this marriage was clearly dependent on her finding employment, and she now works as a supervisor in the same plant where she has been working for ten years. She says she would not quit working, even if she found another man, because "*son hombres machistas. De que piensan de que si la mujer trabaja se va a gobernar demasiado, porque así es que se usa aquí en Santo Domingo. De que cuando la mujer trabaja entonces ellos ven que es liberal, un poco más liberal, que no pueden hacerle mucha maldad y no pueden abusar ... Pero muchos hombres cuando la mujer no trabaja, la mujer tiene que esperar obligado, mal pasar, aguantarle al hombre muchas cosas. Pero cuando la mujer trabaja ya ahí cambia, porque estamos trabajando los dos.*" (They are *machistas*. They think that if the woman works, she will

A Dominican head of household with her child. She is a garment worker in the free trade zone. Photograph by the author.

rule too much, because that's the way it is here in Santo Domingo. That when a woman works, they think she is liberal, a little too liberal, that they can't mistreat or abuse her ... But many men when the woman isn't working, the woman is obliged to wait, to have a bad time, to put up with many things from a man. But when the woman is working, then things change, because we are both working.) Teresa clearly expresses fear of the dependence that lack of paid employment imposes on Dominican women.

Households with young children to support are in the most critical stage economically, and this is the period when women are the most dependent on men. Eighty percent of the married women in our sample still consider the man to be head of the household (Table 4.2), and 58 percent consider him the principal economic provider. The man is expected to pay for the basic expenses like the house and food, but an increasing number of Dominican working women are taking over these expenses as well as paying for clothes, schooling, and the baby-sitter as well as their own work-related costs. For example, Luz and her partner live in a single room with a makeshift kitchen and a communal bathroom and laundry. Their two young children live with her mother in the rural area, and she only sees them every two or three weeks. Luz's partner has nine children from four previous consensual unions, but has no regular income since he works at occasional jobs doing construction work or driving a cab or even fishing. He would like to get married, but Luz is not interested, claiming marriage would give him more rights over her. She notes: "*Ellos cuando son casados tienen como más derechos en uno. 'No, porque tú eres la esposa y tú tienes que obedecerme,' que sé yo qué ... Los que sólo están unidos se comportan como mejor, mas si las mujeres trabajan, se portan mejor todavía.*" (When they [men] are married, they have more rights over you. "No, because you are my wife and you have to obey me," and so on ... Those who are only *unidos* [in consensual union] behave better, better yet if the women are working, they behave even better.) While legal marriage confers more legal rights on a woman and should be more stable than a consensual union, its rejection may be seen as another form of resistance to male authority.

Women involved in consensual unions often carry more financial responsibility for the household than legally married women. It would seem that legal marriage confers greater responsibility on a man to support his family than more unstable consensual unions. Women in consensual unions have no right to their partner's social security or property and may be left without anything if the union dissolves. In addition, women in consensual unions have often had more than one partner and are likely to have children from previous unions, for whom their current

TABLE 4.2

Women Workers in the Free Trade Zones of the Dominican Republic
by Marital Status and Declared Head of Household

Declared Head of Household	Single		Married and Consensual Unions		Widows, Divorced, and Separated	
	No.	Percentage	No.	Percentage	No.	Percentage
Herself	5	0.8	14	11.0	40	64.5
Husband	--	--	92	80.0	2	3.2
Both	--	--	7	6.0	--	--
Mother	14	27.5	1	0.9	9	14.5
Father	17	33.3	2	1.6	5	8.1
Other	15	29.4	2	1.6	6	9.7
Total	51	100.0	118	100.0	62	100.0

Source: Ricourt 1986:96.

partner is not expected to assume financial responsibility. They are also not likely to receive economic assistance from their previous partners, so they are left with the primary responsibility of raising these children. As we noted earlier, Hilda continued to work after she had two children with her second partner, although he wanted her to quit. Hilda said she felt more secure working, especially since she had two children from a previous union, noting: "*Me sentía bien segura porque sabía si él se va por lo menos mis hijos no van a pasar hambre, porque yo los puedo ...*" (I felt very secure because I knew that if he goes my children at least would not go hungry, because I could ... [support them].) Like Hilda, many women in consensual unions feel insecure in their relationships with men and have come to depend on themselves for supporting their family.

In our sample, the number of women in consensual unions is twice as high as those legally married, which corresponds to the high level of consensual unions nationally in the Dominican Republic, which reached 28.2 percent in 1981 (Báez 1991: 3). Legal marriages are more stable, and both in our sample and at the national level, the proportion of women who have had more than one partner is much higher among those living in consensual union than among those legally married. Consensual unions are also linked to lower educational levels and lower socio-economic status, indicating that the type of union may be a less important factor in marital stability than general class characteristics (Duarte et al. 1989: 40–42). In our sample, for example, 49 percent of those legally married have a secondary education, compared to 23 percent of those in consensual unions.

The lower educational level of women in consensual unions may help explain their greater receptivity to patriarchal norms. There is a curious contradiction between behavioral norms and ideological beliefs among women in consensual unions in our sample. At the behavioral level, as we have seen, women in consensual unions often assume greater responsibility for the household and are less economically dependent on men than legally married women. In our sample, women in consensual unions are more likely to pay the bills, to make major household purchases, to decide how many children to have and how to educate them than legally married women. Brown (1975) has argued that the greater authority and responsibility of Dominican women in consensual unions make them less subordinate to men and less dependent on them economically. However, our data suggest that women in consensual unions ideologically subscribe to patriarchal norms more than legally married women. For example, in our sample, 58 percent of the legally married women compared to 39 percent of women in consensual unions think that the husband should share important domestic decisions with his wife. Women were also asked their opinion (as opposed to their actual behavior) about matters such as whether women should work outside the home, whether domestic concerns should be left entirely to women, and whether men and women should enjoy equal access to education and equal rights at work. In almost all these questions, women in consensual unions consistently favored less autonomy and equality for women than legally married women, though the majority of respondents in both cases were in favor of more egalitarian relationships. These attitudes reflect not only the class and educational differences noted earlier but also suggest the insecurity Dominican women feel in their increasingly fragile relationships with men. By subscribing to patriarchal norms, women in consensual unions may be rejecting their heavy financial responsibilities and voicing their desire to share the responsibility for raising a family with a stable male partner. In order to oblige a man to assume this responsibility, a woman cannot directly challenge his role as head of the household and thus she is forced to support the maintenance of patriarchal authority patterns. This persistence of traditional gender ideology reflects the constraints women feel in raising a family on their own.

It is difficult for women to support a family on their low wages, particularly since they have no state supports like welfare or unemployment insurance, as is the case in Puerto Rico and advanced industrial countries like the United States. Half of the households in our sample have other relatives living in the household, generally siblings who are looking for work and who are expected to contribute to the household once they are employed. The addition of adult working members becomes another way of enlarging the household income, and 30 percent of the households in our sample reported receiving financial assistance from relatives. The majority of those receiving assistance are single women, who are most likely to be living with immediate family or other relatives. However, aid or support from relatives left behind in the rural area has been attenuated because of rapid rural-urban migration and the poverty of the older generation. Older parents are often poor subsistence farmers, who cannot afford to live in the city because of the high cost of living, particularly housing. They also cannot help support their children, although occasionally they send some fresh vegetables or help them build a place to live in the city. The most important assistance they provide is in terms of child-rearing. Young children are often left with grandparents in the rural area while their mother or both parents work in the free trade zone. For example, Dolores now lives in La Romana with her two grown sons who work in the free trade zone of San Pedro de Macorís. They pay their own expenses, including those for their studies, and contribute what they can to the household. When Dolores separated from her husband, she left her four children with her father in the country, and the youngest child still lives there. She came to work in the free trade zone of La Romana ten years ago but sent her children money regularly. She has thought of remarriage but notes: *"Es muy bueno tener un compañero para ayudarlo en el hogar, uno sentirse con mayor apoyo, de cualquier cosa, cualquier problema fuerte así. Pero fíjate, mis hijos son varones todos, ya no son niñitos chiquititos, que ya son hombrecitos. Yo no doy mis hijos por un hombre, y mucho menos por lo que aparecen hoy."* (It is good to have a companion, to help you in the house, to feel you have more support, for whatever thing, whatever tough problem. But look, my children are all men, they are no longer little boys, they are young men. I wouldn't give up my sons for a man, and much less for those who are around now.) Despite her reluctance to remarry, however, Dolores still thinks that it is the man *"que manda en la casa"* (who gives the orders in the house).

Resistance to male authority has been heightened by the increasing inability of men to fulfill their role as breadwinner. Male unemployment in the households interviewed in 1986 appears to have increased from the time of the original 1981 survey, when it stood at only 11 percent compared to 18 percent nationally. Increased male unemployment reflects the crisis and the subsequent decline in government jobs and employment in the sugar industry, which fell drastically during the early 1980s and is a principal source of male employment in La Romana where these in-depth interviews were conducted. Most of the men like

A Dominican man delivering food at a factory in the free trade zone, an activity typical of informal-sector employment. Photograph by the author.

Luz's partner were *chiriperos,* doing odd jobs in the informal sector like selling cooked food, driving cabs part-time, working at temporary jobs in construction, and participating in *sans* or *rifas.* A few who had the capital to start their own businesses were doing quite well.

The erosion of the man's role as economic provider has led some men to tighten their control over women. Many Dominican men are threatened by their wives' employment and may even forbid them to continue working. One woman had to stop working because her husband objected so strenuously and even refused to buy anything for the house. Men may exert economic pressure in this way to keep women dependent on them. Adolfina, who is working, notes the difficulty her employment causes with her husband: *"Ahora a veces como yo trabajo, sucede que a veces me acusa de que yo ... es decir, que como que me gobierno, que yo hago lo que yo quiero. El me acusa de que yo me gobierno porque yo trabajo y yo hago con ese dinero lo que yo quiero ... Y hay muchos hombres no les gusta que la mujer trabaje por eso."* (Now that I work, it happens that he accuses me of ... that is, that I rule myself, that I do what I want. He accuses me of ruling myself because I work and I do with that money what I want ... And there are many men who don't like a woman to work for that reason.) However, there are also men who wait on Fridays outside the gate of the free trade zone to collect their wives' or girlfriends' paychecks, that is, they live off of women's wages. When I asked if men felt threatened by women working, one of our respondents laughed, *"Se aprovechan."* (They take advantage of it.)

This kind of male irresponsibility is leading some women to reject marriage or remarriage. For example, Josefina is 33 years old and lives with another woman in a nicely furnished house provided by her roommate's relatives in New York. She has no plans to marry, because she thinks men today are too irresponsible, noting: *"Ellos ahora no se ocupan de la mujer como se ocupaban antes. Que antes un hombre se llevaba una mujer o se casaba con una mujer y sabía que a esa mujer tenía que comprarle zapatos, vestidos, o sea todo lo que necesitaba. Pero ahora no, ahora ellos, 'Ah no, tú trabajas, cómpratelo tú.'"* (They [men] don't take responsibility for a woman the way they used to. Before, a man took a woman or married a woman and knew that he had to buy that woman shoes, dresses, everything she needed. But now no, now they say "Oh no, you work, buy it yourself.") In short, increased employment has brought women greater financial responsibility as men abdicate their role as economic provider.

Some younger women have succeeded in negotiating a more egalitarian relationship with their husbands, partly through the independence that paid employment has given them. For example, Eva and her husband both work and have two children after nine years of marriage, and they make most decisions jointly: *"El siempre lo ha dicho, 'que aquí tanto mando yo como mandas tú.' Que él no se siente como esos hombres que dicen, 'allí en la casa mando yo.' El siempre comparte conmigo, igual que yo con él."* (He always has said, "that here I give the orders as well as you." He is not like those men who say, "here I give the orders." He always shares with me, and I with him.)

Fertility is one area where most Dominican women in our sample are clearly challenging male authority. Many women in both legal and consensual unions are now making their own decisions regarding the use of contraception and how many children to have, although an equally high percentage of legally married women share this latter decision with their husbands. Very few women expressed a desire for more than three children, and some have stopped at two. Many of these women came from families with ten or more children, indicating a rapid fertility decline in one generation, as can be seen as well at the national level. Our sample survey reveals that 30 percent of the women use contraceptives (primarily pills), while 18 percent have been sterilized. However, our in-depth interviews suggest that sterilization is more frequent, and it is possible that it has increased due to economic pressures during the early 1980s. Young children are a burden to working women because paid child care in the free trade zones is very expensive, and many women complain that their children are not well taken care of. Women who leave their children in the rural area with their parents or other relatives must contribute to their support, and they may not see their children more than once a month or less.

Married women still do most of the housework alone, which again increases the burden of young children, although female relatives or children may help out. Men never do routine domestic tasks except for occasional shopping, although 63 percent of the women sampled would like men to assume more household responsibilities. Only two men in our sample regularly looked after their children. Men tend to dominate financial matters, like paying the bills or making major household purchases, since this gives them control of the family purse strings, although married women now have a greater voice in the family budget. Several factors inhibit Dominican women workers from asserting more authority in the household. The need to support young children, the increasingly high cost of living, and the inability of extended kin who remain behind in the rural area to provide more support, combined with their low wages and precarious jobs, make it very difficult for Dominican women workers to support a family on their own. Even when both the man and woman are working, they can barely make ends meet and cannot save to buy a home of their own or meet an emergency like illness. The high rate of consensual unions and of marital instability coupled with the pressures of the economic crisis heightens the woman's insecurity and her fear of challenging male dominance. The crisis has also threatened the man's role as provider and made households all the more dependent on the woman's wages. This marginalization of men combined with apparent male irresponsibility is leading many Dominican women working in the free trade zones to question the legitimacy of marriage and, in the case of female heads of household, to resist remarriage.

Conclusion

It is clear that paid employment has had an impact on gender roles in the Dominican Republic, and that this impact is greater at the level of the household than in the workplace or in the polity, where women are still regarded as supplementary wage earners. In part, women's exploitation as workers reflects the weakness of labor generally in the Dominican Republic, due to a long history of labor surplus, fragmentation of the labor movement, and state repression. But women workers receive even less attention than men from political parties and labor unions, at the same time that their wages are lower, their unemployment higher, and many are not provided with social security, health care, or other basic needs. Recent changes taking place in the Dominican free trade zones also suggest that gender hierarchies are being reestablished very rapidly with men occupying the better-paid, more highly qualified jobs, despite the higher educational level of women. The proportion of women employed in the free trade zones also appears to have been reduced, although this reflects a shift toward heavier fabrics such as that used in pants, for which women's "nimble fingers" are not as necessary.

For women workers to gain greater legitimacy in the workplace and the polity, they would have to organize collectively, but most attempts to unionize in the free trade zones have been suppressed and have failed to receive government support. In the 1980s women have been more successful in organizing at the neighborhood level, where they protest cuts in government services, the high cost of living, and other economic problems through national strikes, marches, pickets, and other public protests. These neighborhood forms of mobilization cut across age and gender lines and constitute a challenge to traditional political parties and labor unions as the legitimate mechanisms of social mobilization (Cela et al. 1988; Báez 1993).

At the household level, however, women have always had more legitimacy, and here they are able to negotiate individually. Paid employment, as well as higher educational levels and declining fertility, offer women a basis for exerting greater authority in the family, although many women still cling to the traditional notion of the man as the head of the household. Their forms of resistance to male dominance take several forms, including the rejection of marriage or remarriage, greater control over the budget and a greater share in household decisions, and control over their own fertility. It is clear that Dominican women are conscious of subordination and even exploitation by men and are attempting to gain as much leverage as possible in household decisions without totally undermining the man's authority. Most would prefer to maintain a stable conjugal relationship, while they struggle to make it more egalitarian, because they realize the difficulty in maintaining a family on their own. They recognize the increasing burden of children in a wage economy, but are still heavily identified with their maternal role, which remains the prime source of female identity in Latin American society. This continued identification with their role as wife and mother suggests that Dominican women workers still function on the basis of separate spheres for men and women, despite the increasing importance of their public role as workers.

The Dominican data also underline the importance of examining the man's role as economic provider in analyzing gender inequalities. Some Dominican women workers are acquiring more authority in the household not just because they are employed but because of the importance of their economic contribution. As a result of the economic crisis and the collapse of an economy based on sugar and import substitution industrialization, men's capacity to fulfill their role as economic provider has been seriously eroded. Unemployment and underemployment are increasing, and many men are seeking survival in the informal sector, while the rates of female labor force participation are rising. This pattern holds true for many third world countries undergoing the economic crisis and affected by global restructuring and is becoming more relevant as well in advanced industrial countries like the United States. As Safilios-Rothschild (1990: 227) notes: "When male breadwinning inadequacy becomes chronic and women become co-breadwinners on a permanent basis, men are no longer able to maintain their superior and authoritarian position vis-a-vis their wives."

The degree of dependence on a male provider changes over a woman's life cycle, however, so that her age and marital status become critical determinants of her capacity to resist male dominance at the household level. Women with young children to support are most dependent on a man's support. This is one reason why female heads of household are often found among older women who do not have young children to support, and who may even be able to call on their children to contribute to the household. However, older women often maintain more traditional gender roles than younger women, who generally have higher levels of education and fewer children. As a result, young, better-educated women are also less likely to subscribe to patriarchal norms and more likely to expect to share responsibility and authority with their conjugal partners than older women, who were raised in an agrarian society in which the man's dominance in the household was unquestioned. Patriarchal norms have eroded in Dominican society as a whole with the move to a wage economy and increasing urbanization and education.

A recent study of rural Dominican women in the agro-industrial zone of Azua confirms that the changes in gender roles documented in this study are not confined to women workers in the free trade zones. Comparing women workers in this agro-industrial complex with largely nonemployed women in the community, Finlay (1989) concludes that workers had more power and control over resources within the family and were more likely to limit their fertility, which closely parallels our own findings. Among Dominican women immigrants to New York City, increased employment and the importance of their contribution to the household have also led to a more egalitarian division of labor and distribution of authority, with a greater sharing of household tasks and control over the budget. Dominican women are beginning to define themselves as co-partners in heading the household. However, the struggle over domestic authority has also led to marital breakup and may help account for the rising percentage of female-headed house-holds in the Dominican community in New York City (Grasmuck and Pessar 1991: 148–156). In contrast, among Dominican rural women limited to unpaid labor on family farms or to supplementary sources of income through the informal sector, a strong patriarchal gender ideology and dependence on a male breadwinner still prevail (Pou et al. 1987; Jansen and Millán 1991; Georges 1990). A national-level study of Dominican rural women conducted in 1983 by CIPAF concludes: "*Está tan interiorizado en la mujer de la zona rural que el hombre es el principal proveedor que, de hecho, concibe su participación en las actividades generadoras de ingreso como transitorias y las justifica mientras perdure la crisis de reproducción de su unidad familiar*" (Pou et al. 1987: 204). (The woman in the rural area has so internalized the man as principal breadwinner that she, in fact, conceives her participation in income-generating activities as transitory and justifies them as long as the reproductive crisis in her household lasts.) That is, these rural Dominican women have not even begun to see themselves as permanent wage earners and continue to view men as the principal breadwinners.

In short, our empirical analysis of Dominican women workers in export-led industrialization suggests several additional factors that condition the impact of paid employment on gender subordination. The importance of the woman's contribution to the household economy in itself is partially determined by the number of other contributors to the household, which varies by life cycle and marital status. It is also affected by the levels of male employment and wages, which largely determine how well men can carry out their breadwinner role. The woman's age and educational level as well as the type of work women do (permanent wage labor vs. unpaid family labor and informal sector work) also influence her ability to challenge male domination. Legally married women appear to subscribe less to patriarchal norms than women in consensual unions, which are more subject to marital instability. In general, more egalitarian relations seem to be found among young couples who are both working, are better educated, have lived in the city longer, have not married very young, and are legally married rather than living in consensual unions.

Have Dominican women benefited from their increased wage labor? Here again the results are complex and contradictory. By taking advantage of women's inferior position in the labor market, export-led industrialization may reinforce their subordination through poorly paid, dead-end jobs. On the other hand, women's increased ability to contribute to the family income may challenge traditional patriarchal authority patterns and lead to more egalitarian family structures. This is particularly true where, as in the Dominican free trade zones, women have become critical contributors to the household economy. This more egalitarian pattern is the result of a gradual process of negotiation, in which women use their earnings and the family's increased dependence on them to bargain for increased authority and sharing of responsibilities within the household (Roldán 1985: 275). Gender consciousness grows as the contradiction between women's increasingly important economic contribution to the household and their subordination in the family, in the workplace, and in the polity becomes more apparent.

Notes

1. Unless indicated otherwise, the category of married women includes women in consensual unions, who in our sample are twice as numerous as legally married women. At the national level as well, according to a 1980 survey, the percentage of women in consensual unions is 34.6 percent, compared to 21.4 percent in legal marriages (Duarte et al. 1989: 35).

2. Twenty percent of the sample refused to answer this question, indicating the degree of intimidation about unions among women workers in the free trade zones.

5

Cuba: Revolution and Gender Inequality

Rosalía Hernández's life reflects many of the changes in the lives of Cuban women brought about by the Cuban revolution. Now 55 years old, she was born in Oriente into a poor family of 13 children and only finished first grade. She is still illiterate; although a teacher lived with them after the revolution, Rosalía had too many children to concentrate on studying. Rosalía was married at a young age to a man who became active in the Revolutionary Army and fought with Fidel in the Sierra Maestra. He is still active in the Communist Party and now works in agriculture. They had four children before moving to the Havana area after the revolution in 1959.

When they first arrived, Rosalía and her family lived three years in a *rancho* (shack) made of makeshift materials on the outskirts of Havana, near her husband's military base. With the Camarioca airlift in 1965, the government gave them a house in Bauta vacated by an exiled family. It was an old-fashioned wooden row house with a large *sala* (living room) and patio in the rear, but the Hernández family had never lived in such "luxury." The children then numbered eight, and their father confined them to one area of the house, and as Alicia, their daughter recounts: "*Nosotros nunca nos salimos del terreno éste, parecíamos gallinas.*" (We never left that spot, we were like chickens.) As the children grew and married, they built separate living quarters for each family in the patio until in 1987, when this interview was conducted, the household contained 26 people, including Rosalía, seven of her children, their spouses, and grandchildren. The housing was built gradually out of a common construction fund to which all the children have contributed 50 Cuban pesos a month, but each family cooks separately in a tiny kitchen, apparently to accommodate individual wishes and retain some sense of independence. Only Rosalía does not cook, but eats with one of the other family members.

Rosalía's husband no longer lives with them. They separated 15 years ago, but as Rosalía explains: "*Estamos separados de nada más de dormir, porque nos llevamos bien. Sí, acabamos de criar los muchachos, cualquier problema lo resolvemos él y yo, y él está aquí. Es igual que si estuviera aquí.*" (We are only separated for sleeping, because we get along well. Yes, we finished raising the children, whatever problem, he and I resolve it, and he is here. It's the same as if he lived here.) Clearly the father is still considered the head of the household, although he has been living with another woman nearby for about six years. He comes by frequently, is consulted on all major decisions, directs the housing construction, and when the children were younger contributed to the household economy. Rosalía feels that with so many children, they could not afford to go their own ways, and even now that the children are older, it is better to stay united. They wanted their children to study, and most of them completed the ninth grade, while two of the children have become teachers. One of these teachers, a son, was sent with his family to Oriente to teach.

Four of the children and two sons-in-law work in the textile factory in Ariguanabo. Rosalía has worked in the factory for 15 years as a winder (*torcedora*), which requires lifting 10- to 14-pound spools of yarn. This strenuous work has given her severe pains in her shoulders and legs, for which she has been operated upon several times, and she was once absent from work for a year and a half. Cuban women are entitled to retire at 55, and Rosalía would like to but has been unable to obtain official permission because of problems with her birth certificate, which does not give her accurate age. She has made several appeals, including calling three witnesses and paying a lawyer 100 Cuban pesos to fix her papers, but to no avail. Still Rosalía likes her job, especially working with machines, and prefers factory work to the poultry farm on which she worked before.

Her children also like their work, but Rosalía and her daughter Alicia complain of the lack of child care for working mothers. The day care center at the factory and two in the town cannot accommodate the increasing demand, which is much greater than when Rosalía's three small children attended many years ago. Alicia has a newborn baby and thinks she is going to have to take an unpaid leave if she cannot place her child when her current 12-week maternity leave expires. She and Rosalía complain that women workers in Ariguanabo are not given preference in placement and that the daytime hours of the day care center do not fit the needs of women production workers like Alicia who work rotating shifts. State day care worked well for Rosalía's other daughters, who are office workers, but the lack of adequate child care has caused absentee-ism among women production workers in Ariguanabo. Rosalía and her daughter do not see the FMC as a resource for solving these problems and view it as quite ineffective. They think the FMC is only interested in collecting its monthly fee of 25 Cuban cents and should be more dy-namic in attending to the needs of working women.

Though Alicia defers to her father as "*el papá de la casa*" (the father of the house), she is still less subordinate than her mother to male author-ity. Alicia was married at age 18 to a man 13 years her senior, but di-vorced at age 22 because he would not allow her to work or to be active in mass organizations such as serving as the president of the Commit-tees for the Defense of the Revolution (CDR). Her current husband is more open, and they make joint decisions and undertake most activities together. For example, she does not allow him to repeatedly go to the movies alone and leave her at home alone with the baby. Her mother ob-jects, saying: "*Déjalo que él es hombre, que los hombres son de la calle*" (Leave him, he's a man, and men belong on the street), whereupon Alicia responds: "*No, no son de la calle, nosotros también somos de la calle y esto que está aquí es de los dos.*" (No, they don't belong on the street, we also belong on the street, and this [baby] here is from both of us.) Her re-sponse indicates that the old *casa/calle* distinction referred to in chapter 2 by which status was conferred on women who were confined to the home is no longer accepted by the younger generation of Cuban women, who have learned a different set of values during the Cuban rev-olution. Higher educational levels, better job opportunities, lower fertil-ity, and public support for women's equality have given this younger fe-male generation greater autonomy and self-confidence with which to challenge male dominance.

Rosalía and her family illustrate many of the achievements of Cuban women resulting from Cuban revolutionary policy. Cuban women have benefited from a substantial increase in labor force participation, rising educational levels, the establishment of social services to alleviate wom-en's domestic load such as day care centers, and the development of mass organizations such as the CDR and the FMC, which is specifically designed for women. All of these policies were designed to promote women's equality, which became a key element of revolutionary policy. These policies have helped to promote a change in household authority patterns, which can be seen in the differences between Rosalía and her daughter in their attitudes toward male authority. Rosalía's husband is still the patriarch who rules the house (though he no longer lives there), while Alicia and her husband share a more egalitarian relationship.

Though Alicia continues to believe in gender differences in the physical and emotional nature of men and women, she is also cognizant of her rights in both the private and public spheres. She and her mother demand more from the state and mass organizations such as the FMC, which has recently been publicly criticized for losing touch with its grassroots constituency. While fiercely proud of the revolution and its achievements, Cuban working-class women like Rosalía and Alicia are also critical of certain state policies that fall short of the revolution's own goals in promoting gender equality.

This chapter will examine the impact of the changes in gender roles brought on since the Cuban revolution on a small sample of women textile workers. The focus will be on women's participation in the full-time, salaried labor force, which increased rapidly in the postrevolutionary period, from 13 percent in 1955 to 34.8 percent in 1990 (Table 1.7). Under socialism, paid employment is seen as the key to women's equality, because it is supposed to raise their class consciousness and reduce their isolation within the home and their dependence on a male wage. Critics charge socialist states with a productionist bias, which emphasizes economic changes such as increasing labor force participation to the neglect of women's reproductive role, the division of labor, and gender ideology (Kruks, Rapp, and Young 1989: 10). Cuba and other socialist states have attempted to socialize women's domestic role through day care centers and other support services provided by the state, but these are expensive and they never fill total demand. As a result, many working women remain burdened with a "double day," especially onerous in a less-developed society where domestic tasks are even more time-consuming. The Cuban state recognized this problem as a prime factor in the high turnover and absenteeism of employed women in the early years of the revolution and attempted to address it through the Family Code adopted in 1975. The Cuban Family Code is unique in socialist societies in requiring men and women to share household tasks and child-rearing as well as financial responsibility. This study examines the extent to which paid industrial employment and other policies of the Cuban revolutionary government have succeeded in promoting the equality of Cuban women in the postrevolutionary period.

Critics have also charged that high rates of female labor force participation in socialist societies arise out of necessity as well as principle; that is, women are employed to meet the state's need for their labor power rather than for their own liberation (Molyneux 1981). Undoubtedly there was a need for women's labor force participation in the early years of the Cuban revolution, but toward the end of the 1970s, this need appeared to lessen and there was even fear of lack of sufficient employment for women (Nazzari 1983: 260).

However, the percentage of Cuban women in the labor force continued to grow, reaching 34.8 percent in 1990 (Table 1.7), propelled not only by the state, but by changes taking place among women themselves. As noted in chapter 1, women were motivated by state policies such as the greater availability of consumer goods through the SDPE, the new economic management and planning system introduced in the late 1970s. Rising educational and occupational opportunities for women also played a part, since the 1970s were the period in which women began to make substantial advances into higher-level technical and managerial jobs (Larguia and Dumoulin 1986). Most growth in women's labor force participation took place after 1970 and does not appear to have leveled off until the "special period" began in 1990,[1] when the drastic decline in trade with and aid from the former Soviet Union caused severe economic problems, including increased unemployment. In 1993, Ariguanabo was operating on two rather than four shifts, due to shortages of fuel and raw materials. Displaced workers continue to receive 60 percent of their salary and many are now working in agricultural activities, including several of Rosalía's children, while Rosalía has retired and moved to live with another man in a nearby town.

The increasing rate of Cuban female labor force participation prior to this special period weakens Nazzari's (1983) argument that the shift from moral to material incentives in Cuba under the SDPE in the 1970s hindered women's employment opportunities. Nazzari argues that this shift required firms to become more cost effective and therefore less likely to hire and promote women, who need more support services than men and who may also be subject to higher rates of turnover and absenteeism. Our data on women textile workers show that the need under the SDPE to increase productivity and cost effectiveness does appear to favor skilled male workers over less-skilled women production workers. At the same time, however, the wage and consumer policies promoted by the SDPE increased the attractiveness of wage labor for Cuban women.

As in Puerto Rico and the Dominican Republic, our analysis of the impact of paid employment on women's status in Cuba will not be limited to the household, but will also examine changes at the level of the workplace and in political participation, particularly in mass organizations. Our data demonstrate that there have been significant gains for Cuban women in the postrevolutionary period at all three levels, but that as in Puerto Rico and the Dominican Republic, working women in Cuba are still regarded as supplementary wage workers. Despite Cuba's public support for women's equality, there is still resistance to regarding women as full breadwinners on a par with men.

Methodology

Though there have been other studies on Cuban women's labor force participation, both by Cuban[2] and non-Cuban authors, based mainly on census data, this is the first attempt to analyze with primary data qualitative changes in the lives of Cuban women resulting from paid employment in the postrevolutionary period.[3] The study was initiated in May 1986 with the collaboration of the FMC, which provided a team of researchers to carry out the survey research and analysis and worked with me on the preparation of the final report. They also participated in the in-depth interviews conducted in 1987.

The study focuses on the textile industry, because it provided greater comparability with the previous studies on women garment workers in Puerto Rico and the Dominican Republic and because of its importance as a source of industrial employment for women in Cuba in the postrevolutionary period. In the mid-1980s, there were 13 textile factories in Cuba with a total labor force of 32,886, of which 46.2 percent were women. Although there are considerable differences between the garment and textile industries, they both represent entry-level jobs for a relatively unskilled female industrial labor force. The greater male participation in the textile industry actually makes for better possibilities of comparison between the occupational mobility of male and female workers than the virtually total female labor force in the garment industry.

Since we were interested in comparing the prerevolutionary and postrevolutionary periods, we deliberately chose the oldest textile factory in the island, Ariguanabo, which was started with North American capital in 1931 and which as early as the 1940s employed more than 4,000 workers, almost all men. The factory was nationalized in 1960 and underwent an extensive process of modernization, which boosted productivity considerably.[4] It is located in the province of Havana about seven miles from the capital.

A study of one factory cannot attempt to be representative of the entire female industrial labor force in Cuba. This is why this study must be considered exploratory and its results interpreted with great caution. However, Ariguanabo has certain characteristics that make it particularly worthy of study. For example, in the prerevolutionary period Ariguanabo had an almost exclusively male labor force, despite the prevalence of women in other Cuban textile plants.[5] Women did not begin to enter the factory in massive numbers until 1973, when women's labor force participation began to rise. Since that time their percentage has steadily increased, so that at the time of this study in 1986, they represented approximately 33 percent of the labor force. A year later, following a change in the shift hours from eight to six hours, which resulted in additional workers being hired, Ariguanabo had a total of 5,211 workers, with women representing 35.6 percent. Women are well represented in production, administration, and technical positions but constitute only 6.7 percent of management, a point I shall return to later.

In selecting the sample, administrative, service, and managerial employees were eliminated in order to focus on workers and technicians directly involved in production. A total of 168 respondents were chosen at random from a sample of 1,289 women workers stratified according to age. All of the women in the sample were production workers, except for 14 women working as *técnicos* or technicians. Since we were interested in obtaining an adequate sample of women workers with employment experience in the prerevolutionary period, we over-sampled women over 50 years of age, of whom there were only 93 in the factory in 1986. A 50 percent sample of these women plus a 10 percent sample of women 50 years of age or younger gave us a total sample of 168 women. There were 33 cases of substitution for respondents who could not be located, who were also chosen from a random list. The over-sampling of older women workers gave us a large enough number to examine generational differences among Cuban textile workers, which turns out to be one of the more interesting aspects of the study.

The interviews were conducted in workers' homes by the Cuban team of researchers, most of whom are professional staff of the Federation of Cuban Women. The author trained this special research team in interview techniques and assisted them in adapting the interview schedule used in the study of Puerto Rican garment workers to the Cuban situation, after careful pretesting with randomly selected women workers from Ariguanabo. For example, we found it useful to obtain educational and employment information for both the prerevolutionary and postrevolutionary periods, in order to obtain an accurate measure of the changes that had occurred. In addition, questions were asked about participation in several Cuban mass organizations that are unique to socialism. The interview schedule, which lasted about two hours, covered work experiences, family life, political attitudes, and participation in mass organizations. In addition, a year after the completion of the survey the author, with the assistance of the Cuban team, conducted in-depth interviews with a sub-sample of 17 women of different ages and marital status to obtain more qualitative information. We also had several lengthy interviews with representatives of management and the union in Ariguanabo to obtain data and to discuss the results of the study, and some of this information is included here.

In analyzing the data, it turned out that the sample divided almost equally between three age groups: 17–29; 30–44; and 45 and over. However, since the latter category includes the women over 50 who were overrepresented, the sample does not reflect an accurate breakdown of the ages of women employed in Ariguanabo, the majority of whom were under 30. It would have been preferable to keep this over-50 category separate rather than lumping them with women 45 and over, but it is impossible to redo the analysis at this time. At any rate, we are concerned less with a representative sample of women workers in the factory than with how these ages, which represent different stages in the life cycle, are correlated with differences in household composition, attitudes toward work, and political participation.

Household Composition and Authority Patterns

The area around Ariguanabo has experienced considerable population growth in the postrevolutionary period, due partly to industrial development. In our sample of women workers, 45 percent were born in the area of Ariguanabo, while the remainder came from other areas, some from as far away as Oriente. Many came to work in the factories established in the area, including another large textile factory located only a few kilometers from Ariguanabo opened in 1965 as part of the revolution's import substitution strategy. Still, half the sample population have lived in their present residence for over ten years, a few for their entire lives. So, though Ariguanabo is close to Havana, we are dealing with a fairly stable, not highly urbanized population.

Population growth has contributed to a severe housing shortage, which is evident in the fact that 38 percent of our sample households have five or more members (Table 5.1). The women workers interviewed cite housing as their most important domestic problem, although the state provides housing both as *viviendas vinculadas,* through which workers can purchase their homes by paying monthly installments for up to 20 years, and as a *medio básico* or company housing allocated to workers so long as they are employed. The homes of those sampled are quite well equipped, with 68 percent having a washing machine and refrigerator, while 90 percent have a television and radio.

In an attempt to provide more housing for its workers, in 1974 Ariguanabo opened an apartment housing complex called Pueblo Textil, which in 1985 housed 346 families. Though the Pueblo Textil is located close to the factory and the apartments are very modern and well equipped, some residents feel isolated because they are located eight ki-

TABLE 5.1

Number of Persons in Household by Women's Age
in Ariguanabo Sample
Percentages

| | Number of Persons in Household | | | |
Age	*1*	*2-4*	*5+*	*Total*
17-29	4.9	37.7	57.4	100.0
30-44	8.9	68.9	22.2	100.0
45 and over	24.2	45.2	30.6	100.0
Total N	22	82	64	168
%	13.1	48.8	38.1	100.0

Source: Data compiled by Helen I. Safa and the Federation of Cuban Women.

lometers from Bauta, the nearest town, where they must go for shopping and all other amenities, except for a small *bodega* (grocery store) and medical clinic opened recently in the complex. Most workers live in Bauta, long the residence of most Ariguanabo workers, while some come from as far away as Havana. Ariguanabo has its own buses, which transport workers to and from the various areas in which they live.

As in Puerto Rico and the Dominican Republic, age and marital status have a profound impact on how women dispose of their earnings and the way in which their contribution affects household authority patterns. Almost half of the total female labor force in Ariguanabo is under 30.[6] Born after 1956, they represent the new generation of Cuban women workers raised in the postrevolutionary society. In our sample, over half of these young women live in large families of five or more persons (Table 5.1), where many adults are working. As a result, half of the single women in our sample contribute less than half their salaries to the household (Table 5.2). Sometimes single women pay their parents a fixed amount and reserve the rest for their expenses, as well as saving towards a home of their own.

Single women living with their parents generally defer to them to make the major decisions at home and administer the expenses (Table 5.3). Young women are clearly subordinate members of the household, even if they are married and have children of their own. Young women are especially close to their mothers, who often take care of their children while they work, and with whom they consult on personal problems and share household chores. For example, Odalys relies completely on her mother to take care of her three-year-old twins while she works in Ariguanabo. She receives no assistance from their father, and doesn't want any, "*porque ahora son míos nada más y no tiene derechos*

TABLE 5.2

Women's Contribution to Household Expense by Marital Status
in Ariguanabo Sample
Percentages

| | *Percentage of* | | |
| | *Women's Salary Contributed to Household Expenses* | | |
Marital Status	*All*	*50% or More*	*Less than 50%*	*Total*
Married	65.6	26.9	7.5	100.0
Female Head	50.8	30.5	18.6	100.0
Single	25.0	25.0	50.0	100.0
Total N	95	47	26	168
%	56.5	28.0	15.5	100.0

Source: Data compiled by Helen I. Safa and the Federation of Cuban Women.

ninguno" (because now they are only mine and he has no rights at all). By law she could make him pay, but she does not want him to have any authority over the children or even to see them. They never married or lived together and broke up when Odalys was three months pregnant at the age of 20. He wanted her to have an abortion, but she says first children should not be aborted, and she always wanted twins. Her family was quite upset initially but now have grown very fond of the children and even spoil them. She makes enough money to support the children with her parents' help and gives her mother all of her salary except for occasional expenses like clothes and dances. Her mother administers expenses for the household, which consists of eight members, including her parents, the twins, and three younger brothers and sisters. Her father and brother also work, and she considers her parents to be the heads of the household. Although she still goes dancing every week, Odalys has no interest in remarrying for the moment, *"porque es mejor, te diviertes más … puedes salir, no tienes quien te vele ni te mande, nada más que mis padres"* (because it's better, you enjoy yourself more … you can go out, you don't have anyone watching or ordering you, only my parents). In effect, Odalys continues to live much like a single girl, though because of the children she was forced to interrupt her studies and was denied a scholarship to the Soviet Union to study engineering. Perhaps this helps explain why she has little interest in remarrying and does not want to have any more children. Resistance to marriage indicates the degree to which even single mothers have become less dependent on a male partner for support, especially if they live in extended families.

Contrary to common demographic patterns, increased educational and occupational possibilities have not increased the age of marriage

TABLE 5.3

Who Makes Decisions in Household by Marital Status
in Ariguanabo Sample
Percentages

Marital Status	Respondent	Husband	Both	Other[a]	Total
Married	12.9	17.2	52.7	17.2	100.0
Female Head	49.2	—	1.7	49.2	100.0
Single	18.8	—	6.2	75.0	100.0
Total N	44	16	51	57	168
%	26.2	9.5	30.4	33.9	100.0

[a] Usually refers to parents or in-laws.
Source: Data compiled by Helen I. Safa and the Federation of Cuban Women.

and pregnancy for Cuban women, who continue to enter unions and have children at an early age. In our sample of textile workers, women under 30 have much higher educational levels than older women, reflecting the educational advances of the postrevolutionary period (Table 5.4).[7] Nevertheless, nearly two-thirds of the younger women sampled had their first child under the age of 20, and 28.6 percent have had more than one partner. At the national level, between 1981 and 1987, the average age for first unions[8] in Cuba declined from 19.7 to 18.4 years, while the percentage of consensual unions increased from 23.1 percent to 28.4 percent among women aged 15 to 49, principally among the young. A national-level study of women in consensual unions showed that they have lower educational and occupational levels and lower participation in the labor force than legally married women (Catasús 1992). Consensual unions are also more fragile than legal unions, and the percentage of separations (from consensual unions) doubled to over 10 percent of the female population aged 15 to 49 years from 1981 to 1987. Divorce also increased rapidly after the revolution, and in 1987, 42 out of every 100 marriages ended in divorce (Catasús 1992).

The high rate of teenage pregnancies combined with the severe housing shortage in Cuba contributes to the increasing rate of three-generation households, which constitute 40 percent of our sample.[9] Single mothers, often living in three-generation households, like consensual unions are more prevalent among the young (Dominguez et al. 1989: 44–53). Extended, three-generation families often have the highest income because of the large number of wage earners per household and also provide valuable assistance in child care and other tasks to working mothers.[10] However, three-generation households also tend to increase the authority of the older generation and maintain a more traditional sexual division of labor in the home, as in the case of Odalys described

TABLE 5.4

Educational Level by Women's Age in Ariguanabo Sample
Percentages

Age	Primary Grade 1-6	Secondary Grade 7-9	Grade 10 or more	Total
17-29	6.6	75.4	18.0	100.0
30-44	35.6	48.9	15.6	100.0
45 and over	74.2	19.4	6.5	100.0
Total N	66	80	22	168
%	39.3	47.6	13.1	100.0

Source: Data compiled by Helen I. Safa and the Federation of Cuban Women.

above. The presence of several women decreases the pressure on men to share in household tasks.

There appears to be a more egalitarian household pattern among better-educated women, more skilled workers in our Ariguanabo sample, who are legally married and living apart from kin. Yodalys is 23 and has been working as a draftsman in the factory for five years while she studies mechanical drawing to improve her position. She and her husband had been married only two months at the time of the interview, but they already had their own home, for which they had saved during their five years of courtship after they met in school. Neither of them have close relatives living nearby and her parents live in Oriente, and she sees them only about once a year. They do not plan to have children for two years until Yodalys completes her studies and they have finished furnishing their house. At present her husband helps her considerably with shopping and cooking, because she attends classes after work and often arrives late, and she hopes this will continue when they have children. Although Yodalys knows that children will increase her burden, she thinks she can manage with her husband's help, even in a supervisory position. Yodalys attributes the high divorce rate among young couples to the fact that they often live with their parents and never learn responsibility. She notes: "*Cuando se casan, deben de construir su hogar, vivir solos, y tener sus obligaciones, tanto la mujer como el hombre, que cada cual se sienta responsable del matrimonio en todo sentido.*" (When they marry, they should build their home, live alone, and have their obligations, the woman as much as the man, that each feels responsible for the marriage in every sense.)

Except for certain upwardly mobile couples like Yodalys and her husband, in most working-class families, men do not share in household tasks nor do women put much pressure on them to do so, even though they are also employed. Among most older couples in our sample, the wife continues to do most of the household work. The only household tasks in which men actively participate are paying the bills, doing the shopping, and taking out the garbage. Women are partly to blame, because they turn for help to other female relatives who live with them or nearby rather than increasing pressure on their husbands to take on additional chores. Raquel, who has been married for 33 years and works the same shift in Ariguanabo with her husband, claims it is too late to get her husband to change, *"porque es que nunca yo lo he adaptado a que lo tenga que hacer"* (because [it's that] I've never adapted him to do anything). She contrasts their traditional pattern with that of the younger generation of *"matrimonios modernos"* (modern marriages) such as her daughter and son-in-law, who share cooking and other household tasks while they both work in the factory on alternate shifts.

As in Puerto Rico and the Dominican Republic, however, paid employment has had a significant impact on authority patterns. Over 65 percent of married women contribute all of their salary to the household expenses (Table 5.2), and this contribution has clearly increased their bargaining power in the household. More than half of the married women in our sample administer expenses and make decisions jointly with their husbands (Table 5.3), which constitutes a real change from a traditional patriarchal pattern common to previous Cuban working-class households, in which the husband was the primary authority. For example, 28-year-old Zoila has been married for seven years to a college professor and they have two small children. She has worked at Ariguanabo for eight years, and though both of her children are in the day care center in Bauta, she still has a lot of work to do bathing, feeding, and playing with her children when she returns from work. She says her husband, who now teaches nights, helps considerably with cooking and picking up the children and does not object to her working. She notes: *"Yo pienso que si los dos estudiamos, trabajamos y los hijos son de los dos y la casa y todo, debemos ayudarnos, no? en todo."* (I think that if we are both studying and working, and the children are both ours and the house and everything, we should help each other, no? in everything.) The emphasis Zoila places on both the children and the house being a joint responsibility reflects her egalitarian views.

Almost none of the husbands have asked their wives to stop working, representing another radical change from the prerevolutionary period. This reflects both economic need and the greater social acceptance of women working, which is reinforced by state policy. As Ana María's 30-year-old daughter remarked: *"Hay algunos todavía que le hacen un rechazo a eso, pero la mayoría … la mayoría están de acuerdo conque la mujer trabaje. No es que estén de acuerdo que es, la vida la necesita, la vida está cara, tienen hijos. Y uno siempre pa' los hijos quiere lo mejor."* (There are some who still reject that, but the majority ... the majority agree that the woman should work. It is not that they agree, but life requires it, life is expensive, they have children. And one always wants the best for one's children.) Like Ana María, women often legitimate their paid employment by reference to their children's welfare.

The marked decline in fertility among Cuban women suggests another area in which women have more control, although their input into fertility decisions was not questioned directly. Few middle-aged women under 45 in our sample have more than three children compared to 29 percent in the older age group (Table 5.5), reflecting the overall decline in fertility in Cuba in the postrevolutionary period. Most of our respondents who have one or two children do not plan to have any more, even among women under 30 who are in their prime child-bearing age. From 1975 to 1988, the total Cuban fertility rate fell from 2.74 births per woman to 1.88 births per woman, an extremely low figure for Latin America and comparable to that of many advanced industrial countries. However, the rate of fertility decline has been lower in younger age groups, reflecting the relatively high rate of teenage pregnancies (FMC 1990: 14).

Our data suggest clear generational differences in gender roles between younger and older women industrial workers in Cuba. As a result of the revolution, younger women have much higher educational levels and lower fertility levels than older women, and expect to participate in the labor force most of their lives. Like the older generation, they are making a substantial contribution to the household economy, which has given them more authority in the household and greater control over the family budget, especially if they live apart from their relatives. Young women also expect more from their husbands in terms of sharing housework and child care, as in the case of Yodalys, while still maintaining differences in gender roles. On the other hand, despite lower fertility levels, the age at marriage and particularly the age at which women have their first child remain very young and help account for the relatively high rate of marital instability.

Early pregnancy and consensual unions are principal factors behind the formation of female-headed households, which doubled nationally from 14 percent in 1953 to 28.1 percent in 1981 (Valdés and Gomariz 1992: 33).[11] Female heads of household constitute 35 percent of our sample, and most are separated or divorced, although a few older women are widows. In our sample, while age at marriage and educational levels do not differ greatly, 57.4 percent of female-headed house-

TABLE 5.5

Number of Children by Women's Age in Ariguanabo Sample
Percentages

Age	1	2	3	4	5 or more	Total
17-29	67.6	29.7	2.7	–	--	100.0
30-44	30.0	45.0	20.0	2.5	2.5	100.0
45 and over	18.2	23.6	29.1	14.5	14.5	100.0
Total N	47	42	25	9	9	132[a]
%	35.6	31.8	19.0	6.8	6.8	100.0

[a] Excludes those women who have not had children.
Source: Data compiled by Helen I. Safa and the Federation of Cuban Women.

holds had their first child under age 20 compared to 42.1 percent of married women. Race is also a significant factor, since 56 percent of the black women in our sample are female heads of household, compared to about 30 percent of white and mulatto women.[12] This corresponds to national-level data, which show that in the 1981 census, black women and men had a higher rate of marital dissolution than either white or mulatto women (de la Fuente 1995: Figure 3), which was also true historically. In the 1981 census, although consensual unions are highest among mulattoes, whites also show a marked increase over censuses taken prior to the revolution, suggesting a racial convergence in mating patterns (de la Fuente 1995: Table 6).

The Cuban government is clearly not pleased with the high rate of marital dissolution to which its policies of greater economic equality for women have indirectly contributed. Thirty percent of all the women in our sample have been married more than once, while among female-headed households, the rate is 39 percent. One explanation for this may be the greater economic independence of Cuban women and the existence of support services such as day care, which have made it easier to raise children without dependence on male support, particularly in three-generation households. Ana María recalls how difficult it was for her when her husband left her with three small children, the youngest of whom was only six months old. This happened in the early years of the revolution, but now, she says: *"Ahora actualmente, cualquiera mujer, para mí, cualquiera mujer cría un hijo sola, porque hay mucho trabajo, hay más facilidades para la mujer."* (Now actually any woman, for me, any woman can raise a child alone, because there is a lot of work, there are many facilities for women.)

Contrary to capitalist countries like Puerto Rico or the Dominican Republic, marital instability in Cuba does not appear to result from high levels of male unemployment and other signs of economic stagnation that make it more difficult for the man to carry out his role as principal breadwinner. All of the husbands of the married women in our sample were employed, 58 percent in the same textile mill where their wives worked. Nearly 90 percent of these husbands contribute more than half of their salary to the household (the great majority contribute their entire salary), showing they fully share the responsibility for economic support with their wives. In our sample, 45 percent of the husbands earn 200 Cuban pesos or more a month compared to 68 percent of their wives, although in the factory as a whole, men generally earn more than women. This is a relatively high wage for Cuba, where the average monthly wage in 1986 was 188 Cuban pesos (Comité Estatal de Estadística 1986: 198). Although respondents complain of the rising cost of living and more than half cite economic need as the principal reason for their present employment, they are generally referring to amenities such as household appliances or furniture rather than basic necessities. As Zoila, a young mother married to a university professor, notes: "*No es lo mismo un solo salario que dos. Podemos vivir más cómodos. No es indispensable porque yo, con el sueldo de mi esposo yo no me voy a morir de hambre ni mis hijos no van a estar desnudos ni nada de eso.*" (One salary is not the same as two. We can live more comfortably. It is not indispensable because, with my husband's salary, I am not going to die of hunger nor are my children going to go naked nor anything like that.) While Zoila recognizes the importance of her salary and plans to continue working, she feels they could manage on her husband's income. Because of the prestige of her husband's occupation, Zoila may also feel the need to minimize her contribution to the household. However, she is not typical of most of our respondents, most of whom are very conscious of the importance of their contribution to the household economy.

The pressure to earn money increases in female heads of household, 62 percent of whom have only one or two persons working in the household, and half of them give all their salaries to the household (Table 5.2). Those contributing less are generally younger women living with their parents, to whom they give a monthly allowance for food and housing, while they pay their other expenses for themselves and their children on their own. For example, 20-year-old Alina gives her mother 40 Cuban pesos biweekly for herself and her 19-month-old son. Her mother administers the expenses out of the pooled income of various household members, including her cousin and her former stepfather, who has now broken up with her mother but continues to live with them until he can find adequate housing. Alina's brother also visits on weekends from boarding school, but because he is studying he does not contribute. The house, for which there is no charge, is in her mother's name, and the mother is clearly the head of the household and does most of the chores, although Alina helps with the cooking and other tasks when she can.

Like other young single mothers, Alina has had to give up a great deal for her son. Although she left school in ninth grade, she was about to receive a four-year scholarship to study in the former German Democratic Republic when she became pregnant. She thinks women should study and not have their children so young, but now she has to work to support her son. Alina notes: *"Porque yo puedo atender al niño, pero si no trabajo, no tengo quien me sostenga a mí."* (Because I can attend to the child, but if I don't work, I don't have anyone to support me.) She does receive 20 Cuban pesos monthly from the son's father, who is now married, and he comes to see his son every weekend. Now that they are working shorter shifts, she and her mother, who both work in Ariguanabo, are able to share the care of her child. But previously she paid 50 Cuban pesos monthly for someone to look after him. Alina says that many women with children working in Ariguanabo are obliged to pay this amount, underlining the need for more day care. She tried to enroll her son in the day care center, but there was no room. As a result, Alina has repeatedly had to ask for unpaid leaves of absence from work because she has no one to take care of her son.

Like Alina, some divorced or separated women receive minimal child support from the fathers of their children, while widows receive a pension. However, many single mothers do not receive child support, and in some cases, such as that of Odalys referred to earlier, prefer to support their children on their own because this limits the authority fathers have over their children. Female-headed households in Cuba do not receive special welfare payments from the state as in the United States or Puerto Rico, although female heads are given preference in employment and enjoy the other subsidies in education, health, and other areas that the Cuban state provides. Given the high divorce rate, particularly among the young, it could be argued that the Cuban state wishes to avoid encouraging the formation of female-headed households.

Another factor promoting marital instability (and three-generation households) is the housing shortage, which forces families to double up and may lead to problems with in-laws or even parents. Over half (55.9 percent) of the female-headed households in our sample consist of three generations and are composed both of younger women with children living with their parents and older women living with children and grandchildren, as in the case of Rosalía described earlier. Catalina at 36 has returned to her parents' house with her four-year-old son because she could not get along with her mother-in-law. Her mother-in-law only had one child and although he is now 42, apparently she never accepted Catalina and kept interfering in their lives. Apparently, women have greater problems with their mothers-in-law than with their own mothers because, as Catalina remarked, "*No es familia, tú me entiendes, no es la misma sangre, porque yo puedo discutir con mi mamá por cualquier bobería y después no pasó nada, pero con la suegra es distinto, tú entiendes? Por eso es que uno debe vivir solo.*" (It is not family, do you understand me, it is not the same blood, because I can argue with my mother over any little thing and afterwards nothing happens, but with the mother-in-law it is different, do you understand? That is why one should live alone.)

Catalina is very upset about the breakup, especially since her son misses his father and has become very fearful, though his father visits him regularly. Her greatest desire is to be reunited with her husband in their own house, but she is not sure he will ever leave his mother. Catalina says: "*A mí me gustaría vivir sola y tener al padre del niño al lado porque yo sé que a él le hace mucha falta, no lo pienso por mí sola, vaya, a mí también me hace falta un compañero, pero más por él.*" (I would like to live alone and to have the father of the child at my side because I know that he misses him very much. I don't think about it only because of myself, well now, I also miss a companion, but more for him.)

Catalina and her son now sleep in her parents' living room, and she has requested her own housing but has not been accepted because others with apparent greater need have been given priority. The large number of female heads of household living doubled up with relatives suggests that they are not given any preference in housing, even when, as in Catalina's case, they have worked many years in Ariguanabo. She has worked for 20 years in the textile industry, including four initial years in Alquitex, a factory nearby. Although she left secondary school to help her parents, she has worked at several jobs in the factory, and until recently was the only woman working in the die vats, a very heavy, tiring job. However, Catalina never complains and is proud of her work and the *primas* (bonuses) she earns and often works double shifts. She plans to go on working "*hasta el final*" (until the end) or till she retires. Thus, her desire for reunification with her husband is clearly not motivated by need for money. Her husband, who also works in Ariguanabo, gives her 60 Cuban pesos a month for the child, the same amount she gives her mother, but Catalina manages her own expenses for herself and her child. Her mother takes care of her son while she works and did so even when she was living with her husband.

Children of dissolved unions generally remain with their mother, although in exceptional cases, the father may have custody. Noemí, for example, is 53 years old and started working in Ariguanabo 23 years ago, shortly after her daughter was born, but the daughter has lived with her paternal grandparents since she was two years old. Noemí and her former husband separated before their daughter was born, but the grandparents convinced Noemí to let them raise her child, probably because they are clearly of higher socio-economic status and could provide more for her. Noemí sees her daughter regularly, who now works in a government ministry, and is very proud of her and is always buying her things. Though Noemí is pleased with the independence her daughter's job has given her, she disapproves of young women who use their salaries foolishly, buying dresses and going out and forgetting their domestic obligations. For Noemi, *"tienen confundido la liberación con el libertinaje. Porque yo no entiendo que una mujer porque trabaje se tenga que ... que ser un libertín"* (they confuse liberation with licentiousness. Because I don't understand why a woman who works has ... has to be licentious). She went on to refer specifically to the case of some women who were unfaithful to their husbands who went abroad to participate in *misiones internacionales* (international missions) such as Angola.

As Noemí suggests, Cuban women in the postrevolutionary period have more sexual freedom, and this has also contributed to increased marital instability. Women's incorporation into wage labor has reduced women's dependence on a male breadwinner and made it easier for women to raise children on their own. However, an increase in teenage pregnancy, consensual unions, and separations, especially among the young, contributes to a high percentage of three-generation households that maintain traditional patterns of authority and domestic labor.

Occupational Mobility and Job Discrimination

As we noted in chapter 1, Cuban women have made significant occupational advances in the postrevolutionary period, as can be seen in the marked shift out of unskilled service occupations into higher-level technical and professional jobs. Forty percent of the women who entered the labor force between 1976 and 1980 were technical, skilled, or professional personnel (Pérez-Stable 1987: 61), and this trend continued in the 1980s. By 1988, women constituted 58.3 percent of all technicians in Cuba and 26.5 percent of managers (FMC 1990: 73). However, occupational segregation has persisted, as women continue to be most heavily represented in fields such as education, public health, and finance and insurance, while they represented less than 30 percent of all workers in industry (see Table 1.8). How can we explain the persistence of occupational segregation by gender in Cuba? Is it related to women's household responsibilities described above or is there also resistance in the workplace to women's occupational mobility? How is this resistance manifest and what is the state doing to overcome gender discrimination in the workplace? These are some of the questions this section will address.

Women's increase in the labor force in Ariguanabo since the revolution is undeniable. Before the revolution, Ariguanabo had an almost exclusively male labor force. Only 140 women were employed, representing about 5 percent of the labor force. In fact, the male workers were considered a labor aristocracy because of their high level of skill and pay. Women did not work in the factory in massive numbers until 1973, when 800 women were employed. This was also the period in which women began entering the labor force in larger numbers in Cuba as a whole. Since then, the number and percentage of female workers in Ariguanabo have increased steadily, from 31.5 percent in 1980 to 37.3 percent in January 1989.

Two older sisters who were formerly employed in Ariguanabo and are now retired described the strict work discipline in the prerevolutionary period, when the factory was owned and administered by Americans. All supervisors were white men, except for a few black Jamaicans, who were the only blacks then employed in the factory. Older workers were often discharged, and there was no retirement plan with pay such as these sisters and their husbands now enjoy. Workers were not permitted to eat or smoke on the job and had to fulfill their quotas or they were replaced. Despite what the sisters describe as a *sindicato patronal* (company union), there were several massive strikes in the 1930s and 1940s, principally for wage increases. Both these sisters were married to factory supervisors and lived quite well, but they claim conditions have improved a great deal since then. In the prerevolutionary period, the factory provided housing for some workers (in which these sisters continue to live) and also had a school for the children of factory workers. Children were encouraged to attend school by receiving a one-cent-a-day bonus from management for each child who attended. Many of the children of factory workers in the prerevolutionary period continue to be employed at Ariguanabo, and the son of one of these sisters currently works as a supervisor. The few women who were employed were entitled to a 12-week maternity leave, which was mandated by Cuban law. The sisters explain the low number of women employed at that time as partly due to the resistance of male workers, but they say this situation now has changed completely, noting, "*Porque si la mujer está trabajando, él no la va a quitar del trabajo. Ya ese tiempo se acabó ... Aquí los hombres no le quitan nada a las mujeres."* (Because if a woman is working, he is not going to take it from her. That time is over ... Here men don't take anything away from women.) However, other respondents suggest that male resistance to female employment and occupational advancement in Ariguanabo is greater than these sisters acknowledge.

The increasing number of women workers represents a conscious strategy on the part of the Cuban government to encourage female employment. As early as 1968, the Ministry of Labor adopted a kind of affirmative action policy (Resolution 47 and later 511), whereby in each workplace certain jobs would be declared *puestos preferentes* (preferential positions) for women. The decision as to the number and type of jobs for women is made by the management and union officials in each workplace in consultation with the FMC and is supposed to be approved in a worker assembly. According to data provided by management, at the time of our study almost half of the production jobs in Ariguanabo had been declared *puestos preferentes* for women, but about 35 percent of these were actually occupied by men. The number of women in technical, administrative, and service jobs generally met the designated goals, but women fell short in certain production jobs and particularly in management. In 1987, only 7 out of 169 *dirigentes* (managers) in Ariguanabo were women, though previous to our research, the general manager of the factory was a black woman, who left to become vice minister of light industry.

One reason for women's lack of advancement into supervisory positions in Ariguanabo is the way female production workers are inserted into the labor process. The most numerous jobs for women as production workers are as winders, spinners, and weavers, to the extent that there are comparatively few men left in either of the former two occupations, suggesting a possible new form of occupational segregation. There are no women working as mechanics, who have the best chances for promotion because they are more aware of all phases of the production process. Mechanics also earn more and often become heads of sections or shifts for one of the new integrated brigades. In 1986, at the time of our research, while there were no female heads of shifts or sections, 13 of the 94 heads of brigade were women, but it appears that these elected positions have been eliminated with the change to a six-hour shift.

Although women themselves have shown little interest in becoming mechanics, management has also made little effort to train them. Management is still governed by traditional sexist principles that underestimate a woman's physical ability and magnify her concern for her appearance (for example, greasy hands). As the plant director noted: "*Las*

A Cuban woman winder in a textile mill. Courtesy of the Federation of Cuban Women.

manos de una mujer no son iguales que las de un hombre, para cortar caña, la mecánica, para andar con el martillo, muchas cosas las pueden hacer y la están haciendo las mujeres." (The hands of a woman are not the same as those of a man, to cut sugar cane, for mechanics, to work with a hammer; women can do many things and are doing many things.) Yet women do other dirty and heavy jobs in Ariguanabo such as cleaning or oiling machines, working in the die vats, or lifting heavy spools of yarn. The Ministry of Labor also bars women from certain jobs that it maintains present health hazards, particularly to women's reproductive functions. This policy has been strongly contested by the FMC and by the mid-1980s, the number of such positions closed to women was sharply reduced (Pérez-Stable 1993: 139–140).[13]

One policy to enhance women's occupational advancement suggested by the FMC is placing qualified technicians or university graduates in these management positions, but this still would not give women in lower-level production jobs an opportunity to advance. In Ariguanabo, in 1987 women comprised more than half of the technicians or *técnicos* at the factory and about one-third of the engineers, all of whom have received advanced degrees, often in the Soviet Union or other East European countries. Digna, for example, began working as a technician in Ariguanabo six years ago immediately after completing five years of study in Tashkent in the Soviet Union. She is now 31 and has been married for two years to a man who also works in the factory and has two children from a previous marriage. They would like to have children, but they now live in the old part of Havana about two hours' distance from the factory. All of her family lives near the factory and both her mother and father worked in Ariguanabo.

The primary reason given by our Cuban sample for why women are not promoted is that management prefers men, and several of the younger and middle-aged women say that the women workers are not valued, indicating that some women are conscious of gender discrimination in the factory. Rosalía's daughter quotes older men in the factory saying, "*No, si una mujer me manda a mí en el trabajo, me voy y dejo el trabajo.*" (No, if a woman gives orders to me at work, I'll leave and quit the job.) Rosalía claims there are many higher-level jobs requiring less physical effort, such as head of personnel, that could be carried out by a woman. Ana María spent several years working as a domestic after the revolution, until in 1963, she finally got a job in Ariguanabo with the help of the president of the local CDR. Ana María claims it was more difficult then for women to work in Ariguanabo because there was a lot of unemployment, adding: "*Tú sabes que el hombre no siempre ha querido que trabajen las mujeres.*" (You know that the man did not always want women to work.) This suggests that men may have initially resisted the entry of women in the factory labor force and may help explain continuing patterns of gender discrimination.

Younger women are generally more optimistic about advancement in the factory, since they are better educated and have fewer household responsibilities. Many of the older women are burdened by domestic responsibilities and feel they are not qualified for supervisory positions or are afraid of assuming positions of authority. Juana, a divorced woman who has worked in Ariguanabo for 26 years and has raised two daughters on her own, has served as a substitute head of brigade in the factory but doesn't like having to reprimand people. She also claims that women's heavy domestic responsibilities do not permit them to take on additional responsibilities. "*Nosotras las mujeres tenemos mucho problema, mucho problema en la casa y a veces los jefes, si no viene el que lo releva tiene que quedarse. Tenemos muchos problemas en las casas con los hijos, las escuelas, y todo eso ...*" (We women have a lot of problems, a lot of problems at home, and sometimes the supervisors ask you to stay if the person who is to relieve you doesn't come. We have a lot of problems at home with the children, the schools and all that.)

Education would not appear to be a barrier to advancement, since the educational level of women in Ariguanabo is equal or superior to that of men. According to data provided by the factory, at the end of 1985, the percentage of women at the preuniversity level and especially at the technical level was higher than that of men, while the percentage with just primary education was much lower. However, the length of time employed may be a deterrent because women have not been employed at the factory for the same length of time as men, since women did not enter in large numbers until after 1973. Though data on length of time employed were collected on only about half our sample, among these respondents over 65 percent have been employed ten years or less.[14]

Another fundamental factor explaining women's lack of advancement in Ariguanabo is shift work. Shifts change weekly, so that workers are always working different hours. While shifts are necessary in order to use the expensive physical plant to full capacity, they pose more of a problem to women who already have heavy domestic responsibilities and also make it difficult to attend classes for advanced training, union meetings, and other events. Although shifts have recently been reduced from eight to six hours, women still cite shifts as a primary cause of absenteeism and one of the things they like least about working in the factory.

With the change to a six-hour shift, the factory was open six days a week and produced more than previously with three eight-hour shifts daily. In addition, 700 new workers were employed. Though in 1988, Ariguanabo surpassed its quota for the third year in a row, management claimed that they still needed to improve efficiency, which then stood at about 70 percent, especially in weaving. Part of the problem is due to a high rate of turnover, which with the change to six-hour shifts, was reduced from 30 to 25 percent. Management claims that the majority of those leaving are young, new recruits who quit before they have been working six months, which represents a heavy investment in training for about 1,200 people annually. Some of the older workers complain that discipline was stricter when Ariguanabo was owned by Americans, who did not hesitate to fire workers for any reason. Zoila, whose father has worked in Ariguanabo for 43 years, has overheard older workers comment: "*Si estuvieran los americanos no pasaba esto porque en seguida lo botaban.*" (If the Americans were here, this wouldn't happen because they would be thrown out immediately.) Although moral and material sanctions may be applied, management claims that it is very difficult to fire anyone from their job in the factory despite repeated absences.

Undoubtedly, labor turnover and absenteeism may be more of a problem in a socialist society than under capitalism since the incentive to work is not as great where workers are not forced to seek paid employment to meet all their needs (Lindenberg 1993: 35). In our sample, illness (personal and familial), the lack of day care, and shift work are cited by women as the primary reasons for absenteeism. Women often suffer higher levels of absenteeism because they must take off work for family reasons, because their children are ill or need to be taken to the clinic. Until recently, only women could accompany sick children in the hospital, but with pressure from the FMC, this regulation has recently been changed to include men. However, Rosalía's daughter claims that the father would take leave only when he is the single parent, *"pero mientras que esté la mujer, siempre es la mujer"* (but while the woman is around, it is always the woman). Although her husband shares in household tasks, she said she would never ask him to take off work if their child was ill. Here again we can see how women workers adopt a different standard for men and women and always place their domestic responsibilities above their work role, even when state policy attempts to reduce such restrictions.

To counter the problem of absenteeism and turnover, management is placing more emphasis on stability as a criterion for recruitment, seeking people who are not only qualified but demonstrate responsibility. They are also trying to reward good workers, especially in highly skilled jobs for which it is difficult to recruit, by placing them on fixed shifts and providing them with housing and other amenities. *Escalafones,* or pay scales based on seniority, may also be relaxed to reward particularly productive workers. However, nearly three-fourths of our sample say that pay scales are respected in the factory. Cuban state law requires that men and women receive equal pay for equal work, and as we have seen, our female respondents often make more money than their husbands who work in the same factory. However, this is not representative of the factory as a whole, in which men are generally better represented in skilled and managerial jobs that pay more. In addition, men earn more by working longer hours and double shifts, which is more difficult for women with domestic responsibilities. It would seem that men in highly skilled jobs also receive preference in housing. Only one of our respondents has received housing as an incentive, despite the clear need among married women and single mothers who are doubled up with their parents or in-laws. The need to stabilize the labor force in order to cut costs and boost productivity apparently takes precedence over meeting women's special demands in areas such as housing, day care, and fixed shifts.

Ariguanabo provides workers with a full array of support services that far surpass those found in the prerevolutionary period and among industrial workers in Puerto Rico, the Dominican Republic, and other countries (Humphrey 1987). These include transportation to and from work, a day care center, a medical clinic, a pharmacy, housing, a lunchroom, and recreational facilities including a baseball field and a workers'

club with a bar, where dances are held periodically. Cuban law also provides all workers with 30 days of vacation at full pay each year, maternity
leave of 12 weeks, sick leave, accident coverage, and pensions for retired
workers, who at one time received full pay (Lindenberg 1993: 28). Nevertheless, it would seem that some of the facilities offered by the factory
such as the lunchroom and the day care center are better suited to the
needs of white-collar workers in administrative, service, or even technical jobs than to production workers who rotate shifts.

The day care center, for example, is open from 6 AM to 6 PM, and cannot accommodate women on shift work. Almost 30 percent of our respondents sent their children to the day care center, particularly among
middle-aged women, while more of the younger women rely on their
mothers to take care of their children. Though this reflects the fact that
younger women are more likely to live with their mothers, it also reflects
the scarcity of day care facilities in recent years. In 1975, day care centers
were projected to expand to a capacity of 150,000 children, but by 1980,
the number had only reached 90,000 (Pérez-Stable 1987: 63). However,
as part of the rectification campaign started in 1986, day care centers received renewed emphasis, and by 1988, there were a total of 1,021 day
care centers in Cuba with a total matriculation of 142,073 children (FMC
1990: 47). Under the "special period," however, day care construction
has again declined.

Over 80 percent of our sample think more day care centers are
needed, and a number of our respondents suggested that the day care
center accommodate to women who work rotating shifts. Lourdes, an
older single mother, was forced to stop working for seven years when her
son was born. She was then working at Alquitex, a nearby textile factory,
and requested a transfer to Ariguanabo because it was closer to her
home, but her request was refused. She supported herself by sewing at
home until her son started school, when she started working at
Ariguanabo. She has been separated from the father of her son since before the child was born, and he has since married and never comes to
see his son. The seven years she worked at home were difficult finan-
cially, but she managed with the assistance of her family and eventually
secured some child support from the father because she took him to
court. Several women also claim that the day care center on the grounds
of the Ariguanabo plant is not reserved exclusively for the children of
factory workers, since admission depends on the Ministry of Education
which apparently gives them no preference.

Women workers receive paid maternity leave for 12 weeks and can
take off another year without pay. However, once they resume working,
they must also work shifts. The difficulty of shift work combined with

the lack of child care forces many women to extend their maternity leave or to leave work entirely for a few years, as we have seen in the case of Lourdes. The factory management also attempts to place women with young children on fixed shifts but claims it has not been able to accommodate demand. A total of 1,400 persons or about one-fourth the labor force are on fixed shifts. However, nearly 10 percent more men than women are on fixed shifts, and only half of the 400 women on fixed shifts work in production. Most of the 20 percent of our sample who do not rotate shifts are technicians and other specialized personnel.

The lunchroom also caters to white-collar workers on fixed shifts, and its hours cannot accommodate those who rotate shifts, particularly with the change to six hours. Even the snack that was formerly sold to them during working hours has been eliminated, except for a small piece of bread or pancake (*la cegueña*). Few of the production workers use the lunchroom, and most prefer to eat at home before leaving for work or take a snack with them to eat while they are working. With the six-hour shift, rest periods have been reduced to ten minutes and some workers complain that they have to work under greater pressure in order to fulfill their quotas, which at the time of the study in 1986 were still being adjusted to the shorter hours.[15] Still they all prefer the six-hour shift, because the work is less tiring and it gives them more free time.

Despite its problems, factory work is a distinct improvement over the jobs most older women had in the prerevolutionary period. Many women over 30 in our sample first worked in agricultural work or in domestic service[16] (Table 5.6), reflecting its prevalence in the prerevolutionary period. Many came from large families and were sent to work at an early age. Ana María's family, for example, was desperately poor because her father died when she was nine, leaving nine children, including a newborn. Ana María, the oldest daughter, was taken out of school in fourth grade and sent to work as a domestic for a family in Bauta, where they have always lived. She earned ten Cuban pesos a month, half of which was paid by giving her family half a liter of milk daily with which to feed the younger children. Her mother worked taking in wash and is still alive at age 82. Carmen, another 40-year-old woman worker from a poor, large family, started working at age ten selling hot coffee and candy in the street, and then at 15 went to Oriente to pick coffee and work in agriculture. She has worked in Ariguanabo only four years and is trying to obtain housing through the factory, because she now lives with her current partner and son and 12 other people, including her parents, five brothers, their wives, and children. Though the house is quite large, they are very crowded and she and her current partner practically live in one room.

TABLE 5.6

First Job of Respondents by Age in Ariguanabo Sample
Percentages

	First Job						
Age	*Ariguanabo Factory*	*Other Factory*	*Agri-culture*	*Service*	*Other*	*N*	*%*
17-29	72.1	8.2	3.3	4.9	11.5	61	100.0
30-44	33.3	8.9	20.0	22.2	15.5	45	100.0
45 or more	19.4	11.3	21.0	27.4	20.9	61	100.0
Total N	71	16	24	30	27	168	
%	42.3	9.5	14.3	17.8	16.1	100	

Source: Data compiled by Helen I. Safa and the Federation of Cuban Women.

Better jobs are also linked to higher educational levels, which many of our older respondents acquired after the revolution. Before the revolution, more than half of the women over 45 in our sample had never completed primary school (sixth grade), mostly because of economic problems. But 60 percent of these women continued their education after the revolution, and now nearly three-fourths have completed primary school (Table 5.4). Many middle-aged women also continued studying, and nearly half went to secondary school. Currently many are not studying because it conflicts with their shift work in the factory and with their heavy burden of domestic responsibilities.

The dramatic increase in educational levels among younger women and their children is one of the most notable effects of the revolution. This can also be seen by comparing the educational level of our respondents with that of their children. In our sample as a whole, among those children who have completed their schooling, more than half the daughters and over two-fifths of the sons have gone beyond secondary school, including some who have gone to the university. Many of these better-educated young people have entered technical fields, while a few have become professionals. Ana María, who is almost illiterate, has a son who is a naval engineer and studied in Bulgaria, and her daughter is a teacher. Ana María is very proud of her children's achievements, which would not have been possible without the revolution: "*Yo miro a mis hijos y le agradezco lo que son a la Revolución misma, porque quien me iba a decir a mí que a un hijo mío iba a estudiar fuera, si él me lo decía a mí, yo le decía eso es mentira.*" (I look at my kids and I am grateful to the revolution for what they are, because who would have said to me that a son of mine would study abroad, if he said it to me, I would have said that is a lie.) Twice as many sons as daughters in our sample have continued as factory workers, which may reflect their lower educational level or may also reflect the greater attraction of factory work for men. Nearly 70 percent of our respondents do not want their sons or daughters to do factory work,[17] though several families had three generations working in Ariguanabo.

Sixty percent of the husbands of the women interviewed are also factory workers, and 58 percent of them work in Ariguanabo, primarily also as production workers. Husbands have educational levels similar to their wives, although more of them have gone beyond secondary school. Many of them also started to work before they were 17, most often as factory or agricultural workers. In some cases they met working in the factory, and many women also have fathers, brothers, sisters, or other relatives who are currently or were previously employed in Ariguanabo, reinforcing the strong sense of a worker community in the area. Raquel's father, for example, worked in Ariguanabo since its founding in 1931 until 1967. Both she and her husband have worked in production for 17 and 30 years, respectively, while two of her daughters have office jobs and one son-in-law is also employed at the factory. When husband and wife both work in Ariguanabo, they often work different shifts in order to share child care responsibilities. This policy is promoted by management to encourage men to share more in child care and also relieves the demand for day care facilities.

Occupational mobility can also be seen in the way the fathers of our respondents have improved their occupational status since the revolution. In the prerevolutionary period, nearly 42 percent of their fathers were agricultural workers while another 25 percent were factory workers, which increased to 46 percent for those fathers living and working after the revolution. This reflects not only the shift out of agriculture into industrial employment but the tendency for the children of Ariguanabo workers to remain in the factory, which now affects women as well as men. The most startling change, however, is in the level of employment, since 32 percent of fathers were unemployed much of the time in the prerevolutionary period, while after the revolution, almost all of those not retired or deceased were employed full-time. The changes among the mothers of our respondents were not so dramatic, with the percentage of housewives being reduced from 62 to 53 percent.

Almost all the women in our sample plan to continue working indefinitely, unlike most women in the prerevolutionary period who did not work after marriage. The strong commitment to work stems both from economic need and a strong work ethic, which is reinforced by state policy. Despite the strain of the double day, most women like their jobs, because they find their work stable and interesting, they like their fellow workers, and they think their work is useful to society. The contribution that individual work makes to the collective good is emphasized in Cuba as part of the socialist ethic of *conciencia,* and workers are expected to contribute extra unpaid work on occasional Sundays and do other forms of volunteer labor. Lindenberg (1993: 32) notes that in 1987 there were more than 2,000 Ariguanabo workers pledged to work more hours than they were paid for.

Women also feel that paid employment has improved their self-concept. Over 90 percent of the women interviewed feel that work has had a positive impact on them, that it has made them feel more independent, experienced, and capable. Work has also contributed to a change in attitude toward gender roles. Three-fourths of our sample are in favor of women working even if they have young children, which again suggests a major change from the prerevolutionary period. Almost all agree that education is equally important for boys and girls, which is reflected in the high educational attainment of their sons and especially daughters.

The increasing percentage of women in the labor force, the high proportion in technical or professional positions, their relatively high wage levels, and their strong commitment to work contradict Nazzari's assertion that women in Cuba are used as a labor reserve (Nazzari 1983: 260).[18] However, it seems that unions and management continue to undervalue women workers because of their failure to address women's needs adequately, such as the shortage of day care and other facilities and the problems of advancement for women in the factory. These are problems that the union should address. Women are well represented in the union, which is part of the Confederation of Cuban Workers (CTC). In Ariguanabo in 1987, there were 467 union *supervisores* or delegates, of whom women constituted 42 percent (Lindenberg 1993: 30), which is higher than their percentage in the factory labor force. A woman administrator also heads the *Frente Femenino* or Feminine Front of the union, but most of the respondents in our in-depth interviews had no knowledge of its activities, and Lindenberg does not even mention the *Frente Femenino* in her analysis of the union in Ariguanabo. Hostility toward the *Frente Femenino* was voiced by the male head of the CTC union at the factory, who said he saw no need for a separate female unit and thought that the needs of working women could be attended to through a single integrated union.

Despite the weakness of the *Frente Femenino* in Ariguanabo, nearly 61 percent of the sample feel that the union has improved the work situation for women, particularly in regard to recent changes regarding shorter shifts, better working conditions, and the renovation of the day care center. Still it would appear that the CTC and the *Frente Femenino* are not responding adequately to working women's needs in Ariguanabo. Women complain that they are not listened to in union meetings, and there is considerable dissatisfaction with the union, particularly among older women. Ana María, who has worked in Ariguanabo for 25 years, is very critical of the union and says that it does not defend the workers and always supports management. She claims it has been that way most of the time, although when Ariguanabo had a female manager, women had greater access to management. She recalls that one time in a workers' assembly run by the union, the head of a brigade announced new regulations, and when he finished, the union delegate added: "*Ustedes oyeron al jefe de brigada lo que dijo. El que no se rija por eso a mí no me vengan a ver.*" (You heard what the head of the brigade said. He who doesn't comply need not come to see me.) Union delegates are elected but, according to Ana María, only one was responsive to the workers, and he was suddenly dismissed. She claims many workers do not want to pay their union dues.

Both union and management are also heavily influenced by the Communist Party. According to Lindenberg (1993: 30) nearly 40 percent of the union delegates in Ariguanabo are members of the Communist Party and Communist Youth, about double the percentage in the population as a whole and in our sample. Representatives of the party as well as the CTC and *Frente Femenino* and management also sit on the *Junta Directiva* or executive board of Ariguanabo, which suggests party representatives have considerable control over factory management, as the party does over unions and production generally (Fuller 1992: 62–63). However, when asked to choose who has done more for working women, more women indicate the union (where they are better represented) than management or the Communist Party. Still most women present their problems at work to management rather than to the union or the party, although unions are supposed to be the normal route for worker complaints in Cuba.

It seems that the passage of the SDPE in the late 1970s weakened the power of unions in favor of management. Management was given greater power over worker discipline with the passage of a law in 1980 restricting the rights of work councils to settle grievances. Work councils are elected directly by workers in a secret ballot, but problems of worker discipline and the need for tighter control with the institution of the SDPE severely restricted their power (Fuller 1987: 146–147). In her study of the role of unions at the Cuban workplace, Fuller (1992) indicates that since 1970 unions have more autonomy, but that it is commonly acknowledged that they still serve primarily to transmit orders downward rather than serving as vehicles through which workers can voice their

complaints and suggestions. Unions are expected to play a nonantag-
onistic counterpart role as management overseers but are not permitted
to strike. Fuller reports that workers complain that some managers
thwart the union in this overseer role, which appears to be the case in
Ariguanabo (Lindenberg 1993: 36).

The new management system instituted by the SDPE may also have
made it more difficult to address women's needs. The SDPE put firms
under increased pressure to reduce costs and show a profit, which could
make firms more reluctant to hire women workers who require special
support services and may experience higher rates of turnover and absenteeism, as Nazzari (1983: 262) claims. The emphasis on productivity
under the SDPE also demanded stabilization of the labor force, which
may have weakened support for the needs of women production workers, particularly if priority is given to highly skilled jobs in which men
predominate. However, as we have seen, the percentage of women employed in Ariguanabo has increased steadily, although some of these
women are also in technical jobs. State support services for women were
also cut, particularly the construction of day care centers, which revived
after *rectificación,* but with the special period have again been cut.
Housing construction diminished as well under the SDPE and the volunteer micro brigades that assisted in construction were abolished, but
with the change to *rectificación* in 1986, they have been reinstated. Little
housing construction is taking place during the special period due principally to a shortage of building materials.

I would argue that women in Cuba do not constitute a cheap labor reserve comparable to that in capitalist countries such as Puerto Rico or
the Dominican Republic, because of the measures the state has undertaken to reduce gender discrimination in the workplace. They have provided women with access to higher educational and occupational levels,
with equal pay for equal work, and with a wide array of support services
to reduce the burden of the double day. Although these services are still
inadequate, they also increase the cost of employing women, even if the
costs are provided by the state rather than the firm. This may help explain why Cuban working women are still subject to gender discrimination in terms of occupational segregation, possibilities of advancement,
and the addressing of their special needs in day care, fixed shifts, housing, and other privileges reserved for more highly valued, skilled male
workers. In all three countries, male workers resist women's occupational advancement, and men are favored for more highly skilled and
supervisory positions, while union and management are also male
dominated. This suggests that gender discrimination in employment
persists in Cuba despite a socialist ethic that professes greater gender
equality.

Political Participation and Consciousness

The mass organizations in a socialist society are the primary vehicle for expressing democratic participation. They are simultaneously a mechanism through which people can voice their decisions and through which the socialist state can mobilize specific groups in support of the revolution. Critics of the Cuban revolution have generally emphasized the mobilizing function, but an important shift toward greater decentralization and participation took place with the institutionalization of the Cuban revolution in the 1970s and can be seen in the strengthening of unions (Fuller 1992) and the institution of *Poder Popular* or Popular Power, an elective body with broad responsibilities for local economic and social development. Our data do not lend themselves to a systematic evaluation of the extent of democratic participation. But we can try to measure the extent to which working women are participating in and benefiting from these mass organizations to see whether the participatory or mobilizing function is being emphasized.

The most important Cuban mass organizations for working women are the CDR or Committees for the Defense of the Revolution, which operate primarily at the neighborhood level; the CTC or Cuban Confederation of Workers at the workplace; and the FMC or Federation of Cuban Women, which is specifically charged with representing women. Almost all the women interviewed belong to these three organizations, but their participation varies (Table 5.7). They report the highest degree of regular attendance at union meetings, which may reflect the growing importance they attach to their work activity. Participation in all three organizations is quite high, considering the time pressures and heavy responsibilities these women are already facing. In addition, over half the women in our sample have held office in one of these organizations in the past, especially the FMC and CDR, but the number of those currently holding office is considerably smaller (Table 5.7). Younger women have a particularly poor record of holding office: 70.5 percent of them currently hold no office and 57.4 percent of them never have. Although it is likely that younger women have not acquired the requisite years of experience to hold office, their low rates of holding office may also indicate a waning interest in participation in mass organizations among the young. The aging bureaucracy of mass organizations has been recognized as a problem, and as a result, the FMC has adopted a policy of encouraging younger women to assume professional leadership positions in the organization, which has resulted in an increase of professional cadres of women under 28 from 16 percent in 1985 to 34 percent in 1988 (FMC Statistical Office). In 1989, 40 percent of the membership of the FMC was under 30 years of age (FMC 1990: 99).

TABLE 5.7

Women's Current Participation in Mass Organizations in Ariguanabo Sample
Percentages

| | Level of Participation | | | | |
Organization	Participate Regularly	Participate Occasionally	Don't Participate	Total	Hold Office
C.D.R.	42.8	56.0	1.2	100.0	11.9
C.T.C.	87.5	10.1	2.4	100.0	10.7
F.M.C.	41.7	56.5	1.8	100.0	14.3

Source: Data compiled by Helen I. Safa and the Federation of Cuban Women.

Seventy percent of our sample thought the FMC had done the most for working women nationally, compared to much lower percentages for the Communist Party and the CTC.[19] The major accomplishments of the FMC are seen to be day care and employment, both of which are former functions of the FMC that have now passed to other government ministries. Day care continues to be seen by far as the most important benefit the FMC could provide for working women, followed by employment and support services for the home (such as laundries, special shopping hours for working women, and so on). Although these services are undoubtedly important to working women, they tend to identify the FMC as a service organization designed primarily to tend to women's domestic needs.

In part this image stems from a change in the focus of the FMC mandated by the Cuban government. The FMC did play a major role in the initial incorporation of women into the labor force in the 1970s, but as the number of working women grew, its role has been limited largely to housewives.[20] In 1974, responsibility for working women was taken over by the *Frente Femenino* of the CTC, although there are joint FMC and CTC commissions to coordinate policies on women and work. This shift in focus to housewives may have contributed to the FMC's current identification with more domestic needs. Like Rosalía and her daughter, many women feel the FMC needs to be more dynamic and to do more at the neighborhood level than give inoculations, hold *fiestas,* and collect dues.

The FMC also carries out important ideological work through lectures, reading, and other activities, which are designed both to raise women's consciousness and to disseminate the goals and achievements of the revolution. However, they seem to be more successful at dissemination than at consciousness raising. Although the FMC has forcefully defended women's interests in employment and other areas, it has to struggle within and not against the state to press their demands. This

A meeting at the Federation of Cuban Women headquarters in Havana. Courtesy of the Federation of Cuban Women.

lack of autonomy from the state impedes the growth of gender consciousness among working women and creates a socialist form of *asistencialismo* (aid dependency) that stifles creativity and self-empowerment. Even the Family Code, which received overwhelming approval from the women in our sample, has done little to change the attitude of our respondents to the household division of labor. Instead, women look to the state to provide more day care and other services. Vilma Espín, president of the FMC, has criticized women for not being more conscious of issues such as job discrimination against women and the sharing of household and child care responsibilities. Espín (1986: 61) complains that women (and men) often speak of men "helping" with the household chores when they should speak of "sharing." Espín adds: "*Las costumbres arraigadas no pueden justificar actuaciones incorrectas. Tales tradiciones, tales atrasos deben ser enfrentados con valentía, y hacer prevalecer la razón sobre semejantes injusticias que atentan contra los principios de la revolución.*" (Deep-seated customs do not justify incorrect actions. Such traditions, such delays must be confronted with courage, to make reason prevail over all such injustices that weaken the principles of the revolution.) However, it is not just tradition that impedes women's desire for greater equality, but also a top-down approach that has led women to look to the state as the source of this equality rather than themselves.

While women's equality is seen as one of the major accomplishments of the FMC and the revolution, it is identified primarily with increasing state services such as day care or employment rather than with ideological changes in gender roles. It would seem that as in capitalist societies, working-class women are concerned primarily with women's immediate, practical needs rather than with strategic gender interests such as gender equality (Molyneux 1986). Women feel strongly that increased employment has freed women from dependence on men and brought about greater gender equality. Reflecting on the changes in relationships between men and women since the revolution, Rosalía remarks: "*Antes la mujer a penas trabajaba, porque antes era esclava de la casa … Entonces uno tenía que vivir esclava ahí del marido y de los hijos, usted comprende? Pero como vino la revolución y le dio la libertad a la mujer para trabajar, ya no tiene que ver, ya no tiene que pensar en que tengo que estar con Carlos* [her husband], *porque me tiene que mantener. Tiene que mantener a mis hijos, no, si yo trabajo yo los puedo mantener igual.*" (Before the woman barely worked, because she was a slave of the house … Then one had to live as the slave of the husband and the children, do you understand? But the revolution came and gave a woman freedom to work, now it doesn't matter, now I don't have to think of staying with Carlos because he has to support me. He has to support my children, no, if I work, I can support them as well.)

Cuban women do not identify equality with the eradication of differences between men and women. As Rosalía's daughter so eloquently states: "*Somos iguales que los hombres, tenemos los mismos derechos, pero somos mujeres, siempre somos mujeres, con los mismos derechos y todo pero siempre mujer.*" (We are equal to men, we have the same rights, but we are women, we are always women, with the same rights and everything but always a woman.) Alicia thinks women require special attention, because they are not as strong as men, but that this does not imply inferiority. To illustrate her point, Alicia went on to recount how a man on a bus refused to give up his seat to a woman with a small child, claiming, "*No se dice que los hombres y las mujeres tienen los mismos derechos, que vaya de pie.*" (Don't they say that men and women have the same rights, let her stand.) Other men on the bus were so outraged they pulled him out of his seat and told the woman to sit. In short, equality does not mean that women are not entitled to special privileges, particularly as wives and mothers. The man's statement also suggests the resentment some Cuban men feel at the state-supported struggle for greater gender equality.

While our Puerto Rican and Dominican respondents complain of discrimination at the hands of political parties, 87 percent of our Cuban respondents feel the Communist Party has shown a concern for the needs of working women. The party is credited with much of Cuba's progress as well as their own improvement in living standards and that of their children. However, they were not very knowledgeable about the initiatives for women adopted at the Third Party Congress in 1986, such as the special platform for women or Vilma Espín's election to full membership in the Politburo (a position she no longer occupies). Only 11.9 percent of the women interviewed belong to the Cuban Communist Party, while another 9.5 percent belong to the UJC, or the Union of Communist Youth (for persons under 30). Membership in these political organizations is only by nomination and is based primarily on performance in the workplace. The party pledged in 1980 to increase membership to reflect women's labor force participation, and since then, women's party membership nationally has increased from 18.8 percent to 24 percent in 1988 (FMC 1990: 94).

Women's participation and leadership in mass organizations have also increased in recent years, partly due to the initiatives of the party and the FMC. However, there is still a low representation of women leaders in *Poder Popular,* particularly at the municipal level, where delegates are elected directly (FMC 1990: 90–91). This reflects both the reluctance of women to run (because of their heavy domestic and work responsibilities) and the popular lack of confidence in their political leadership. Only one of our respondents has held office in *Poder Popular,* but nearly half the women said they attend the meetings regularly. *Poder Popular* is soon as the main resource for solving neighborhood problems such as housing or lack of water, both cited by women as major problems in Ariguanabo. However, 35 percent of our respondents report that they do not go to anyone with these neighborhood problems, which suggests *Poder Popular* is not seen as a particularly effective mechanism for addressing these problems. The severe economic shortages of the special period have made its ability to respond even more difficult (Roman 1993: 11).

The Cuban government's efforts to decentralize decision making and to incorporate more women in the Cuban leadership have diminished but not eradicated the hierarchical relationship between the mass base and the state and party elite. This became very clear to me in the one FMC Congress that I attended in 1990. The proposals prepared for the Congress after a year of discussion at the municipal and provincial level addressed many of the problems discussed here such as women's double day, the lack of day care and sharing in household tasks, and the preference shown to men for occupational advancement. However, the Congress coincided with the electoral defeat of the Sandinistas in Nicaragua and with the rapid disintegration of the Soviet Union and Eastern Europe. As a result, the proposals were scrapped and the FMC Congress

President Fidel Castro addressing the Fifth Congress of the Federation of Cuban Women in 1990. Vilma Espin, president of the federation, is seated at his left along with other Cuban high officials and foreign visitors. Photographs from *Granma* (Cuban official newspaper), courtesy of Center for Cuban Studies, New York, N.Y.

turned into a rallying cry for national and party unity. Fidel's speech to the Congress, which he attended in its entirety, warned Cuban women to expect even more consumer shortages and lack of support services than they had experienced before and to forget their needs in defense of the fatherland (*patria*). This was hardly a display of democratic participation but a desperate call for women once again to support a revolution under siege.

Conclusion

Has the increasing incorporation of Cuban women into the labor force integrated women into the revolutionary process and raised their consciousness of gender discrimination? Women are clearly making an important contribution to the household economy, which has raised their self-esteem and is manifest in greater authority in the household and the erosion of the *casa/calle* distinction. Women have a strong commitment to work and no longer expect to stop working and rely on their husbands' wages when they marry or have children. They expect their children to study and work at better jobs than they have, and this applies equally to boys and girls. All of this implies a fundamental change in gender roles from the prerevolutionary period.

However, despite the Family Code and the massive incorporation of women into the labor force, men's household role has changed little. The only families that approach the ideal conceptualized in the Family Code are younger nuclear families who are relatively independent of their kin, and where the husband and the wife are stably married, better educated, and often in technical or supervisory positions. While men accept the idea that their wives work and probably also welcome the added income, most of them do not share in the housework or child care, nor do their wives appear to encourage them. In part, this stems from the high percentage of three-generation households in our sample, which reinforces traditional patterns of authority and domestic labor. Additional women in the extended family may provide working mothers with important assistance in child care and other household tasks, but they discourage men from taking more responsibility.

The absence of much household help from men leaves working women with a heavy burden of domestic responsibilities, especially if they have young children. This is the prime reason our respondents constantly reiterate the urgent demand for day care along with other support services for working women. It is interesting that these women look to the state to provide these services rather than expecting their husbands to take more responsibility, as mandated by the Family Code. This may emanate from all of the services the state has provided for women, which has led them to depend on the state to solve their problems rather than requiring more from their husbands. Most women in our sample seem to identify gender equality with more opportunities for employment and greater services from the state rather than with a transformation of gender roles at the household level.

Although women's equality is officially recognized and supported by the state, it is contained within defined limits (Molyneux 1986). Women are encouraged to participate in mass organization and have increased their membership in the Communist Party, but their activities are circumscribed by party directives designed to fulfill state goals. This has constrained the formation of gender consciousness and contributed to women's continued identification with their domestic role. Although women now see paid employment as a lifelong commitment, which does not cease with marriage or motherhood, they continue to identify as mothers first and as workers second. Even one of the female managers in Ariguanabo argues: "*Aquí nosotras mismas las mujeres nos discriminamos un poco, yo te lo digo, a punto de que ya yo soy dirigente y no sé qué, pero en un momento determinado con mis hijos, mira primero mis hijos y primero es mi casa, primero es esto.*" (Here we women discriminate against ourselves a little, I tell you, to the point that I am a manager and I don't know what, but at a certain point, with my children, look, my children first and first my house, that is first.) As long as women continue to view paid employment as having lesser importance than their domestic role, they are likely to continue to assume major responsibility for household tasks, which weakens their possibilities of achieving equality with men in the workplace.

But part of the reason women continue to identify with their domestic role stems from policies at the workplace that reinforce women's secondary status as workers. While there have been efforts in Ariguanabo to recruit and promote women through the creation of *puestos preferentes*, training programs, and the hiring of women technicians and engineers, the women we interviewed complain that they do not have equal chances for advancement and that their needs in terms of support services are not adequately addressed. In part this reflects the need to cut costs with the implementation of the new economic management and planning system in the late 1970s, which forced management in Ariguanabo to give top priority to the stabilization of the labor force, particularly among skilled workers where men predominate. This appears to contribute to women workers receiving lower priority in housing than men, resulting in many young mothers (particularly single mothers) being doubled up in cramped quarters with relatives. It also means fewer working women with young children are placed on fixed shifts, which would ease their child care problems and make the day care center more accessible to them. Occupational segregation in Ariguanabo still persists, as seen in the lower percentage of women in management and other highly skilled jobs. Despite the high percentage of female technicians and engineers, women production workers appear to be recruited primarily for lower-level jobs and are not given certain jobs like mechanics that offer the best salaries and the most possibilities for advancement.

These problems do not simply stem from management or the union's neglect of women workers, but from male workers' resistance to incorporating women at higher ranks and to giving them special privileges. Women are relatively recent recruits to the labor force in the factory, which has a strong male worker tradition. As Humphrey (1987: 198) points out in his study of industrial workers in São Paulo, where the proportion of women workers also grew rapidly in the 1970s, male workers try to defend their superior status in the factory by barring women from more prestigious jobs and by devaluing the work women do. Although I have no systematic evidence that this is happening in Ariguanabo, it could be one factor in management's protection of male privileges in terms of access to higher-level jobs and other incentives.

Despite the revolution's remarkable achievements, gender inequality persists in Cuba, due in part to state and workplace policies that continue to undervalue women as workers in comparison to men. Socialist states should be in a better position to combat gender discrimination on the job because they do not have to face resistance from the private sector. The problem is less a lack of political will on the part of the Cuban state to promote women's equality in the workplace than the pressure of competing demands. Under socialism, there is a constant tension between productivity and equity, between an increase in output such as in industry and the provision of social services. The same tension is evident with regard to the family. While the Cuban state applauds the increasing economic autonomy of women, it is distressed by rising divorce rates and an increasing percentage of teenage pregnancies and female-headed households, to which this autonomy has contributed. The state's image of women as mothers is seen in policies that emphasize women's reproductive role, such as barring women from certain hazardous jobs, which in turn reinforces a traditional division of labor. According to Bengelsdorf (1985) even the Family Code, though designed to share responsibility within the household, is also aimed at strengthening the family and relieving the state from the burden of total socialization. A major reason for socialist support for the family is the state's lack of resources to meet all the needs of social reproduction. In socialist as well as capitalist societies, the contribution the family makes to social reproduction greatly alleviates the role of the state in this regard. Under the economic crisis that Cuba now faces, this role of the family is intensified as the state is forced to withdraw or reduce many services formerly provided free of charge to all citizens.

There has been an increase in female-headed households in all three countries studied here, but for different reasons. In Puerto Rico and the Dominican Republic, this is primarily a result of increasing male marginalization with the move away from male-dominated agricultural products (principally sugar) to export-oriented light industry and a service economy, which have opened greater opportunities for women. Cuba's focus on import substitution industrialization and sugar exports continued to provide jobs for men, while occupational opportunities for women grew with their higher educational qualifications and an expanding state bureaucracy. However, dependence on a male breadwinner was reduced as Cuban women acquired increasing economic autonomy and were supported by the redistributionist policies of the state. Private patriarchy was replaced with public patriarchy, which the centralization of the state and services under socialism made all the more powerful. Single mothers do not need to marry or even require men to provide for their children, because they can work and count on the support of the state and the extended family. No special privileges are given to female heads of household, perhaps out of fear that their number will increase even further, but free health and education, day care, and other state services have reduced the cost of rearing children. Cuban youth enjoy a sexual freedom new to the postrevolutionary generation, and despite free access to birth control, abortion, and sex education programs, teenage pregnancy has increased. Though the birthrate has fallen dramatically, the age of marriage and first birth has fallen rather than increased, as is the case in most countries with growing educational and occupational opportunities for women. Certainly the Cuban state did not anticipate such an outcome from its policies, which it hoped would lead to stable, nuclear families, as some of the more upwardly mobile young couples in our sample have achieved. Marital instability can be traced to several contemporary features of Cuban society, such as women's greater economic autonomy, the housing shortage, and greater sexual freedom among the young. But as I have shown in chapter 2, marital instability and female-headed households have a long history in Cuba, particularly among the Afro-Cuban working class, and cannot be attributed solely to factors brought on by the revolution. Nevertheless, the reasons why the Cuban revolution reinforced these marital patterns rather than promoting more stable nuclear families, as the Cuban state sought, bear further scrutiny.

The severe economic crisis Cuba is now facing is likely to increase the percentage of female-headed households because men as well as women are subject to increasing unemployment and job instability. The burden of the crisis is falling heavily on women as they wait in line for scarce consumer goods and try to manage to feed and clothe their families with increasingly meager resources. The implications of this special period for women's equality in Cuba remain to be seen, but certainly the need for women to contribute to the household has become even more critical.

Notes

1. Accurate figures are not available on labor force participation for the special period, although the FMC (Aguilar and Pereira 1994: 31) maintains that women's *share* of the civilian labor force was maintained at about 39 percent from 1989 to 1992. Labor force participation and unemployment may be disguised because of the government's policy of maintaining workers on partial (60

percent) salary until they are relocated from industries that have closed (such as textiles) to other areas.

2. Cuban studies on the changes among women in the postrevolutionary period have been carried out by the FMC; the Center for Demographic Studies and the Development Studies Group of the University of Havana; and the Center for Sociological and Psychological Research of the Cuban Academy of Sciences.

3. Osmond (1993) conducted an unofficial study on a small sample of 61 women garment workers near Havana.

4. Due to the blockade following the revolution, the lack of parts to replace machinery produced a total stagnation in the textile industry, requiring modernization as well as the establishment of eight new plants. Although these measures more than tripled textile production, in 1987 the textile plants were still not working at full capacity due to the high rates of turnover and absenteeism.

5. In the 1950s, the percentage of women in industry was nearly equal to that of men (around 20 percent) (Pérez-Stable 1993: 33). Women's exclusion from Ariguanabo may be due to its relatively advanced technological level, so that workers constituted a form of "labor aristocracy."

6. By January 1989 the percentage of women under 30 had increased to 54.5 percent. The total number of women had increased to 2,106 out of a labor force of 5,639, representing 37.3 percent of the whole.

7. Between 1976/1977 and 1988/1989, the percentage of Cuban women enrolled in seventh to ninth grade (*enseñanza media*) increased from 45.2 to 51.5 percent, while those enrolled in post-secondary education (*enseñanza superior*) increased from 40.4 percent to 57.1 percent (FMC 1990: 53).

8. The term "union" as used in this chapter refers to both legal marriages and consensual union.

9. In Cuba as a whole, according to the 1981 census, extended families (who are often three generations) represented 32.5 percent of all private households and contained an average of 5.3 persons compared to 3.8 persons in basic nuclear families. Extended families became more predominant in the 1970s, especially in urban areas where they are associated with the housing shortage (Reca et al. 1990: 423).

10. Unfortunately, data on total family income were not collected.

11. The figures for female-headed households published by the Academy of Sciences (Reca et al. 1990: 30) are lower, 9.6 percent in 1953 and 19.7 percent in 1981. The difference may be due to differences in interpretation of who is considered a female head of household, since many young single mothers live with their parents in male-headed households. In our sample, I classified as female heads all separated, divorced, and widowed women, even if they are not the head of the household in which they are living. The aging of the Cuban population may also be contributing to the increase in female heads of household, and the percentage of widows among Cuban women in 1981 was 7 percent of the female population, similar to the percentage divorced (Catasús Cervera 1992: 4).

12. Unfortunately, this is the only tabulation done by race in this study, because we did not become aware of its importance until later, and it is now impossible to retrieve these data. Two-thirds of our sample population are white,

reflecting the racial composition of the province of Havana, while blacks, who number 15 percent, are often migrants from Oriente like Rosalía.

13. The number of positions closed to women was reduced from 300 to about 25, but the principle of prohibition was maintained. Pérez-Stable (1993: 139) contends that the earlier prohibition in 1968 was also designed to curb unemployment and open up jobs for men.

14. Unfortunately, data on length of time employed in Ariguanabo were inadvertently omitted from the interview schedule, but were collected on 81 respondents on which this estimate is based. Since we overrepresented older women workers in our sample, the average length of time all women workers in Ariguanabo have worked is probably lower.

15. According to management, when the working day was reduced from eight to six hours, production quotas were increased 9 or 10 percent an hour to help make up this loss.

16. In the last census before the revolution (1953), one-fourth of all employed women were in domestic service (Larguia and Dumoulin 1986: 346), which is still the most numerous occupation for women in most of Latin America. Domestic servants in Cuba were trained after the revolution for more skilled jobs, and today they no longer exist as an occupational group.

17. The generational study in Cuba carried out by the Academy of Sciences also notes the low prestige of worker occupations and the tendency for occupational mobility to slow down in the younger generations, resulting in the class reproduction of the manual worker vs. white-collar wage labor force (Dominguez et al. 1989: Part 2, pp. 23–25).

18. Nazzari claims that as long as Cuba's policy of full employment applies only to men and not women, women can still be regarded as a labor reserve (personal communication).

19. At the workplace, the CTC was considered to have done the most for working women, but the FMC was favored at the national level. The identification of interviewers with the FMC could also have influenced results.

20. At the national level in 1989, the percentage of working women and housewives among the FMC membership was almost equal (40 percent), which corresponds to the percentage of Cuban women in the labor force (FMC 1990: 98).

6

Conclusion: Economic Restructuring and Gender Subordination

The increased importance of women's contribution to the household economy in Puerto Rico, the Dominican Republic, and Cuba has led working women to redefine their domestic role and challenge the myth of the male breadwinner. This myth is built on the assumption that men are the principal economic providers for the household and that women are at best supplementary wage earners. However, economic restructuring has overturned this order through changes in the gender composition of the labor force in all three countries, as well as in other developing and advanced industrial countries, with increases in female labor force participation and declining or stagnating rates for men (Standing 1989). Between the 1950s/1960s and the early 1980s, the male participation rate declined in all Latin American and Caribbean countries, while the female rate went up. Female employment rates rose by 140 percent in this period compared to 60 percent for men (Psacharopoulos and Tzannatos 1992: 38–44).

These changes in the gender composition of the labor force in Puerto Rico and the Dominican Republic are the product of three main forces: 1) development strategies focusing on export-led industrialization, which favor women workers over men; 2) an increase in the supply of women workers brought about by improvements in educational levels, lower fertility, and accelerated urbanization; and 3) the economic crisis, which forced women to enter the labor force to meet the rising cost of living and the decreased wage-earning capacity of men. Cuban women's incorporation into paid employment was directly promoted as a result of conscious state policy but did not have much effect until the wage and consumer policies instituted under the new economic and management system known as the SDPE in the 1970s made female employment more attractive. The growing supply of well-educated women workers in professional and technical fields also contributed to an increase in female employment, particularly in the tertiary sector, which has grown steadily in all three countries.

The negative impact of state development strategies on male labor force participation has been particularly devastating in Puerto Rico, where male participation rates have fallen more than 20 percent. Despite changes in development strategies from labor-intensive to capital-intensive to high-tech firms favoring male workers, overall activity rates have fallen, as out-migration and federal transfer payments try to make up for rising unemployment rates among both women and men. In the Dominican Republic, male labor force participation has leveled off but not declined as precipitously as in Puerto Rico, because the Dominican working class has no alternative way of earning a living (except international migration). More Dominican men are entering the informal sector as formal wage jobs in agriculture and domestic industry diminish. Until recently, Cuban men displaced as a result of the mechanization of agriculture (chiefly sugar, which continues to be the primary export) were absorbed into import substitution industrialization and other sectors, and male labor force participation, after an initial rise in the 1970s, remained quite high, at least until the economic crisis. The economic crisis in Cuba started in 1990, after this study was completed, and appears to have had serious negative effects on labor force participation.[1] This crisis resulted from the collapse of Cuba's trade with the former socialist countries of Eastern Europe and the Soviet Union and is similar to that in capitalist countries, with a loss of foreign exchange, with heavy foreign debt, and the introduction of austerity measures, which have severely cut domestic production and consumption.

Changes in the supply of women workers in all three countries were also partly the result of state policies that promoted educational expansion, family planning programs, and redistributionist policies that lessened the dependence of women on male wages. In all three countries, women's educational levels are equal or superior to men, while fertility levels have declined dramatically, particularly in Cuba, where they are below replacement levels. Cuba's socialist state instituted the most sweeping redistributionist mechanisms in terms of free education, health care, social security, and subsidized food and housing, making the household less dependent on wages and purchasing power to assure it of basic needs and lessening the woman's dependence on a male wage. It has also gone the furthest in terms of trying to relieve women's child care responsibilities through day care for working women, though demand exceeds supply. The array of support services provided to workers (men as well as women) including transportation, lunchrooms, sick

leave, pensions, housing, and recreational facilities has substantially increased the social wage and reduced the use of women as a cheap labor
reserve. These support services are already being cut as Cuba's economic crisis forces the state to cut expenditures, but redistribution policies have helped stem mass unemployment and generalized malnutrition (Zimbalist 1992: 411).

The effects of the economic crisis on female employment are clearest
in the Dominican Republic, where in the early 1980s sharp currency devaluations decreased labor costs and increased the attractiveness of the
free trade zones to foreign investors. This led to an increased demand for
female labor at the same time that women were forced to seek additional
household income to offset the rising costs of living and declining wages
brought on by structural adjustment policies. In Puerto Rico, the economic crisis hit earlier around 1973, due to the sharp increase in the
price of fuel imports and the consequent collapse of the capital-intensive industrialization strategy, which contributed to mounting government debt and increasing unemployment. The crisis was alleviated by
increasing out-migration and federal transfer payments and a shift to
high-tech industries and financial operations, which have converted
Puerto Rico into a postindustrial service economy.

The economic crisis, particularly in the Dominican Republic, is similar to the one that hit most of Latin America and the Caribbean in the
1980s, where it also resulted in economic restructuring emphasizing export-led industrialization and structural adjustment policies. Studies on
the effects of this economic restructuring note that it has been particularly severe on women (Benería and Feldman 1992; Cornia et al. 1987;
Vickers 1991), while at the same time it is increasing the importance and
visibility of women's contribution to the household economy. Economic
restructuring is not confined to Latin America and the Caribbean but extends to other developing areas such as Africa, where the effects of the
crisis and structural adjustment policies have been even more devastating. Women are not only increasing their incorporation into paid wage
labor but seeking alternative sources of income through the informal
sector, migration, and the intensification of agriculture. Even in advanced industrial countries, the loss of jobs due to deindustrialization
and the decline of real wages has forced more women into the labor
force and replaced the concept of the family wage (based on the male
breadwinner) with that of the two wage-earner family (Nash 1989). As I
noted in chapter 2, this massive increase in women's wage labor as a result of economic restructuring has generated intense debate over its effects on women's status. Does wage labor merely exploit women as a

source of cheap labor and add to the burden of their domestic chores? Or does wage labor give women greater autonomy and raise their consciousness regarding gender subordination?

The key to understanding the impact of paid wage labor on women's status is the importance of their contribution to the household economy. As long as women work but still depend primarily on a male wage earner, they are defined as supplementary wage earners. Most women continue to be seen as supplementary wage earners at the workplace, where they are confined to poorly paid, unstable jobs, and by the state, where their domestic responsibilities as wives and mothers are emphasized over their rights as workers or citizens. However, women themselves are becoming more aware of their critical contribution to the household economy, and this has led many to challenge male dominance, at least within the home, where women have always had more legitimacy than in the public sphere of the workplace and the state. This helps explain why, in our study, women have gained more negotiating power in the household than at the level of the workplace and the state, which is still considered the domain of men. Our data confirm that there are various levels of gender subordination; in the family, in the workplace, and at the state level, which, while interrelated, operate independently to maintain the myth of the male breadwinner.

In this final chapter, I shall compare the level of subordination women workers face at these three levels in Cuba, Puerto Rico, and the Dominican Republic and also draw insights from similar studies on the impact of paid employment on women's status in both developing and advanced industrial societies. It is now clear from this and other studies that the impact of paid employment on women's status is contradictory, that paid employment has both negative and positive impacts on women, increasing their work burden while also possibly enhancing their economic autonomy. The impact of paid employment on women is conditioned by both structural and ideological factors that maintain inequalities between men and women and that vary not only cross-culturally but among women of different social strata in each society. Here we shall try to identify those factors, paying particular attention to those that raise women's consciousness regarding gender subordination and lead them to challenge male domination in the household, in the workplace, and by the state.

State Policy and Gender Subordination

As we have seen, state policy has a significant impact on the gender composition of the labor force. In Puerto Rico and the Dominican Republic, development strategies favored the incorporation of women workers as a source of cheap labor reserve for export-led industrialization. The economic crisis in these countries increased women's need to work, while higher educational levels and lower fertility in Cuba, Puerto Rico, and the Dominican Republic facilitated their entry into wage labor. However, despite the undeniable evidence that women have become major contributors to the household economy, the state in all three countries tends to regard them as supplementary wage earners. Even in Cuba, where women and men are guaranteed equal pay for equal work, occupational segregation continues to account for wage differentials and women are barred from certain jobs to protect their reproductive capacities.

The type of export-led industrialization pursued in Puerto Rico and the Dominican Republic also limits the growth potential of these industries and confines women industrial workers to poorly paid, unstable jobs. Dependency on U.S. markets, capital, and technology retards the development of domestic linkages that might facilitate the move into the second stage of high-tech and more capital-intensive export-led industrialization, such as occurred in East Asia (Gereffi and Wyman 1990). This failure can partially be attributed to differential state policies in the Caribbean and East Asian region, which in turn reflects the weak states and tradition of dependent development on the United States in Puerto Rico, the Dominican Republic, and the Caribbean generally. Part of the explanation for this lies in the historically hegemonic role U.S. capital has always played in the region, even in the export of primary commodities such as sugar in the Dominican Republic and Puerto Rico. U.S. economic hegemony also weakened the local industrial elite, particularly in the Caribbean, where size and low purchasing power sharply reduced the size and strength of the domestic market. The state and labor were further weakened by the economic crisis and structural adjustment measures, whereby the IMF and World Bank largely determined the terms of trade, wage increases, currency exchanges, and even state development policy. As Stallings (1990: 80) has noted in an article examining the role of foreign capital in economic development: "In its extreme version, the issue at stake is whether the state's choice of development strategy determines the role of foreign capital or whether foreign capital determines development strategy." A comparative analysis demonstrates that East Asian countries such as Taiwan and South Korea have opted for the first strategy, while the Caribbean and increasingly Latin America have fallen victim to the latter.

Puerto Rico did attempt to shift development strategies away from labor-intensive garment industries to meet rising wages and competition from other areas, but always relied on U.S. investment in branch plants, which were limited to assembly-type operations. Unrestricted profit repatriation in both Puerto Rico and the Dominican Republic also failed to stimulate domestic industry, while U.S. tariff regulations requiring the use of U.S.-made components further hampered domestic linkages in the Dominican free trade zones.

The failure of export-led industrialization in these two countries to move beyond assembly operations further reduced male opportunities in the labor market, forcing more Dominican men into the informal economy while Puerto Rican male labor force participation rates have severely declined. The marginalization of men has contributed to the weakening of the role of the male breadwinner, particularly in Puerto Rico, where this process of industrialization was initiated earlier than in the Dominican Republic and has contributed to greater erosion of male authority. In contrast, the East Asian shift toward capital-intensive industrialization for the domestic as well as the export market has maintained the incorporation of men into the labor force, enabling them to retain their control over the household, despite the increasing employment of women (Chow 1993; Gallin 1990). Full employment in the more developed East Asian countries like Taiwan and South Korea has contributed to greater domestic demand and to some improvement in workers' bargaining power, wages, and working conditions (Lim 1990: 113). The increasing labor shortages in the more fully developed Asian countries, particularly in low-wage industries, contrast with the continued labor surplus characteristic of the Caribbean Basin.

Government response to the economic crisis reveals the differential way in which women and men are viewed as wage earners. International policy approaches toward third world low-income women articulated by AID and the World Bank vary between welfare approaches that view women as mothers and passive aid recipients and efficiency approaches that focus on increased economic participation and totally neglect women's reproductive needs (Moser 1989). Though the crisis has had devastating effects on male employment and wages, cuts in government expenditures on transfer payments or social services such as health and education assume that women in their reproductive role will make up this gap with voluntary, unpaid labor (Safa and Antrobus 1992). Costs are shifted from the paid to the unpaid economy, as women wait in crowded clinics or stand in line for scarce consumer goods. In some developing countries, women have organized to establish *comedores populares* or collective kitchens to distribute food cooked by women to needy families in shantytowns in Lima, Santiago, and other Latin American cities (Blondet 1990; Mujica forthcoming). Yet women's efforts to organize collectively receive little government support, except for occasional food subsidies, or are controlled to garner political support. Hostility rises as women's demands on the government escalate beyond the traditionally defined feminist concerns such as food and public services to encroach on male domains of power in political parties and labor unions (Safa 1990a). This hostility has limited the ability of women's social movements to effectively challenge gender subordination at the state level. As a result, in the Dominican Republic and elsewhere, these movements remain largely localized and are geared toward meeting immediate practical needs rather than challenging gender and class inequality through demands for more global social transformation (Cela et al. 1988; Báez 1993; Jelin 1990). Yet consciousness of gender subordination has grown, as women increasingly recognize government's failure to support their legitimate rights as wives and mothers to ensure the survival of their families.

Gender Subordination in the Workplace

Women's access to a wage and other sources of income is the most commonly acknowledged mechanism of female empowerment, both in developing countries and advanced industrial societies. A greater focus on gender has now introduced several refinements to the general hypothesis that working women have more leverage in the household than housewives. Blumberg's (1991) review of the literature has shown that it is women's *control* of key economic resources such as income, property, and wages relative to the control exercized by men that is the most important variable affecting gender stratification from the household to the state. Benería and Roldán's (1987) study of industrial home workers in Mexico City shows how women's leverage in household decision varies directly with their contribution to the household economy. The collection of articles on third world women and income control in Dwyer and Bruce (1988) destroyed the myth of the unitary household and introduced the intra-household model that forced many researchers to examine more closely cross-cultural variations in men and women's control of income and the implications for child welfare as well as women's autonomy.

This study goes beyond most previous research in attempting to determine the factors at the macro- as well as at the micro-level that determine the importance of the women's contribution. At the macro-level, state policy plays an important role in determining women workers' access to resources through its effect on the gender composition of the labor force and on wages and working conditions (through the minimum wage, currency devaluation, and other mechanisms); its support of unions and their freedom from state control; and state redistributive mechanisms, which range from social services and transfer payments to socialist control of the means of production. In a socialist state such as Cuba, where almost all workers are employed by the state and where virtually all sectors of the economy have been nationalized, state power is clearly stronger than in capitalist societies such as Puerto Rico and the Dominican Republic, where the state is restricted by the private sector in defending workers' rights.

Occupational segregation and wage differentials play an important role in maintaining gender subordination in the workplace in the three countries studied at both the national and factory level. As I argued in chapter 2, occupational segregation has come to replace the former prohibition on women working outside the home or the *casa/calle* distinction, as it is known in Latin America. Occupational segregation in turn explains a large degree of wage differentials between women and men, as demonstrated by a recent World Bank study on women's employment and pay in 15 Latin American countries (Psacharopoulos and Tzannatos 1992). In all three countries studied here, women are overrepresented in the tertiary or service sector of the economy, which has grown enormously in the last three decades but is also often the worst paid. This is particularly true where, as in the Dominican Republic, domestic service is still a primary source of employment for women and is not subject to minimum wages or control of working conditions. The huge wage differentials between Dominican women and men certainly surpass those in Puerto Rico, where they have declined substantially since 1960, and Cuba, where state policy mandates equal pay for equal work and wage differentials between sectors are much smaller than in capitalist countries.[2] As more highly educated women have begun to move into higher-level jobs in the professions and the public sector (including technical jobs in Cuba), occupational segregation appears to be weakening, though wage differentials may still be maintained at this higher level.

Occupational segregation within the garment industry is evident in the split between female production workers and male management. In Puerto Rico, this makes for a very paternalistic setting, in which even older women are treated as "girls" and loyalty to the company is promoted over worker solidarity. The Puerto Rican plants are unionized, but most women workers in our sample regard the ILGWU as a company union that works in close alliance with management as well as the government to retard the garment industry's decline as plants move to cheaper wage areas elsewhere.

Wages and working conditions are much worse in the Dominican export-manufacturing plants, with brutal discipline, long working hours, and forced overtime. At the rate of exchange then operating, the minimum wage in the Dominican free trade zones in December 1992 was U.S.$101.52 monthly compared to the average *hourly* earnings of $4.03 for Puerto Rican apparel workers in 1988 (Economic Development Administration 1989: 8). Workers are subject to the intense pressure of high production quotas and to the constant threat of dismissal. Gender hierarchies are evident not only in the split between male management and female workers but in the predominance of men among technicians, who are paid over twice the wage of production workers (Consejo Nacional de Zonas Francas 1993: 31–33). Discontent is expressed in turnover or eventual withdrawal, rather than through labor organizing. Legally recognized unions have only begun operating in the Dominican free trade zones, and workers receive little support from the government in their struggle for better wages and working conditions.

The Cuban state has undoubtedly gone the furthest in trying to reduce gender discrimination in employment through training programs, the creation of preferential positions for women, and a wide array of support services as well as equal pay for equal work. Still women production workers in the textile mill studied are recruited primarily for lower-level jobs, and are not hired for certain occupations like mechanics that offer the best salaries and the most possibilities of advancement. In Ariguanabo as well as nationally, women are severely underrepresented in managerial positions, but contrary to the Dominican Republic, they represent over half the technicians, which indicates a real weakening of gender discrimination in education as well as employment. Unions are state-controlled and particularly after *rectificación*, allow little room for worker participation in decision making, while strikes are not permitted. Women workers complain that they do not have equal chances for advancement and that their needs for support services, especially day care centers and housing, are not adequately addressed. Male resistance to female employment in Ariguanabo, which has a strong male worker tradition, may underlie union and management's devaluation of women workers in comparison to men. The need to appease male workers was made more critical by the SDPE economic management and planning system instituted in 1976 (and discontinued a decade later), which put pressure on management to reduce costs and increase productivity, leading them to favor more highly skilled male workers.

In none of the countries studied, then, do women share equal access to employment with men, who still dominate the more highly skilled, better-paid jobs and enjoy greater possibilities of advancement. This cannot be explained by gender differences in educational levels, since in all three countries women's educational levels are superior or equal to men. Occupational segregation and wage differentials are greatest in the Dominican Republic, where women enjoy the least protection from the state and there are few legally recognized labor unions in the free trade zones, despite a new labor code passed in 1992. State support of women workers is greater in Puerto Rico and especially Cuba, but worker solidarity in both countries is reduced by male-dominated unions and a paternalistic state, which attempts to control any labor unrest. Repression in the Dominican Republic and cooptation in Puerto Rico and Cuba have produced a weak labor movement, which fails to support the grievances of women workers.

The Household Economy

Dominican, Puerto Rican, and Cuban women industrial workers have begun to assume more authority in the family, although they are relatively weak at the level of the workplace and the state, where power must be exercised collectively. In all three countries, the majority of married women now maintain that they share household decisions with their partners and that men no longer have exclusive budgetary control. Their authority in the home is derived from their increased economic contribution to the household, but as we have seen, this varies by the number of contributors to the household economy and the life cycle of the women employed. Daughters contribute less to the household than married women or female heads of household, who often bear sole responsibility for their family's survival. A daughter is also less likely to challenge her father's authority in the household and does not threaten his role as breadwinner in the way that a wife may (Lamphere 1987). This is particularly true if they are obliged to turn over their salaries to the household, as studies of young women workers in Hong Kong and other newly industrializing countries in Asia demonstrate (Salaff 1981, 1990).

Differences in household authority patterns occur both within the sample in each country and cross-culturally. In both the Dominican and Cuban samples, more egalitarian relationships appear to be found among young legally married couples, who are both working and better educated and are clearly the most mobile group. A similar group could be identified among stably married couples in Puerto Rico, who identify themselves as middle class, have relatively high incomes, and live in their own home, and where the husband has a steady job and is a regular contributor to the household. Thus, it is not the erosion of the man's role as economic provider but his ability and willingness to share this role with his wife that make for the most egalitarian conjugal relationships.

This upwardly mobile group, where men as well as women have been able to secure stable jobs, has benefited the most from the industrialization process. A study of working-class and middle-class employed and non-employed women in Mexico also found that age, educational level, and type of work are associated with differences in authority patterns both within the same class group and between class groups, although more egalitarian relationships are generally found in middle-class families. Working-class Mexican women are more likely to consider their husband the principal breadwinner, even when their own contribution to the household is critical. However, in the Mexican study, all the husbands were stable providers, so their occupational status did not emerge as an important determinant of authority patterns (García and Oliveira 1995).

In my study, the economic marginality of men is crucial in understanding household dynamics. Not only does it contribute to the importance of the woman's contribution to the household, but where male marginalization is severe, as in some sample households in Puerto Rico and the Dominican Republic, it often results in marital instability or dissolution. The inability to carry out the role of economic provider may actually drive men from the home or make them reluctant to marry and also increases resistance to marriage or remarriage among women. As we have seen among some of our informants, women see little need to marry or remarry if men cannot or will not support the household adequately and simply add to their domestic burden. The same pattern of a poor "marriage market" is evident in the United States, especially among African Americans and Puerto Ricans living on the mainland where the rate of non-marriage and single mothers has increased dramatically. The research by William J. Wilson (1987) attributes this decline in marriage rates to high male unemployment brought about by capital flight and deindustrialization in the United States, reducing the pool of economically stable or "marriageable" men. Amott (1993: 101) adds that increased female employment may have given women more choice whether to marry or not, while the social stigma of single motherhood has also been reduced. Welfare payments such as AFDC are often cited as a major factor in the increase of single mothers in the United States, but research suggests that it may have made these households more visible by permitting them to live independently rather than in the households of parents or other relatives, as in Cuba. This research also suggests that welfare has a small but significant effect on remarriage rates in the United States, giving women the option not to marry or remarry (Garfinkel and McLanahan 1986). My study provides additional evidence that high male unemployment brought about by restructuring reduces the option of marriage for both men and women, particularly among single mothers and female heads of household.

The percentage of female heads of household is increasing nationally in each of the countries studied, reaching around 25 percent. In Cuba, the major increase in female heads of household coincides with the period after 1970 when female employment was also sharply increasing (Valdés and Gomariz 1992: 33), suggesting that greater female economic autonomy may be a factor independent of male marginalization, which was not important in the Cuban sample. The increase in female heads of household also reflects demographic forces such as the high rate of teenage pregnancies and rising divorce rate in all three countries and the persistence of consensual unions in Cuba and the Dominican Republic. The rate of consensual unions nationally is much higher among Cuban and Dominican women (about 28 percent) than among Puerto Rican women, where the percentage has declined to about 4 percent. Consensual unions are generally more unstable than legal unions, and in all three countries are associated with lower educational and occupational levels than are found among legally married women (Duarte et al. 1989; Catasús Cervera 1992; Díaz Temorio 1992; Vásquez Calzada 1988). Dominican women in particular hold very contradictory viewpoints regarding the advantages of legal vs. consensual unions. Some argue that consensual unions provide more autonomy to women than legal unions, but the Dominican women in consensual unions sampled here appear to subscribe more to patriarchal norms than legally married women. This suggests that consensual unions may also make poor women feel more vulnerable and heighten their fears of challenging male dominance.

In our sample, female heads of household are predominantly older in Puerto Rico, while in Cuba and the Dominican Republic, they are about equally divided between younger and older women. It is harder for women with young children to separate, because this is the period when women are the most dependent on men. Older women are more able to support themselves on their own, because they are less likely to have young dependents and may even have adult children contributing to the household. Older female heads of household are also in a less precarious economic position than younger women, even where, as in Puerto Rico and Cuba, they receive some support from the state. In all three countries, there is also an increasing percentage of widows, as life expectancy increases and is higher for women than men.

Increasing marital instability may also be a product of women's rising expectations of men, although some of our informants suggest that men are now more irresponsible. There has clearly been a generational change in each country, which is especially evident in Cuba because of the marked impact of the revolution. Younger women have greater confidence and self-esteem and expect more from men, in terms of sharing household responsibilities and decisions, including control over their own fertility. Older women in each country even criticize younger women for having too much sexual freedom and lack of familial responsibility, which partly reflects their own more patriarchal values. Men also resist giving up authority, even when they expect a woman to work, and may devalue her contribution to the household. In none of the countries studied do men help much with household chores or child care, to which there appears to be great cultural resistance worldwide, in advanced as well as developing countries (Blumberg 1991). My research suggests that women also identify housework and child care as female tasks and do not pressure men to share these responsibilities, although some younger women are changing here also. Among young working mothers of Anglo and Mexican-American working-class households in Albuquerque, men's level of participation in household and child care was found to be directly linked to the importance of the woman's contribution to the household (Lamphere et al. 1993), while Nash's (1989) study of blue-collar workers in Pittsfield, Massachusetts, noted distinct generational changes, with younger men being more flexible. Generational change was also true in the Caribbean families studied here, but the presence of other women in extended family households also alters the gender division of labor in the household.

Household composition alters authority patterns as well as the division of labor. This can be seen most clearly in the Cuban case, due to the prevalence of three-generation households in the sample, which is much higher than in Puerto Rico or the Dominican Republic. Three-generation households increase the influence of the older generation, particularly since many of them include single mothers with their children, who tend to regard their parent(s) as the head of the household. While parents provide assistance to young working mothers, they also perpetuate traditional gender roles and discourage any change in the household division of labor or authority patterns. These larger Cuban households, like the larger Puerto Rican rural households, are also more likely to have a large number of wage earners, which increases household income but reduces the importance of the woman's contribution.

On the other hand, the support of the extended kin group and especially female kin can be critical to working women, particularly in female-headed households. Cuban women depend heavily on kin and neighbors for help, and non-working grandmothers often are responsible for child care, whether they live in the same household or not. In

Puerto Rico, though the nuclear family form is dominant, rural households in particular live in a tightly knit network of kin and neighbors, who help each other out in child care, house building, shopping, and transportation. Female heads of household often live with their mothers, who provide child care while their daughters work and continue to live with them after the children are grown. Extended family patterns are also prevalent in the Dominican Republic but have been disrupted in the free trade zones because of the high cost and shortage of housing and child care. As a result, women workers often leave their children with their mother, father, or other relative in the rural areas. Though they visit when they can and contribute to their children's upkeep, these Dominican women are deprived of the close support of female kin, which Puerto Rican and Cuban women enjoy. Migration has also had an impact on the female support networks of working mothers in Albuquerque, with kin more important to Mexican-American women who had relatives in close proximity than to Anglo women, who had migrated more recently and often substituted friends for kin (Lamphere et al. 1993: chapter 8).

To summarize, there are clear variations both within and among the samples in Cuba, Puerto Rico, and the Dominican Republic in terms of household composition, number of wage earners in the household, age and marital status of the household head, marital stability, and support from kin, all of which affect household authority patterns as well as the importance of the woman's contribution. The fear of challenging male dominance increases with factors that add to the woman's vulnerability, such as young children, consensual unions, and the lack of support from kin, as well as vulnerability on the job, which clearly puts Dominican women in the worst negotiating position. This helps explain why most Dominican men are still regarded as head of the household, while joint headship is more common in Puerto Rico and Cuba.

Gender Ideology and Gender Subordination

It is apparent from the results of this study that paid employment only empowers women under certain specific conditions, which vary with state policy, access to resources, and the nature of the household economy. These variations help us to resolve some of the contradictions apparent in the literature on the impact of paid employment on women's status. In general, I would argue that the impact of paid employment is greatest where women have become critical contributors to the household economy and where there is a substantial participation of married women in wage labor, because they feel more acutely than single women the contradiction between their economic and domestic role.

Both of these factors may lead women to challenge the myth of the male breadwinner, but the outcome can be radically different, depending on the gender composition of the labor force and the relative contribution of women and men in the household. Two contrasting tendencies have been identified in each of the countries studied here:

1. Women gain little from increased employment if they are merely substituting their earnings for those of men. The assembly-type export manufacturing promoted in Puerto Rico and the Dominican Republic has contributed to this change in the gender composition of the labor force by providing more jobs to women than to men. Where women have to assume the role of breadwinner, this may produce conflict and lead to higher levels of marital instability and female-headed households, as we have seen here. While this form of economic restructuring may challenge the myth of the male breadwinner, it also shifts the burden of family survival from men to women.

2. The most egalitarian and stable relationships are found among young couples where both women and men are securely employed and are better educated. Both partners contribute to the household and share in household decisions and in the control of the budget, though housework and child care still tend to be largely the woman's responsibility. Paid employment is clearly not the only factor that contributes to these more egalitarian relationships, since higher educational levels, lower fertility, and legal unions are also factors that strengthen a woman's negotiating power in the household. Cuban women also benefited from state support of women's equality, as more egalitarian conjugal relationships were encouraged through the Family Code and other measures. The increase in female-headed households in Cuba after the revolution, despite such measures, is clearly of concern to the Cuban state, since they violate the nuclear family norm on which Cuba has modeled its family policy. Although the Cuban state does not provide any direct benefits to female heads of household, it may have indirectly contributed to their increase through redistributionist policies that reduced the dependence of women on a male breadwinner.

The great majority of the women studied here are somewhere between these two extremes, negotiating for greater authority and autonomy in the household while still trying to maintain a stable, conjugal relationship. The centrality of women's domestic role in Latin America helps explain their efforts to keep the family intact. As Stolcke (1984) notes, the family provides women with a social identity that proletarianization as wage workers has not diminished. Despite women's increasing incorporation into the labor force, they still define gender roles differently. Men are seen as workers with family responsibilities, while women view themselves as wives and mothers with economic responsibilities; that is, women place their domestic responsibilities over their economic responsibilities. Women continue to identify primarily with the family, whereas men are more closely identified with their economic role. In fact, most women in our sample now consider paid employment part of their domestic role, because they are working to contribute to the household economy rather than for their own self-esteem or personal autonomy.

Most women are trying to renegotiate the marriage contract under which women depended on men as the primary breadwinner. Even in the United States, where the notion of separate spheres for men and women has apparently given way to individual rights, Nash's study in Pittsfield suggests that white working-class women until very recently accepted the authority of men as fathers and husbands in return for a guarantee of economic support (Nash 1989: chapter 9). The generational changes that Nash describes as women became fully employed, such as changes in the administration and allocation of the household budget, are also evident among the Caribbean families studied here. These Pittsfield women are similar to the white, working-class garment workers I studied earlier in New Jersey, most of whom continued to regard their husbands as the primary breadwinners and themselves as supplementary wage earners, even though many had been employed for more than 20 years. Only among single unmarried women and female heads of household, most of whom were older widows, were women the major source of income, so that no woman supported a family on her meager earnings as in the Caribbean (Safa 1987). As long as working mothers continue to depend on a male breadwinner, they will not experience the fundamental change in gender roles and gender ideology that we have observed in the Caribbean. The Caribbean pattern is more similar to black and Hispanic low-income women in the United States, where the need to work and the importance of the woman's contribution is also greater.

However, the lack of recognition of women as workers and breadwinners is not simply the fault of women themselves, but also reflects resistance on the part of male-dominated institutions such as labor unions and political parties to regard women as workers on a par with men. Even in Cuba, where the most radical measures have been undertaken to establish gender equality, women's domestic or reproductive roles are still emphasized. However, women's consciousness of gender subordination is growing, as the contradiction between their increasingly important economic contribution and their subordination in the family, in the workplace, and in the polity becomes more apparent. Women now recognize that they have rights as well as responsibilities—as housewives, workers and citizens—and they are more willing to challenge male domination, especially within the household. This suggests that the family is not the central site of women's oppression, but that the myth of the male breadwinner is preserved by public forms of patriarchy, which continue to profit from women's subordination.

Notes

1. Statistics show that women's share of the labor force has not decreased since the onset of the crisis, but do not give unemployment or overall activity rates (Aguilar and Pereira 1994: 9).

2. Women still tend to earn less than men because they are less likely to be employed in sectors where wages are above the national average (Pérez-Stable 1993: 141–142).

References

Abreu, Alfonso, Manuel Cocco, Carlos Despradel, Eduardo García Michel, and Arturo Peguero. 1989. *Las Zonas Francas Industriales: El Éxito de una Política Económica.* Santo Domingo, Dominican Republic: Centro de Orientación Económica.

Acevedo, Luz de Alba. 1989. "El Desarrollo Capitalista y la Nueva División del Trabajo: El Empleo de la Mujer en los Servicios en Puerto Rico." Paper presented at the 15th Congress of the Latin American Studies Association, Miami, FL.

Acevedo, Luz de Alba. 1990. "Industrialization and Employment: Changes in the Patterns of Women's Work in Puerto Rico." *World Development* 18(2): 231–255.

Acevedo, Luz de Alba. 1993. "Género, Trabajo Asalariado y Desarrollo Industrial en Puerto Rico: La División Sexual del Trabajo en la Manufactura." In *Género y Trabajo: La Industria de la Aguja en Puerto Rico y el Caribe Hispánico,* edited by María del Carmen Baerga. San Juan, Puerto Rico: Editorial de la Universidad de Puerto Rico.

Acker, Joan. 1988. "Class, Gender, and the Relations of Distribution." *Signs* 13(3): 473–497.

Aguilar, Carolina, and Rita María Pereira. 1994. "El Período Especial y La Vida Cotidiana: Desafío de las Cubanas de los 90." Paper presented at the 17th International Congress of the Latin American Studies Association, Atlanta, GA.

Alternative Women in Development (Alt-WID). 1992. *Reagonomics and Women: Structural Adjustment U.S. Style—1980–1992.* Washington, DC.

Amott, Teresa. 1993. *Caught in the Crisis: Women and the U.S. Economy Today.* New York: Monthly Review Press.

Amott, Teresa, and Julie Matthaei. 1991. *Race, Gender and Work: A Multicultural Economic History of Women in the United States.* Boston: South End Press.

Arrom, Silvia M. 1985. *The Women of Mexico City, 1790–1857.* Stanford, CA: Stanford University Press.

Baerga, María del Carmen. 1987. "La Articulación del Trabajo Asalariado y no Asalariado: Hacia una Reevaluación de la Contribución Femenina a la Sociedad Puertorriqueña." In *La Mujer en Puerto Rico,* edited by Yamila Azize Vargas. San Juan, Puerto Rico: Ediciones Huracán.

Baerga, María del Carmen. 1992. "Puerto Rico: From Colony to Colony." In *Creating and Transforming Households: The Constraints of the World Economy,* edited by J. Smith and Immanuel Wallerstein, with M. C. Baerga. New York: Cambridge University Press; Paris: Editions de la Maison des Sciences de L'Homme, pp. 121–144.

Baerga, María del Carmen, ed. 1993. *Género y Trabajo: La Industria de la Aguja en Puerto Rico y el Caribe Hispánico.* San Juan, Puerto Rico: Editorial de la Universidad de Puerto Rico.

Báez, Clara. 1985. *La Subordinación Social de la Mujer Dominicana en Cifras.* Santo Domingo, Dominican Republic: Dirección General de Promoción de la Mujer/United Nations Research and Training Institute for the Advancement of Women/INSTRAW.

Báez, Clara. 1991. *Mujer y Desarrollo en la República Dominicana: 1981–1991.* Santo Domingo, Dominican Republic: Unedited report prepared for Inter-American Development Bank.

Báez, Clara. 1993. "Democracia y Movimientos de Mujeres." *Género y Sociedad* 1(1):1–21.

Barrett, Michele. 1980. *Women's Oppression Today.* London: Verso Editions.

Benería, Lourdes, and Shelley Feldman. 1992. *Unequal Burden: Economic Crises, Persistent Poverty, and Women's Work.* Boulder, CO: Westview Press.

Benería, Lourdes, and Martha Roldán. 1987. *The Crossroads of Class and Gender: Industrial Homework, Subcontracting, and Household Dynamics in Mexico City.* Chicago: University of Chicago Press.

Bengelsdorf, Carolee. 1985. "On the Problem of Studying Women in Cuba." *Race and Class* 2: 35–50.

Billingsley, Andrew. 1992. *Climbing Jacob's Ladder: The Enduring Legacy of African-American Families.* New York: Simon & Schuster.

Blondet, Cecilia. 1990. "Establishing an Identity: Women Settlers in a Poor Lima Neighborhood." In *Women and Social Change in Latin America,* edited by Elizabeth Jelin. Geneva, Switzerland: United Nations Research Institute for Social Development; London; Atlantic Highlands, NJ: Zed Books, pp. 12–44.

Blumberg, Rae Lesser, ed. 1991. *Gender, Family and Economy: The Triple Overlap.* Newbury Park, CA: Sage Publications.

Boserup, Ester. 1970. *Women's Role in Economic Development.* New York: St. Martin's Press.

Boyer, Richard. 1989. "La Mala Vida, and the Politics of Marriage." In *Sexuality and Marriage in Colonial Latin America,* edited by A. Larrin. Lincoln, NE: University of Nebraska Press, pp. 252–286.

Bradsher, Keith. 1992. "Conferees Agree to Restrict Projects by A.I.D." *The New York Times,* October 4, p. 5.

Brown, Susan. 1975. "Love Unites Them and Hunger Separates Them: Poor Women in the Dominican Republic." In *Toward an Anthropology of Women,* edited by R. Reiter. New York: Monthly Review Press, pp. 322–332.

Brundenius, Claes. 1990. "Some Reflections on the Cuban Economic Model." In *Transformation and Struggle: Cuba Faces the 1990's,* edited by Sandor Halebsky and John M. Kirk, with Rafael Hernández. New York: Praeger, pp. 143–156.

Buvinic, Mayra, and Geeta R. Gupta. 1994. *Targeting Poor Woman-Headed Households and Woman-Maintained Families in Developing Countries: Views on a Policy Dilemma.* Washington, DC: The Population Council and the International Center for Research on Women.

Cabán Catanzaro, Pedro. 1984. "Industrialization, the Colonial State and Working Class Origins in Puerto Rico." *Latin American Perspectives* 42, 11(3): 149–172.

Catasús Cervera, Sonia. 1992. "La Nupcialidad de la Década de los Ochenta en Cuba." In *La Demografía Cubana ante el Quinto Centenario*. Centro de Estudios Demográficos (CEDEM). Havana, Cuba: Editorial de Ciencias Sociales, pp. 30–42.

Catasús Cervera, Sonia, A. Farnos, F. González, R. Grove, R. Hernández, and B. Morejón. 1988. *Cuban Women: Changing Roles and Population Trends*. Geneva, Switzerland: International Labour Office.

Ceara, Miguel. 1987. *Situación Socioeconómica Actual y Su Repercusión en la Situación de la Madre y el Niño*. Santo Domingo, Dominican Republic: Instituto Tecnólogico de Santo Domingo (INTEC) and United Nations Children's Fund (UNICEF).

Cela, Jorge, Isis Duarte, and Carmen Gómez. 1988. *Población, Crecimiento Urbano y Barrios Marginados en Santo Domingo*. Santo Domingo, Dominican Republic: Fundación Friedrich Ebert.

Chow, Esther. 1993. *Women, the Family, and Policy: A Global Perspective*. SUNY series in Gender and Society. Albany, NY: State University of New York Press.

Colón, Alice. n.d. "Mujeres Jefe de Familia en Puerto Rico: Algunas Consideraciones Teóricas en Torno a Su Incremento y Niveles de Pobreza." Río Piedras, Puerto Rico: Proyecto Centro de Estudios, Recursos y Servicos de la Mujer (CERES), Centro de Investigaciones Sociales, Universidad de Puerto Rico.

Colón, Alice. 1993. "Feminist Research and Action in Contemporary Puerto Rico: A Trajectory of Changing Visions of Gender Relations Within the Family." Paper presented at the 1993 Meeting of the American Sociological Association, Miami, FL.

Colón, Alice, Marya Muñoz, Neftalí García, and Idsa Alegría. 1988. "Trayectoria de la Participación Laboral de las Mujeres en Puerto Rico de los Años 1950 a 1985." In *Crisis, Sociedad y Mujer: Estudio Comparativo entre Países de América (1950–1985)*. Havana, Cuba: Federación de Mujeres Cubanas.

Comité Estatal de Estadística (CEE). 1986. *Anuario Estadístico de Cuba 1986*. Havana, Cuba.

Consejo Nacional de Zonas Francas de Exportación, Secretaría de Estado de Industria y Comercio. 1993. *Zonas Francas en la República Dominicana*. Santo Domingo, Dominican Republic.

Cornia, Giovanni A., Richard Jolly, and Frances Stewart. 1987. *Adjustment with a Human Face*. Vol. 1. New York: UNICEF; Oxford: Clarendon Press.

Dauhajre, Andrés, E. Riley, R. Mena, and J. A. Guerrero. 1989. *Impacto Económico de las Zonas Francas Industriales de Exportación en la República Dominicana*. Santo Domingo, Dominican Republic: Fundación Economía y Desarrollo, Inc.

de la Fuente, Alejandro. 1995. "Race and Inequality in Cuba, 1899–1981." *Journal of Contemporary History* 30: 131–167.

Deere, Carmen Diana. 1990. *Household and Class Relations: Peasants and Landlords in Northern Peru*. Berkeley: University of California Press.

Deere, Carmen Diana, and Edwin Meléndez. 1992. "When Export Growth Is Not Enough: U.S. Trade Policy and Caribbean Basin Economic Recovery." *Caribbean Affairs* 5(1): 61–70.

Deere, Carmen Diana, Peggy Antrobus, Lynn Bolles, Edwin Meléndez, Peter Phillips, Marcia Rivera, and Helen Safa. 1990. *In the Shadows of the Sun: Caribbean Development Alternatives and U.S. Policy.* Boulder, CO: Westview Press.

Departamento del Trabajo y Recursos Humanos. 1991. *Serie Histórica del Empleo, Desempleo y Grupo Trabajador en Puerto Rico.* Informe Especial Número E-74. San Juan, Puerto Rico: Department of Labor and Human Resources.

Deyo, Frederic. 1986. "Industrialization and the Structuring of Asian Labor Movements: The 'Gang of Four.'" In *Confrontation, Class Consciousness and the Labor Process,* edited by M. Hanagan and C. Stephenson. Westport, CT: Greenwood Press, pp. 167–198.

Díaz Temorio, Marelén. 1992. "Análisis Preliminar de las Uniones Consensuales en Cuba." Havana, Cuba: Center for the Study of Psychological and Sociological Research, Cuban Academy of Sciences. Mimeographed.

Dietz, James. 1986. *Economic History of Puerto Rico: Institutional Change and Capitalist Development.* Princeton, NJ: Princeton University Press.

Domínguez, María Isabel, María Elena Ferrer, María Victoria Valdés. 1989. *La Formación de la Juventud en Cuba.* Havana, Cuba: Center for Sociological and Psychological Research, Cuban Academy of Sciences.

Duany, Jorge. 1985. "Ethnicity in the Spanish Caribbean: Notes on the Consolidation of Creole Identity in Cuba and Puerto Rico." *Ethnic Groups* 6: 99–123.

Duany, Jorge, ed. 1990. *Los Dominicanos en Puerto Rico: Migración en la Semiperiferia.* Río Piedras, Puerto Rico: Ediciones Huracán.

Duarte, Isis, Clara Báez, Carmen J. Gómez, and Marina Ariza. 1989. *Población y Condición de la Mujer en República Dominicana.* Santo Domingo, Dominican Republic: Instituto de Estudios de Población y Desarrollo, Estudio no. 6.

Dwyer, Daisy, and Judith Bruce, eds. 1988. *A Home Divided: Women and Income in the Third World.* Palo Alto, CA: Stanford University Press.

Eber, Christine, and Brenda Rosenbaum. 1993. "That We May Serve Beneath Your Hands and Feet: Women Weavers in Highland Chiapas, Mexico." In *Crafts in the World Market: The Impact of Global Exchange on Middle American Artisans,* edited by June Nash. Albany, NY: State University of New York Press, pp. 155–180.

Economic Commission for Latin America and the Caribbean (ECLAC). 1992. *Economic Survey of Latin America and the Caribbean, 1990.* Vol. 1. Santiago, Chile.

Economic Development Administration. 1989. *Selected Socio-economic Statistics.* San Juan, Puerto Rico: Office of Economic Analysis, Commonwealth of Puerto Rico.

Espín, Vilma. 1986. "La Batalla por el Ejercicio Pleno de la Igualdad de la Mujer: Acción de los Comunistas." *Cuba Socialista* 6: 27–68.

Espinal, Rosario. 1988. *Torn Between Authoritarianism and Crisis-Prone Democracy: The Dominican Labor Movement.* Notre Dame, IN: The Helen Kellogg Institute for International Studies, Working Paper no. 116.

Etienne, Mona, and Eleanor Leacock, eds. 1980. *Women and Colonization: Anthropological Perspectives.* New York: Praeger.

Federación de las Mujeres Cubanas (FMC). 1988. Personal communication.

Federación de las Mujeres Cubanas (FMC). 1989. *Integración de la Mujer Cubana a las Actividades Socio-Económicas y Políticas.* Havana, Cuba: Editorial de la Mujer.

Federación de las Mujeres Cubanas (FMC). 1990. *Mujer y Sociedad en Cifras 1975–1988.* Havana, Cuba: Editorial de la Mujer.

Fernández-Kelly, M. Patricia. 1983. *For We Are Sold, I and My People: Women and Industry in Mexico's Frontier.* Albany, NY: State University of New York Press.

Fernández-Kelly, M. Patricia, and Saskia Sassen. 1995. "Recasting Women in the Global Economy: Internationalization and Changing Definitions of Gender." In *Women and Development in the Third World,* edited by E. Acosta-Belén and C. Bose. Philadelphia: Temple University Press (in press).

Finlay, Barbara. 1989. *The Women of Azua: Work and Family in the Rural Dominican Republic.* New York: Praeger.

Folbre, Nancy. 1991. "The Unproductive Housewife: Her Evolution in Nineteenth Century Thought." *Signs* 16(3): 463–484.

Frazier, E. Franklin. 1939. *The Negro Family in the United States.* Chicago: University of Chicago Press.

Fuller, Linda. 1987. "Power at the Work Place: The Resolution of Worker-Management Conflict in Cuba." *World Development* 15(1): 139–152.

Fuller, Linda. 1992. *Work and Democracy in Socialist Cuba.* Philadelphia: Temple University Press.

Fundapec (Fundación APEC de Crédito Educativo, Inc.). 1992. *Encuesta Nacional de Mano de Obra.* Santo Domingo, Dominican Republic: Report prepared for Inter-American Development Bank.

Gallin, Rita. 1990. "Women and the Export Industry in Taiwan: The Muting of Class Consciousness." In *Women Workers and Global Restructuring,* edited by Kathryn Ward. Ithaca, NY: ILR Press, School of Industrial and Labor Relations, pp. 179–192.

García, Brígida, and Orlandina de Oliveira. 1995. "Gender Relations in Urban Middle-Class and Working-Class Households in Mexico." In *Engendering Wealth and Well-Being,* edited by Rae Blumberg et al. Boulder, CO: Westview Press.

Garfinkel, Irwin, and Sara McLanahan. 1986. *Single Mothers and Their Children.* Washington, DC: The Urban Institute Press.

Georges, Eugenia. 1990. *The Making of a Transnational Community: Migration, Development, and Cultural Change in the Dominican Republic.* New York: Columbia University Press.

Gereffi, Gary. 1990. "Paths of Industrialization: An Overview." In *Industrialization in Latin America and East Asia.* Princeton, NJ: Princeton University Press, pp. 3–31.

Gereffi, Gary, and D. Wyman, eds. 1990. *Manufacturing Miracles: Paths of Industrialization in Latin America and East Asia.* Princeton, NJ: Princeton University Press.

Gómez, Carmen Julia. 1990. *La Problemática de las Jefas del Hogar.* Santo Domingo, Dominican Republic: CIPAF.

González, Nancie L. 1970. "Toward a Definition of Matrifocality." In *Afro-American Anthropology,* edited by N. E. Whitten, Jr. and J. Szwed. New York: Free Press, pp. 231–243.

Grasmuck, Sherri, and Patricia Pessar. 1991. *Between Two Islands: Dominican International Migration.* Berkeley: University of California Press.

Hartman, Heidi. 1981. "The Unhappy Marriage of Marxism and Feminism: Towards a More Progressive Union." In *Women and Revolution,* edited by L. Sargent. Boston: South End Press, pp. 1–42.

Hartman, Heidi. 1987. "Changes in Women's Economic and Family Roles in Post–World War II United States." In *Women, Households and the Economy,* edited by L. Benería and C. Stimpson. New Brunswick, NJ: Rutgers University Press, pp. 33–64.

Herskovits, Melville J. 1958. *The Myth of the Negro Past.* Boston: Beacon Press.

Humphrey, John. 1987. *Gender and Work in the Third World: Sexual Divisions in Brazilian Industry.* London: Tavistock Publications.

Hyo-Chae, Lee. 1988. "The Changing Profile of Women Workers in South Korea." In *Daughters in Industry: Work, Skills and Consciousness of Women Workers in Asia,* edited by N. Heyzer. Kuala Lumpur, Malaysia: Asian and Pacific Development Centre.

International Labour Organization (ILO), United Nations Centre on Transnational Corporations. 1985. *Women Workers in Multinational Enterprises in Developing Countries.* Geneva, Switzerland: International Labour Office.

Jansen, Senaida, and Cecilia Millán. 1991. *Género, Trabajo y Etnia en los Bateyes Dominicanos.* Santo Domingo, Dominican Republic: Instituto Tecnológico de Santo Domingo, Programa de Estudios de la Mujer.

Jelin, Elizabeth. 1990. *Women and Social Change in Latin America.* Geneva, Switzerland: United Nations Research Institute for Social Development; London; Atlantic Highlands, NJ: Zed Books.

Jenkins, Rhys. 1991. "The Political Economy of Industrialization: A Comparison of Latin American and East Asian Newly Industrializing Countries." *Development and Change* 22 (2): 197–231. Newbury Park, CA: Sage Publications.

Joekes, Susan. 1987. *Employment in Industrial Free Trade Zones in the Dominican Republic.* Prepared for USAID, Dominican Republic. Washington, DC: International Center for Research on Women.

Joekes, Susan, with Roxana Moayedi. 1987. *Women and Export Manufacturing: A Review of the Issues and AID Policy.* Washington, DC: International Center for Research on Women. Prepared for the Office of Women in Development, United States Agency for International Development (USAID).

Justice. 1993. "Fighting Back: 'Union Free' Workers in Trade Zones Begin to Turn the Tables." *Justice* (75) 8: 8. New York: International Ladies' Garment Workers' Union.

Kandiyoti, Deniz. 1991. "Bargaining with Patriarchy." In *The Social Construction of Gender,* edited by J. Lorber and S. Farrell. Newbury Park, CA: Sage Publications, pp. 104–118.

Kessler-Harris, Alice. 1990. *A Woman's Wage: Historical Meanings and Social Consequences.* Lexington, KY: The University Press of Kentucky.

Kessler-Harris, Alice, and Karen Sacks. 1987. "The Demise of Domesticity in America." In *Women, Households and the Economy,* edited by L. Benería and C. Stimpson. New Brunswick, NJ: Rutgers University Press, pp. 65–84.

Kruks, Sonia, Rayna Rapp, and Marilyn B. Young. 1989. *Promissory Notes: Women in the Transition to Socialism.* New York: Monthly Review Press.

Lamphere, Louise. 1986. "From Working Daughters to Working Mothers: Production and Reproduction in an Industrial Community." *American Ethnologist* 13(1): 118–130.

Lamphere, Louise. 1987. *From Working Daughters to Working Mothers: Immigrant Women in a New England Industrial Community.* Ithaca, NY: Cornell University Press.

Lamphere, Louise, Patricia Zavella, and Felipe Gonzáles, with Peter Evans. 1993. *Sunbelt Working Mothers: Reconciling Family and Factory.* Ithaca, NY: Cornell University Press.

Larguia, Isabel, and John Dumoulin. 1986. "Women's Equality and the Cuban Revolution." In *Women and Change in Latin America,* edited by June Nash and Helen I. Safa. South Hadley, MA: Bergin and Garvey Publishers (now Greenwood), pp. 344–368.

Lim, Linda. 1990. "Women's Work in Export Factories: The Politics of a Cause." In *Persistent Inequalities: Women and World Development,* edited by I. Tinker. New York: Oxford University Press, pp. 101–119.

Lindenberg, Gail. 1993. "The Labor Union in the Cuban Workplace." *Latin American Perspectives* 76, 20(1): 28–39; Newbury Park, CA: Sage Publications, pp. 40–56.

Mann, Michael. 1986. "A Crisis in Stratification Theory? Persons, Household/Families/Lineages, Genders, Classes and Nations." In *Gender and Stratification,* edited by R. Crompton and M. Mann. Cambridge, England: Polity Press, pp. 40–561.

Martinez-Alier, Verena. 1974. *Marriage, Class and Colour in Nineteenth-Century Cuba.* Cambridge: Cambridge University Press.

Mesa Lago, Carmelo. 1981. *The Economy of Socialist Cuba: A Two Decade Appraisal.* Albuquerque, NM: University of New Mexico Press.

Milkman, Ruth. 1985. *Women, Work and Protest: A Century of U.S. Women's Labor History.* Boston: Routledge and Kegan Paul.

Milkman, Ruth. 1990. "Gender and Trade Unionism in Historical Perspective." In *Women, Politics and Change,* edited by L. Tilly and P. Gurin. New York: Russell Sage Foundation, pp. 87–107.

Molyneux, Maxine. 1981. "Women in Socialist Societies: Problems of Theory and Practice." In *Of Marriage and the Market,* edited by Kate Young, Carol Wolkwitz, and Roslyn McCullogh. London: Conference of Socialist Economists (CSE) Books, pp. 167–202.

Molyneux, Maxine. 1986. "Mobilization Without Emancipation? Women's Interest, State and Revolution." In *Transition and Development,* edited by R. Fagan, C. D. Deere, and J. L. Corragio. New York: Monthly Review Press, pp. 280–302.

Monk, Janice. 1981. *Social Change and Sexual Differences in Puerto Rican Rural Migration.* Papers in Latin American Geography in honor of Lucia G. Harrison. Muncie, IN: Special publication of the Conference of Latin Americanist Geographers, vol. 1, pp. 28–43.

Moreno Fraginals, Manuel. 1976. *The Sugar Mill: Socioeconomic Complex of Sugar in Cuba,* translated by Cedric Belfrage. New York: Monthly Review Press.

Moser, Caroline. 1989. "Gender Planning in the Third World: Meeting Practical and Strategic Gender Needs." *World Development* 17(11): 1799–1825.

Mota, Vivian. 1980. "Politics and Feminism in the Dominican Republic: 1931–45 and 1966–74." In *Sex and Class in Latin America,* edited by June Nash and Helen I. Safa. South Hadley, MA: J. F. Bergin Publishers (now Greenwood), pp. 265–278.

Moya Pons, Frank. 1990. "Import-Substitution Industrialization Policies in the Dominican Republic 1925–61." *Hispanic American Historical Review* 70(4): 539–577.

Mujica, María Elena. "Meals, Solidarity and Empowerment: *Comedores Populares* in Lima, Peru." In *Women in Groups,* edited by Anne Jennings. Boulder, CO: Westview Press. Forthcoming.

Muñoz Vásquez, Mayra, and Edwin Fernández Banzó. 1988. *El Divorcio en la Sociedad Puertorriqueña.* Río Piedras, Puerto Rico: Ediciones Huracán.

Nash, June. 1978. "The Aztecs and the Ideology of Male Dominance." *Signs* 4(21): 349–362.

Nash, June. 1988. "Cultural Parameters of Sexism and Racism in the International Division of Labor." In *Racism, Sexism and World Economy,* edited by Joan Smith, J. Collins, T. K. Hopkins, and A. Muhammad. New York: Greenwood Press, pp. 11–38.

Nash, June. 1989. *From Tank Town to High Tech: The Clash of Community and Corporate Cycles.* New York: Columbia University Press.

Nash, June. 1993. "Maya Household Production in the World Market: The Potters of Amatenango del Valle, Chiapas, Mexico." In *Crafts in the World Market: The Impact of International Exchange on Middle American Artisans,* edited by June Nash. Albany, NY: State University of New York Press, pp. 127–154.

Nazzari, Muriel. 1983. "The Women Question in Cuba: An Analysis of Material Constraints on Its Solution." *Signs* 9(2): 246–263.

Nelson, Barbara. 1990. "The Gender, Race, and Class Origins of Early Welfare Policy and the Welfare State: A Comparison of Workmen's Compensation and Mothers' Aid." In *Women, Politics and Change,* edited by L. Tilly and P. Gurin. New York: Russell Sage Foundation, pp. 413–435.

Osmond, Marie Withers. 1993. "Women's Status in Contemporary Cuba: Contradictions, Diversity, and Challenges for the Future." In *The Women and International Development Annual,* vol. 3, edited by Rita Gallin, A. Ferguson, and J. Harper. Boulder, CO: Westview Press, pp. 147–180.

Pantojas-García, Emilio. 1990. *Development Strategies as Ideology: Puerto Rico's Export-Led Industrialization Experience.* Boulder: Lynne Rienner Publishers.

Pérez, Louis A. 1988. *Cuba: Between Reform and Revolution.* New York: Oxford University Press.

Pérez Alemán, Paola, Diana Martínez, and Christa Widmair. 1989. *Industria, Género y Mujer en Nicaragua.* Managua, Nicaragua: Instituto Nicaragüense de la Mujer.

Pérez-Stable, Marifeli. 1987. "Cuban Women and the Struggle for 'Conciencia.' " *Cuban Studies* 17: 51–72.

Pérez-Stable, Marifeli. 1993. *The Cuban Revolution: Origins, Course and Legacy.* New York: Oxford University Press.

Picó Vidal, Isabel. 1980. "The History of Women's Struggle for Equality in Puerto Rico." In *Sex and Class in Latin America,* edited by June Nash and Helen I. Safa. South Hadley, MA: J. F. Bergin Publishers (Greenwood), pp. 202–216.

Pou, Francis, B. Mones, P. Hernández, L. Grant, M. Dottin, A. Arango, B. Fernández, and T. Rosado. 1987. *La Mujer Rural Dominicana.* Santo Domingo, Dominican Republic: CIPAF.

Presser, Harriet B., and Sunita Kishor. 1991. "Economic Development and Occupational Sex Segregation in Puerto Rico: 1950–1980." *Population and Development Review* 17(1): 53–85.

Priestland, Carl H., and Smiley Jones. 1985. *Problems Facing the Local Apparel Industry of Puerto Rico.* Study for the Puerto Rican Needle Trades Association and the Economic Development Administration. San Juan, Puerto Rico: Economic Development Administration, Commonwealth of Puerto Rico.

Psacharopoulos, George, and Zafaris Tzannatos. 1992. *Women's Employment and Pay in Latin America: Overview and Methodology.* Washington, DC: The World Bank.

Puerto Rico Planning Board. 1987. *Socioeconomic Statistics.* San Juan, Puerto Rico: Bureau of Statistics, Puerto Rico Planning Board.

Ramírez, Nelson. 1992. "Nuevos Hallazgos Sobre Fuerza Laboral y Migraciones: Análisis Preliminar de los Datos del Cuestionario de Hogar Ampliado de la ENDESA [Encuesta Demográfica y de Salud] '91." In *Población y Desarrollo,* no. 2. Santo Domingo, Dominican Republic: Profamilia.

Ramírez, Nelson. 1993. *La Fuerza de Trabajo en la República Dominicana.* Santo Domingo, Dominican Republic: Instituto de Estudio de Población y Desarrollo.

Ramírez, Nelson, Isidoro Santana, Francisco de Moya, and Pablo Tactuk. 1988. *República Dominicana: Población y Desarrollo 1950–1985.* San José, Costa Rica: Centro Latinoamericano de Demografía (CELADE).

Raynolds, Laura T. 1994. "The Restructuring of Third World Agro-Exports: Changing Production Relations in the Dominican Republic." In *Global Restructuring of Agro-Food Systems,* edited by Philip McMichael. Ithaca, NY: Cornell University Press.

Reca Moreira, Inés. 1992. "Social Policy and the Family in Socialist Cuba." In *The Cuban Revolution in the 1990s,* edited by Centro de Estudios sobre América. Boulder: Westview Press, pp. 147–162.

Reca Moreira, Inés, Mayda Alvarez Suárez, María del Carmen Caño Secade, Gilda Castilla García, Maritza García Alonso, Orlando García Pino, Consuelo Martín Fernández, Alicia Puñales Sosa, Maysú Ystokazu Morales. 1990. *Análisis de las*

Investigaciones sobre la Familia Cubana 1970–1987. Havana, Cuba: Center for Psychological and Sociological Research, Cuban Academy of Sciences.

Ricourt, Milagros. 1986. *Free Trade Zones, Development and Female Labor Force in the Dominican Republic.* Master's thesis, Center for Latin American Studies.

Roldán, Martha. 1985. "Industrial Outworking, Struggles for the Reproduction of Working-Class Families and Gender Subordination." In *Beyond Employment: Household, Gender and Subsistence,* edited by N. Redclift and E. Mingione. New York: Basil Blackwell Inc., pp. 248–285.

Roman, Peter. 1993. "Representative Government in Socialist Cuba." *Latin American Perspectives* 76, 20(1): 28–39; Newbury Park, CA: Sage Publications.

Sacks, Karen. 1989. "Toward a Unified Theory of Class, Race and Gender." *American Ethnologist* 16(3): 534–550.

Safa, Helen I. 1974. *The Urban Poor of Puerto Rico: A Study in Development and Inequality.* New York: Holt, Rinehart and Winston, Inc. (now Harcourt, Brace, Jovanovich).

Safa, Helen I. 1980. "Class Consciousness Among Working-Class Women in Latin America: Puerto Rico." In *Sex and Class in Latin America,* edited by June Nash and Helen I. Safa. South Hadley, MA: Bergin and Garvey Publishers (now Greenwood), pp. 69–85.

Safa, Helen I. 1981. "Runaway Shops and Female Employment: The Search for Cheap Labor." *Signs* 7(2): 418–433.

Safa, Helen I. 1983. "Women, Production and Reproduction in Industrial Capitalism: A Comparison of Brazilian and U.S. Factory Workers." In *Women, Men and the International Division of Labor,* edited by June Nash and M. Patricia Fernández-Kelly. Albany, NY: State University of New York Press, pp. 95–116.

Safa, Helen I. 1986. "Economic Autonomy and Sexual Equality in Caribbean Society." *Social and Economic Studies* 35(3): 1–22.

Safa, Helen I. 1987. "Work and Women's Liberation: A Case Study of Garment Workers." In *Cities of the United States: Studies in Urban Anthropology,* edited by L. Mullings. New York: Columbia University Press, pp. 243–268.

Safa, Helen I. 1990a. "Women's Social Movements in Latin America." *Gender and Society* 4(3): 354–369.

Safa, Helen I. 1990b. "Women and Industrialization in the Caribbean." In *Women, Employment and the Family in the International Division of Labour,* edited by S. Stichter and J. Parpart. London: Macmillan Press, pp. 72–97.

Safa, Helen I. 1992. "Development and Changing Gender Roles in Latin America and the Caribbean." In *Women's Work and Women's Lives: The Continuing Struggle Worldwide,* edited by H. Kahne and J. Z. Giele. Boulder, CO: Westview Press, pp. 69–86.

Safa, Helen I., and Peggy Antrobus. 1990. "Women and the Economic Crisis in the Caribbean." In *Unequal Burden: Economic Crises, Persistent Poverty, and Women's Work,* edited by Lourdes Benería and Shelley Feldman. Boulder, CO: Westview Press, pp. 49–82.

Safilios-Rothschild, Constantina. 1990. "Socio-economic Determinants of the Outcomes of Women's Income-Generation in Developing Countries." In

Women, Employment and the Family in the International Division of Labour, edited by S. Stichter and J. Parpart. London: Macmillan Press, pp. 221–228.

Salaff, Janet. 1981. *Working Daughters of Hong Kong.* New York: Cambridge University Press.

Salaff, Janet. 1990. "Women, the Family and the State: Hong Kong, Taiwan, Singapore—Newly Industrialised Countries in Asia." In *Women, Employment and the Family in the International Division of Labour,* edited by S. Stichter and J. Parpart. London: Macmillan Press, pp. 98–136.

Santiago-Rivera, Carlos. 1989. "Industrial Reconversion and Economic Restructuring: The Challenge for the Puerto Rican Labor Movement." *Radical America* 23(1): 91–100.

Santiago-Rivera, Carlos. 1993. "The Puerto Rican Labor Movement in the 1990s." In *Colonial Dilemma: Critical Perspectives on Contemporary Puerto Rico,* edited by Edwin Meléndez and Edgardo Meléndez. Boston: South End Press, pp. 143–156.

Shaiken, Harvey. 1994. "Advanced Manufacturing and Mexico: A New International Division of Labor?" *Latin American Research Review* 29(2): 39–72.

Silvestrini, Blanca. 1980. "La Mujer Puertorriqueña y el Movimiento Obrero en la Década de 1930." In *La Mujer en la Sociedad Puertorriqueña,* edited by Edna Acosta-Belén. Río Piedras, Puerto Rico: Ediciones Huracán, pp. 67–90.

Smith, Raymond Thomas. 1956. *The Negro Family in British Guiana: Family Structure and Social Status in the Villages.* London: Routledge and Kegan Paul, in association with the Institute of Social and Economic Research, University College of the West Indies, Jamaica.

Smith, Raymond Thomas. 1988. *Kinship and Class in the West Indies.* Cambridge: Cambridge University Press.

Stack, Carol. 1974. *All Our Kin: Strategies for Survival in a Black Community.* New York: Harper & Row.

Stallings, Barbara. 1990. "The Role of Foreign Investment in Economic Development." In *Manufacturing Miracles: Paths of Industrialization in Latin America and East Asia,* edited by G. Gereffi and D. Wyman. Princeton, NJ: Princeton University Press, pp. 55–89.

Standing, Guy. 1989. "Global Feminization Through Flexible Labor." *World Development* 17(7): 1077–1096.

Steele, Peter. 1988. *The Caribbean Clothing Industry: The U.S. and Far East Connections.* London: The Economist Intelligence Unit, Special Report no. 1147.

Steward, Julian. 1956. *The People of Puerto Rico.* Urbana, IL: University of Illinois Press.

Stolcke, Verena. 1984. "The Exploitation of Family Morality: Labor Systems and Family Structure on Sao Paulo Coffee Plantations, 1850–1979." In *Kinship, Ideology and Practice in Latin America,* edited by R. T. Smith. Durham, NC: University of North Carolina Press, pp. 264–296.

Stoner, K. Lynn. 1991. *From the House to the Streets: The Cuban Women's Movement for Legal Reform, 1898–1940.* Durham, NC: Duke University Press.

Stubbs, Jean. 1985. *Tobacco on the Periphery: A Case Study in Cuban Labour History.* Cambridge: Cambridge University Press.

Susser, Ida. 1986. "Political Activity Among Working Class Women in a U.S. City." *American Ethnologist* 13(1): 108–117.

Tiano, Susan. 1986. "Women and Industrial Development in Latin America." *Latin American Research Review* 21(3): 157–170.

Valdés, Teresa, and Enrique Gomariz, eds. 1992. "Cuba." *Mujeres Latinoamericanas en Cifras.* Madrid, Spain: Instituto de la Mujer; Santiago, Chile: Facultad Latinoamericana de Ciencias Sociales (FLASCO).

Vásquez Calzada, José. 1988. "Tendencias Recientes de las Uniones Consensuales en Puerto Rico." *Revista de Ciencias Sociales* 27(3–4): 51–66.

Vickers, Jeanne. 1991. *Women and the World Economic Crisis.* London: Zed Books.

Walby, Sylvia. 1986. *Patriarchy at Work.* Cambridge, England: Polity Press.

Walby, Sylvia. 1990. *Theorizing Patriarchy.* Oxford, England: Basil Blackwell.

Waldinger, Roger. 1985. "Another Look at the International Ladies' Garment Workers' Union: Women, Industry Structure and Collective Action." In *Women, Work and Protest: A Century of U.S. Women's Labor History,* edited by Ruth Milkman. Boston: Routledge and Kegan Paul, pp. 86–109.

Whiteford, Linda. 1993. "Child and Maternal Health and International Economic Policies." *Social Science and Medicine* 37(11): 1391–1400.

Wilson, Patricia. 1992. *Exports and Local Development: Mexico's New Maquiladoras.* Austin, TX: University of Texas Press.

Wilson, William J. 1987. *The Truly Disadvantaged: The Inner City, the Underclass, and Public Policy.* Chicago: University of Chicago Press.

Zimbalist, Andrew. 1990. "Cuba's Economic Diversification: Progress and Shortcomings." In *Transformation and Struggle: Cuba Faces the 1990's,* edited by Sandor Halebsky and John M. Kirk, with Rafael Hernández. New York: Praeger, pp. 131–142.

Zimbalist, Andrew. 1992. "Teetering on the Brink: Cuba's Current Economic and Political Crisis." *Journal of Latin American Studies* 24: 407–418.

Zimbalist, Andrew, and S. Eckstein. 1987. "Patterns of Cuban Development." *World Development* 15(1): 5–22.

About the Book and Author

Today there is a growing debate about the effects of paid employment on women. Some observers argue that paid employment is the key to gender equality because it raises women's class consciousness and reduces their isolation within the home and their dependence on male wages. Others suggest that paid employment merely increases women's burden and reinforces their subordination, locking them into poorly paid, dead-end jobs.

This book examines the debate through studies of women industrial workers in Puerto Rico, the Dominican Republic, and Cuba. The percentage of women in the labor force has grown rapidly in all three countries since 1970, but each country represents a radically different model of development. Puerto Rico's Operation Bootstrap was a forerunner of other "industrialization by invitation" strategies in the region, and the Dominican Republic represents a classic case of recently initiated, rapidly growing export manufacturing under the Caribbean Basin Initiative. Socialist Cuba continued to rely on sugar exports as a source of foreign exchange and on import substitution industrialization for the domestic economy. However, Cuba has made special efforts to incorporate women into the labor force and has made women's equality a key goal of its revolutionary strategy.

The book focuses on three areas of these women's lives: wages and working conditions; the family, life cycle, and household composition; and political consciousness and participation in unions, political parties, and other mass organizations. Women are now making a critical contribution to the household economy, attributable in part to the growth of labor-intensive industrialization in the region. The increase in women's wage-earning capacity is reflected in authority patterns and in women's greater control over the household budget. However, women continue to be confined to poorly paid jobs and to be marginalized by political parties and labor unions, which persist in regarding them as supplementary wage earners. Women workers have been more effective in challenging their subordination in the home than they have been in the workplace and in relationship to political parties or the state. This finding challenges feminist theories that locate the sources of women's inequality solely in the family and suggests that such theories need to be augmented by studies of subordination at the level of the workplace and of state policy.

Helen I. Safa is professor of anthropology and Latin American studies at the University of Florida. She is author of *The Urban Poor of Puerto Rico: A Study in Development and Inequality,* coauthor of *In the Shadows of the Sun: Caribbean Development Alternatives and U.S. Policy,* coeditor of *Women and Change in Latin America;* and author of numerous other publications on gender and development.

Index